West Baltimore's literary air emanated from Union Square with its fountain circled by plaques naming H. L. Mencken's books. Mencken lived and wrote on the north side, Russell Baker grew up on the south side. Novelists F. Hopkinson Smith and Dashiell Hammett lived nearby.

MARYLAND WITS & BALTIMORE BARDS

A · LITERARY · HISTORY WITH · NOTES · ON WASHINGTON · WRITERS

BY · FRANK · R · SHIVERS · JR

MACLAY & ASSOCIATES · INC · BALTIMORE · 1985

Dedication

This book is gratefully dedicated to the women in my life who have encouraged my love of literature. They include my mother, my wife, my daughters, and most particularly my mother-in-law, Margaret Littlehales Vondersmith, and my maternal aunt, Rebecca Anne Wilkins.

> No work of man's hand but the weary years
> Besiege and take it, comes its evil day:
> The written word alone flaunts destiny,
> Revives the past and gives the lie to Death.
> — Hrabanus Maurus (ca. 835)

"What else endures, of any city, but the memory of the great men it has sheltered? What masonry is half as enduring as a song?"

> — Gerald W. Johnson (1935)

Table of Contents

What is in this book, with up-to-date notes by Russell Baker and Anne Tyler.

A map and character sketch, with fresh views from John Barth, Josephine Jacobsen, Julia Randall, and Adrienne Rich.

Colonial writing — satirical and patriotic at its best — also America's first poet-laureate, her first novel, and the first flowering of George Washington's cherry tree.

Creation of the national song, "The Star-Spangled Banner," and of the myth of the Old South, as well as of a nursery for Poe's genius.

Wizard writer of wonder songs, Edgar Allan Poe: how in Baltimore he found himself — and was found — as a professional author.

List of Illustrations

Aiders and Abettors

It is a pleasure to thank all those good souls who aided in creating this book. My family lived closest to it — and suffered the most. Without them I never could have finished. And without the care and attention to detail of publishers John and Joyce Maclay I couldn't have approached their idea of what this book should be. I am glad that they feel happy with how it turned out.

A covey of other readers joined with the Maclays to help make this history as accurate as possible, and the text as readable as, I trust, it is. Certain people read every page in early versions, a painful task: Alexander Armstrong, H. Chace Davis, Jr., John R. Dorsey, Dorothy Mackinnon, and Natalie Wilkins Shivers, who had to slog through four times. Very valuable indeed were perspectives offered by non-Marylanders, especially Joan Houghton from Cleveland. I give special salutes to Lia Hunt for her professional eye to style, to Anne Healy, who will go to her heavenly reward one Sunday short — a Sunday lost to my manuscript — and to Grace Hodes for laborious creation of the index. Other experts gave generously of time and advice; many read the text for special points: Gertrude Bohmfalk, John E. DeFord, Jr., Ellen Watson Eager, Vincent D. Fitzpatrick III, Richard H. Hart, William K. Jackson, Clarinda Harriss Lott, Phillip McCaffrey, Frances H. Mueller, William R. Mueller, Erik Olson, and Alexander G. Rose.

Surrounding that covey of readers ranges this flock of aiders and abettors: Holmes Alexander, Louis Azrael, Russell Baker, David L. Bergman, Laura Blaustein, Carl Bode, Rev. John W. Bowen, S.S., James H. Bready, Huntington Cairns, Mrs. Brodnax Cameron, Sr., Penny Catzen, Margaret W. DeFord, Diana Digges, Mrs. John Dos Passos, Dr. James R. Duke, Sister Maria Eichner, Richard Flynt, Father Joseph Gallagher, Thomas M. Greene, George H. Hahn, Susan L. Harrell, R. P. Harriss, Lyn L. Hart, Josephine Hughes, Josephine Jacobsen, Jeff Jerome, Teresa Johanson, Gerald W. Johnson, William R. Johnston, Averil Kadis, William B. Keller, Frances Turnbull Kidder, Robin Klein, Mildred Kratavil, Dean Krimmel, Constance Lieder, Walter Lord, Richard A. Macksey, Mrs. Fendall Marbury, Wayne Markert, Ursula McCracken, Marian B. Millard, Dorothy Miner, Gwinn F. Owens, Steven Parks, Richard Parsons, Peggy Patterson,

Alice Piper, Morgan H. Pritchett, Adrienne Rich, Joseph V. Ridgely, Lucy Dos Passos Coggin, David Roszel, Julian Roszel, Lottchen Shivers, Margaret Shivers, Philip Shivers, Eva Slezak, Linell Smith; Summer Session 1984 Communications Department, Loyola College of Maryland, with bows to Dorothy Sharpf, Randall Donaldson, Thomas Schye, Phillip McCaffrey, and Genevieve Rafferty; Henry Y. K. Tom, Michael F. Trostel, Anne Tyler, Christopher Weeks, Wesley L. Wilson, Jonathan Yardley, and Larry Yeatman.

This list names but a few of the many underpaid librarians, archivists, and curators who have helped me for 40 years. To them and to all the helpers listed I send thanks and a wish for a happy read. Thanks also to everyone who gave permission to use words and pictures in their charge. I trust that they will enjoy seeing old gems in a fresh setting.

The best words to end these acknowledgements were written by a contemporary of Poe's, John Van Lear McMahon, of Cumberland, Allegany County. In launching a book of his, McMahon announced:

Alike its author, this work has had no patron to usher it into public view [neither modern publisher nor author had a grant], and it must make friends as it goes. The generous mind will appreciate its difficulties, and make due allowance for its imperfections. To those who look upon the approbation of others' efforts as the office of inferior minds, and the art of finding faults as the evidence of their own superiority, the author has but one admonition to give. If respected, it will relieve him from that class of critics, who, like certain insects, annoy more by their buzz than their sting. It is couched in the language of an old Maryland *poet;*

> *Let critics, that may discommend it,*
> ---------------------------------*mend it.*

As Their Land and Air Is

What is in this book, with up-to-date notes by Russell Baker and Anne Tyler.

"Any body is as their land and air is."[1]
— Gertrude Stein

"Baltimore is permissiveness. The Land of Pleasant Living, according to an old advertising jingle for a local beer. The pleasures of the flesh, the table, the bottle and the purse are tolerated with a civilized understanding of the subtleties of moral questions that would have been perfectly comprehensible to Edwardian Londoners.

"Gross and overt indulgence, however, is frowned upon. The gunned corpses that litter New Jersey are not part of Baltimore life. That sort of thing is a vice. Baltimore does not like vice. Vice leads to cruelty and suffering and, what's more, is in bad taste. Sin is something else. Baltimore tolerates sin. Sin is the human condition, and though it may be deplorable, Baltimore has the intuitive European knowledge that however deplorable sin may be, yet society must live in it."[2]
— Russell Baker

"What is your remembrance of the influences you stood under at the time you began to write? . . . I know that this is difficult ground, for a man can scarcely determine such things himself but it occurs to me that you may remember some enthusiasm of that period. . . . "[3]
— H. L. Mencken

Some Baltimore books, including Griswold edition of Poe's works, first editions of all Fitzgerald's books published during his lifetime, and signed first editions of Mencken. (Publisher's collection.)

Just before Russell Baker published his Pulitzer Prize-winning memoir *Growing Up* (1983), he wrote me that "A very rich and enduring experience of Baltimore must be some element in everything I write."[4] These words gave the reason for writing this book. As literary historian, I first had to find writers like Baker with connections to Baltimore, to Maryland, or to Washington. Next I picked the prominent and the representative ones. And then I put them in order, to open a window for readers on this region's unusually rich literature.

This book offers a focused view of *who* wrote *what* — and *when*. As for the *where*, I include books if the place shows in them, and authors if they have spent some significant time of their lives in Maryland, however brief. These works and authors fall into two groups. Some authors stayed cozily at home enjoying local notice. Examples are writers such as the Bentztown Bard (Folger McKinsey), Sally Bruce Kinsolving, and the 18th-century humorist Dr. Alexander Hamilton. But most of the writers included here made reputations outside Maryland — Christopher Morley, F. Scott Fitzgerald, John Pendleton Kennedy, and Frederick Douglass, to name a few.

Of these Maryland-connected writers, a surprising number pioneered in the forests of national literary history. Edgar Allan Poe comes to mind right away because he invented detective fiction in such stories as "Murders in the Rue Morgue." Later, a native Marylander, Dashiell Hammett, created the hardboiled version of the detective story in *The Continental Op.* (He had been a Pinkerton operative headquartered in the Continental Building in Baltimore.)

Other pioneers freshened language and so pushed both readers and writers in new directions. H. L. Mencken even published the first extensive proof that American English is separate from English English. At the same time, plenty of evidence of that difference as well as of pioneering came from Gertrude Stein, John Dos Passos, and Ogden Nash. Without such adventurous writers, American literature would today be quite different. Two of these pioneers, Poe and Mencken, raised standards; they were like brisk winds blowing away dead attitudes and scattering seeds.

Poe and Mencken were not just national forces: they also entered the smaller world of Maryland. That is why their places in this book divide into (1) what they did in their Baltimore years and (2) what they gained then. Just how important their Maryland years were to their work, I can hint at here. In Baltimore Poe had family roots, found his true family, and invested the first quarter of his career. There Mencken, a native, invested his whole career. Clearly the place sustained them both. There they both found an excellent place to work, there they found themselves as writers, and there they were first found by readers.

Mencken often hymned the advantages of living and working in his native town and away from New York — a third-rate Babylon, he called it. Recently I asked other writers for their views on living and working in Maryland and Baltimore. Josephine Jacobsen, a poet, short story writer, and a native Baltimorean, wrote me: "I think Baltimore *is* a propitious place for writers because it has a distinct personality, does not seem as impersonal as many other cities, and has a heavily mixed ethnic population which, in addition to its being a large port, gives it character."[5]

A contrasting view came from the contemporary poet Adrienne Rich, who grew up in Roland Park, Baltimore, and prepared for Radcliffe at Roland Park Country School there. When I asked what was the chief influence of the place, she wrote me that it was "Probably the fact of growing up as a white person in a segregated, racist city, and as the daughter of a Jew in a city which was also anti-semitic: experiencing at a very young age the treatment of certain people as 'other' — this impression and my need to make sense of it has carried into much of my mature work."[6]

This desire of Rich and other authors to make sense of local impressions runs through this book. How well they succeeded made literary history. To present that history I have told the story chronologically up to 1900. Its narrative span of 350 years begins with an early promotional tract of literary note. The account then moves through the scarce harvest of the 18th century and the abundance of the 19th. Then for the superabundant 20th century I divide the books by theme. Those chapters cover traditionalists as well as experimenters. Central authors are H. L. Mencken and F. Scott Fitzgerald, though others bring the book up into the present.

Quotations from many authors, new and old, aerate the text. Excerpts — and the illustrations — impart a sense of the Maryland place. Photographs of authors' homes and verbal pictures in anecdotes also give authors a local habitation and a name. Certain stories lend local flavor, a flavor then easier for readers to discern in the writings.

Quite apart from any Maryland connection are these general criteria for inclusion: works must have been published for the general reader and have had popular appeal. The early biography of George Washington by Parson Weems is an example. In addition, the writing must have literary merit as recognized and accepted by their contemporaries.[7] Examples are novels by Upton Sinclair and poems by Sidney Lanier and Lizette Woodworth Reese. Usually I let our current critical reputation determine the amount of attention given, but I sometimes go against received opinion, as in the case of William Force Stead.

Though individual authors do dominate the literary landscape, I will notice readers, patrons, editors, publishers, and literary societies. Also significant landmarks in this landscape are non-literary facts, such as Baltimore's being the Southernmost of Northern cities, and thus a haven for Southern writers after the Civil War.

They came for the same reasons that native Marylanders with literary ambitions such as James M. Cain had long been coming: they needed this chief cultural center of the state. In turn, that city needed the outlanders to help make it the center of Maryland writing. That mingling of city and country justifies the conclusion that if there is a Maryland literary tradition of merit, it is Baltimore's.[8]

By contrast, the other major city that grew up on Maryland soil, Washington, made small connection with the literature of that state. The contrast is striking. Baltimore boasts indigenous writers, and Washington can't, though many authors have settled there — Ambrose Bierce, for example. And some have lived in Maryland suburbs of that capital — Rachel Carson and Herman Wouk are two. All the writers were drawn there by politics or perhaps by institutions such as the Library of Congress — or even by the pace of life. Southerners of the literary calibre of Katherine Anne Porter must have liked that pace. And the New Englander Henry Adams fell for the charm of the place, a charm that he said was Maryland's.

Even so, no indigenous literary life has flourished there.[9] Even native Washingtonians such as Jean Toomer and Marjorie Kinnan Rawlings found truer homes elsewhere. And immigrants came dragging their roots from other soils and seldom put down new roots.

By contrast, Baltimore soil allows non-natives to send down roots. The immigrant novelist Anne Tyler told me, "The strongest influence on my writing about Baltimore is simply the city's own unique atmosphere — picked up from conversations overheard; or from the mood at, say, my favorite crabhouse or an Orioles game on a summer evening; and most of all from the sort of trance I fall into when driving past a string of rowhouses where everyone's perched outside on his stoop."[10] Marylanders are as their land and air is.

I
Literary Fames and Domains

A map and character sketch, with fresh views from John Barth, Josephine Jacobsen, Julia Randall, and Adrienne Rich.

"...the fames and the domains, the vistas and the glories of Maryland...."[1]
—F. Scott Fitzgerald

"Baltimore has made a comfortable place of residence for writers of very high rating from Edgar Allan Poe to John Dos Passos, Ogden Nash, and Scott Fitzgerald. Even when he was working in New York five days a week editing the *American Mercury* H. L. Mencken maintained his residence in Baltimore, because, he explained, he could not enter a big restaurant in New York without being spotted by autograph hunters or worse bores, while in Baltimore he could walk into Schellhase's or Miller Brothers' restaurants when they were crowded and nobody would give him a second glance. He did not deny a taste for adulation, but not in his home town.

"One of the great qualities of Baltimore is this ability to incorporate a newcomer into its social structure, using him without hesitation or apology when his particular talent can promote the general welfare, but letting him alone—again without hesitation or apology—when it is not needed. This makes the place intolerable to a man who, as the Apostle puts it, thinks more highly of himself than he ought to think, but gives it a wonderfully comfortable atmosphere for a man who knows that he is good at certain kinds of work, but does not for one minute cherish the delusion that he is Sir Oracle, and when he opens his lips, let no dog bark."[2]
—Gerald W. Johnson

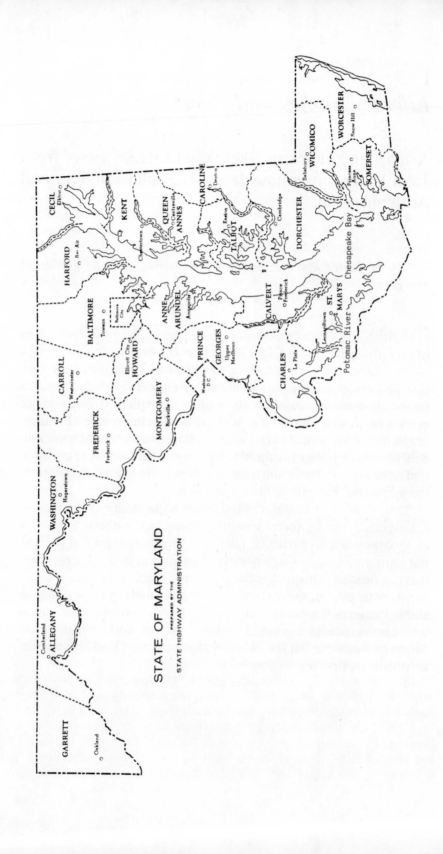

STATE OF MARYLAND

PREPARED BY THE

STATE HIGHWAY ADMINISTRATION

With so many literary fames and domains to examine, readers need a map. And since Marylanders early put their unique stamp on the place, I also provide a history to explain how that happened. To this I add a list of character traits to look for in these literary domains, for definite characteristics stand out in landscapes and people there. H. L. Mencken swore that as his train from New York headed into Maryland, fields always became greener, woods towered, and little towns suddenly grew beautiful. He said that wasn't just imagination, and other writers have agreed.[3]

Let the contemporary novelist John Barth tell about his native Dorchester County on Maryland's Eastern Shore:

In Civil War times Maryland was a Border state. Mason and Dixon's Line runs east-west across its top; and then, appropriately, north-south down the Eastern Shore, which was heavily Loyalist in the Revolution and Confederate in the War Between the States. Marsh country is a border state too, between land and sea, and tide marsh doubly so, its twin diurnal ebbs and floods continuously reorchestrating the geography. No clear demarcations here between fresh and salt, wet and dry: Many, many square miles of Delaware happen to be Delaware instead of Maryland owing to a 17th-century surveyors' dispute about the midpoint of a line whose eastern terminus is the sharp Atlantic coast but whose western peters out in the Dorchester County marshes, where the "shoreline" at high tide may be a mile east from where it was at low, when reedy islets muddily join the main.

To this picture he adds a note about Eastern Shore writers:

Your webfoot amphibious marsh-nurtured writer will likely by mere reflex regard many conventional boundaries and distinctions as arbitrary, fluid, negotiable: form versus content, realism versus irrealism, fact versus fiction, life versus art. His favorite mark of punctuation will be the semicolon.[4]

But marsh country makes up only part of the state. Though the Bay shell-fishing watermen number only a few thousand, they catch the imagination of readers of Pulitzer Prize winners *Chesapeake,* by James Michener (1978), and *Beautiful Swimmers,* by William Warner (1976). By contrast, stories of Western Marylanders remain untold. No wit or bard has yet immortalized their frontier camps and farms. Nor has a poet captured the coal miners or the builders of the railroads or the boatmen on the Chesapeake & Ohio Canal floating up from Georgetown, D.C., into mountain fastnesses.

Our story begins with a map of this diverse topography. The land changes from Atlantic Ocean beaches on the east to Piedmont and the Appalachian Mountains in the west. Separating the two is the nation's largest estuary, Chesapeake Bay. We can see how easily this Bay offered a blue-green path to history.

Sailing up the Bay, Englishmen first permanently settled Maryland in 1634 and made their capital St. Mary's City near the Chesapeake on St. Mary's River. There the proprietor Lord Baltimore had the role of a feudal lord. One of his duties was to impose names on the land. Some he borrowed from the Indians (Chesapeake and Susquehanna). Other names honor his lordship's family, such as Anne Arundel. The colony itself he named Maryland in compliment to the wife of King Charles I, grantor of the land — Queen Henrietta Marie. Luckily for later writers he chose musical names such as these to slide harmoniously into literature.

Another of the proprietor's duties was to attract colonists to work. One way was to force his Maryland Assembly to pass the very first colonial Act of Religious Toleration. In 1649 that was good business because it brought refugees from English religious struggles. Maryland thus became the only colony with Roman Catholics and Puritans (including many Quakers) living together in some degree of harmony.

These colonists cut down the thick woods for the large tobacco plantations that made them rich. They exported hogsheads of tobacco from their own wharves and imported directly those necessities and luxuries that they couldn't grow or make. They saw no need to build towns. Each planter headed his own community; each consciously copied the English aristocrat.

As partners with Virginians of the Chesapeake brand of civilization, wealthy Marylanders looked to London for urban culture. The Maryland Carrolls, like the Byrds of Virginia, sent sons abroad to be educated. By contrast, the New England town fathers provided education at home, as well as communal unity. As the result, Puritan Boston had an urban society a hundred years before Maryland's 18th-century capital Annapolis. Couple this fact with the Puritan emphasis on the Word and on writing as a way of showing that an individual was God's chosen elect, and you see why literary culture flourished earlier in New England than in Maryland. Despite that lag, Mencken believed that a true Baltimorean touched civilization at more places than any other American: "There yet hangs about him some of the repose, the air, the fine superiority of the Colonial planter."[5]

Late in the 18th century two major ports finally grew at the Fall Line of rivers, Georgetown and Baltimore. There ships picked up the products of the hinterland. That western region slowly filled with settlers moving down from Pennsylvania. Since many were German, they had German language presses in Frederick and Hagerstown. These settlers created the province we still call Western Maryland. Exactly where this province begins poses a puzzle. It doesn't appear on the map, but one answer comes by drawing a line dividing creeks emptying into the Chesapeake from those flowing into the Potomac River. That line runs through central Carroll County and western Montgomery County. What life was like in those still sparsely-peopled hills and mountains we find in an early settler's *Forty-Four Years of the Life of a Hunter* (by Meshack Browning, 1781–1859). He killed 50 panthers and catamounts (mostly in Allegany County), 1,800 to 2,000 deer, and 300 to 400 bear and countless wolves and wild cats.

Most 18th-century Marylanders to the south and east of the line followed adjacent Virginia in importing African slaves to grow tobacco. Western Marylanders, like neighboring Pennsylvanians, cultivated wheat without slave labor. To the south, 18th-century Virginians made Williamsburg into an intellectual and yeasty political center. And to the north Philadelphians not only made a city second to London in the British Empire, but also pioneered American institutions, as Benjamin Franklin recorded in his *Autobiography*. Philadelphia was first in everything.

By contrast with these much larger colonies, Maryland remained rural until one big city arose in the early 19th century, Baltimore. Its enterprising leaders sent the Baltimore Clipper ships to trade as far away as China. And in 1832 they pioneered in railroading with the Baltimore & Ohio Railroad. From the back country, they brought wheat, ground it into flour, and exported it to the Caribbean and elsewhere. These merchant princes made fortunes and lived well. Their city reigned as arbiter of style in furniture, in cuisine, and in feminine charms. Baltimore was then the New York of the South. After the Civil War, Baltimore took on even greater metropolitan airs with the full tide of immigrants, both Europeans and freed slaves from the South. Many of them worked in factories refining metals, making clothes, and canning food. By 1900 Baltimore ruled as the commercial capital of the Upper South. It was also the literary capital, as we shall see. Yet all was not well, at least in the view of the Sage of Baltimore: Mencken in 1926 blamed the ruination of his beloved Old Baltimore on the 1904 Fire that turned loose the Babbitts, inventors of the art of enthusing: "They converted a charming, dignified and amusing old town, well-to-do and contented, into a den of go-getters."[6]

The other port on the Fall Line of a Maryland river, Georgetown, didn't boom as either a commercial or literary center. Rather, it eventually became part of Washington. Let us remember, though, that Washington's swampy site on the Potomac River below George-town had been Maryland for 165 years. In 1790 the District of Columbia was taken out of Maryland's side the way Eve was taken from Adam's. Then for decades after George Washington laid the cornerstone for the Capitol there in 1793, the new capital sauntered along, just another sleepy Maryland town, but one with greater preten-sions than any other. Until after the Civil War Washington was a city in name only.

Very important to our literary history are the differences between the two cities that grew up on Maryland soil, Washington and Baltimore. Diverse writings came out of the contrast. That diversity reflects these cities' looks, as different as Venus from Mars.

A world seems to separate the white marble capital on the Potomac where Presidents reigned from the red brick city on the Patapsco which nurtured such streetwise writers as Dashiell Hammett, Upton Sinclair, and James M. Cain. If towns have seasons, it is always spring in Washington as it is always November in Baltimore. By some miracle, too, Washington has always remained not a connexus of commerce or a piece of antiquity entrapped in the modern world, but a place with a character peculiar to itself. Unlike Baltimore, it is not a place where one makes money, or goes when one has money to spend.

Washington has style and intention as if designed for people of sizeable income and some leisure who seek respect and privacy. Its prevailing colors are the whites and beiges that would harmonize with a blue sea and pink sands; and yet there is an urbanity in the style which proclaims the neighborhood of a great city. Even in the 20th century this serenity pervades the Capitol of the United States on its hill. Its large windows still look out upon lawns and trees and foun-tains and barking dogs and couples sauntering arm in arm and pausing there on Capitol Hill to look at the distant domes of Federal City, just as they sauntered and paused and looked when Thomas Jefferson stood there 175 years ago.[7]

Writers such as Jefferson and Henry Adams came to the capital from other places just as politicians have done. Like the third Presi-dent, usually they were one and the same. We shouldn't be surprised that no literary tradition has yet matured there, although Washing-ton has grown into more and more of an urban center. The sole literary genre to develop there was the so-called Washington Novel focusing on politics and being written by transients such as Gore Vidal and

John Dos Passos.

Baltimore's H. L. Mencken often wrote the typical Maryland view of the District of Columbia and its transient population of Congressmen and others. Once he told of how he traveled the 40 miles to the capital with his father who had business at Burkhardt's saloon near the Capitol. Burkhardt, he noticed, treated his Senators and the judiciary with some respect, but begrudged Congressmen common politeness. The reasons, explained Mencken's father, were that they were so numerous, and were given to raising a ruckus in barrooms—caterwauling and wrestling![8]

So much for the glories of high-ranking Washingtonians. A different glory attached itself to the character of the much less transient Marylanders as they developed a character and inspired writers to reflect it in verse and story. In the state center, Baltimore, that character was especially vivid and author-reflectors of it, numerous. For a place to have both character and reflector is a feat, though even more astonishing is its having a *genius loci,* a writer who captured the spirit of a place and perfectly represents it. Baltimore's is H. L. Mencken. Not only did he embody that corner of America for outsiders, but he also caught its spirit in books the way Charles Dickens did London's or James Joyce, Dublin's. Mencken's like is rare in any American city, except Boston. As a prominent Baltimorean recently asserted, "If we're talking about the truly local writer, native, with long residence here, the city showing in his work, and with an international reputation and great influence—we have our monument."[9]

Mencken will be a guide in the pages ahead. Right now he can help list specific Maryland traits to look for. The basis for character there on the Chesapeake, he asserted, was a feeling for the hearth, for the immemorial lares and penates: "A Baltimorean is not merely John Doe, an isolated individual of homo sapiens, exactly like every other John Doe. He is John Doe of a certain place—of Baltimore, of a definite house in Baltimore."[10]

Along with this rootedness we should list a trait that we could call skeptical conservatism. With it come slowness to change and complacency—even smugness. Another offshoot may be the tolerance of sins of the flesh that Russell Baker noticed in 1973. (Baker had grown up and worked in Baltimore and was then a syndicated columnist in Washington.) Here is part of his analysis:

I have always liked the sense of sin that emanates from Baltimore. Coming from Washington with its dull clerk's respectability, its truly monumental criminal operators and its pleasing absorption in large-scale homicide, I feel that I am re-entering civilization when the car enters the yellow smog of South Baltimore and heads into the stately dilapidation clinging to the edge of downtown.

There is a promise of pleasure to come. We will eat well. Conversation will be lighter, racier. Women will be more — what? Provocative. Somebody will talk about horses.

What I anticipate, of course, are the pleasures of sin. They seem so civilized after the vices with which Washington is concerned.[11]

Besides this tolerance of sin, the Baltimorean's (and Marylander's) conservatism makes for a refusal to be carried away by movements, ideologies, or causes. Certain forms of snobbery are engendered there by birth, upbringing, or schooling. This snobbery particularly values the length of time a person and his or her family have been there.

That value naturally led to dynasties and to a citizenry that wants to keep things as they are. And so the daring souls — and writers are daring and restless — leave. The Baltimore poet and advisor to poets Richard Hart recalls that, "Again and again over the years I've had conversations with a young man or woman of which the theme was, 'I've got to get out of here.'"[12] Many of these escapees sought haven in New York. There they found what a literary culture requires: the slashing across lines of race and class.

They left a place where, according to the Maryland-born poet Julia Randall, it is "the environs of the single history that matters and has force." In her poem "Maryland," a true Baltimorean could wear sneakers on the Rue de la Paix but not on Charles Street, where the very buildings looked at her with Grandmother's eyes![13] But whether the emigrant writers move to Paris or just New York, Maryland leaves its mark and appears in their writings. Hart says that the mark is there even in the case of the cleverer folk, though subtly, rather than obviously. The cleverer folk in the 20th century who left include Karl Shapiro, Murray Kempton, Russell Baker, Huntington Cairns, Walter Lord, Leon Uris, and Adrienne Rich.

When I asked the poet Adrienne Rich what picture came to her mind when she thought of Baltimore, she assured me that she hadn't written "about" Baltimore — only out of her early experiences in it. In light of those experiences, which she commented on earlier, readers shouldn't be surprised that the image that came to her mind was of "The Pennsylvania Railroad station, which has changed astonishingly little since I was a child in the 1930s and 40s — gateway to distances, journeys, places of departures and returns in my later years, place of meetings and separations."[14]

In the case of the genius who stayed put, Mencken, the characteristic mark of the place came through admiration for old manners and patriarchal ways. He liked the ideal of aristocracy, and he thought that the South should have won the Civil War. Like Poe, he voted against the mass of democratic readers—their sentimentality, pretentiousness, and superficiality. In other writers too we should expect to find this sensitivity to Maryland's hierarchy of class.

This trait allies Marylanders with the South more than with the North. Some observers find that the foundation of Maryland's charm is Southernness. Certainly 19th-century foreign tourists always noticed swift changes as they journeyed south from Philadelphia. They recognized that Maryland, like neighboring Virginia, had developed its character under the influence of wealth from land cultivated for tobacco. That prosperity had depended upon the humid, mild climate—and on slavery. One English traveller of 1792 found a lack there of what he called individual and national energy. He blamed the inferiority on climate and slave-labor. Since he thought the farming was slovenly and individuals more idle and dissipated than in the North, he advised his English readers to settle in Pennsylvania.[15]

A century later Henry Adams pointed at the Southernness and something more—the Tidewater climate. He described Maryland's springtime this way: "The brooding heat of the profligate vegetation; the cool charm of the running water; the terrific splendor of the June thunder-gust in the deep and solitary woods, were all sensual, animal, elemental. No European spring had shown him the same intermixture of delicate grace and passionate depravity that marked the Maryland May. He loved it too much, as though it were Greek and half human."[16]

Such extravagance of language always broke out in *The Education of Henry Adams* when he talked about Maryland. A Boston emigré, Adams had lived most of his life in Washington and always loved the surrounding Maryland countryside. His lines here make a good introduction for yet another regional characteristic, what F. Scott Fitzgerald called a flair for the fantastic and extravagant. Fitzgerald listed Poe and Dashiell Hammett as examples and could have included himself and James M. Cain. (All these writers also had in common strong Irish genes.) With this flair goes love of words. Russell Baker once contrasted the political flannel-mouths of Washington with Spiro Agnew's revelling in lexicographical exotica.[17] Such revelling we find also in Mencken's prose, as well as in oldtime Southern oratory.

Another Southern connection, the presence of so many descendants

of African slaves, produced another characteristic of the place, awareness of a second culture. Undoubtedly black Marylanders have
influenced literature, particularly through black English and black
songs. A white writer with Maryland ties, Gertrude Stein traced the
beginning of her revolutionary books (as she called them) to her
delivering babies in East Baltimore rowhouses![8] As a medical student
at Johns Hopkins Hospital, she attended poor women, and later
recalled black families and places that she used in her best-known
story "Melanctha," one of *Three Lives*. In it Gertrude Stein caught
the world of the descendants of slaves. Besides that, her use of black
language rhythms inspired black writer Richard Wright. For all the
awareness of black culture, however, black Marylanders wrote little.
And whites in the working classes similarly produced no proletarian
literature. In fact, this region hasn't been the kind of place to nurture
much of that brand of writing.

A final regional characteristic — one including the majority of blacks
— was pointed out to me by the novelist Anne Tyler: "A few years
back, one of the *Sunpapers* published a picture to announce the
coming of spring. It showed a street cleaner, looking very grumpy
and grimy, doggedly pushing his broom, while directly above him
that Mt. Vernon Place statue of a little sprite was dancing away on
one toe. I don't know why this should sum up Baltimore for me, but
it does — perhaps because it combines blue-collar grittiness with a
capacity for enjoyment that I think abounds in Baltimore." Tyler said
that the most Baltimorean of her books was probably *Dinner at the
Homesick Restaurant* (1983), "because I'd lived here longest when
I wrote it and more of the atmosphere had had a chance to soak in."[19]

In this literary history we shall see just how much of Maryland's
atmosphere soaked in during 350 years.

II
Annapolis Wits and Baltimore Bards

Colonial writing — satirical and patriotic at its best —
also America's first poet-laureate, her first novel, and
the first flowering of George Washington's cherry tree.

> "Our fires are wood, our houses are good;
>   Our diet is sawney & Homine.
> Drink, juice of the apple, tobaccoe's our staple,
>   Gloria tibi domine."[1]
>   — Old Maryland song from before 1740

> "There was not a literary man, for aught I could find nearer than
> England; nor were literary attainments, beyond merely reading or
> writing, at all in vogue or repute."[2]
>   — Rev. Jonathan Boucher, Tory
>   Rector of St. Anne's, Annapolis,
>   just before the American Revolution

The Second grand Anniversary Procession.

An 18th-century example of Maryland pioneering in literature was the Tuesday Club, Annapolis, here caricatured by the secretary, Dr. Alexander Hamilton. Members were immigrants from Great Britain, who wrote satires and other neo-classic works. One of them edited *The Maryland Gazette,* oldest newspaper south of Philadelphia. At rear right is a rare view of the state house that preceded the present one.

Colonial Marylanders lagged behind New England and Philadelphia in the race for literary reputation, and natives haven't yet lost their sense of inferiority. No Maryland writer arose to match New England's Jonathan Edwards or Philadelphia's Benjamin Franklin. Even the poems of the fifth Lord Baltimore, proprietor of the colony, came off poorly next to other leaders' writings, such as William Penn's meditations, *The Fruits of Solitude,* or Governor William Bradford's history, *Of Plymouth Plantation.* Lord Baltimore's book was laughed at by critics and never read.

Other works of Maryland's first 150 years surpassed his Lordship's poetry. (Parson Weems's life of George Washington is an example.) But much of merit failed to attract literary historians and anthologists, chiefly New Englanders. To them, Maryland had long seemed a watery waste compared to flowering Boston. Questioning their view is part of the purpose of this chapter—indeed of this whole book. This chapter's main purpose is to survey colonial Maryland writing.

Let us begin with a bird's-eye view. As in other colonies, writing in Maryland began with promotional puffs to lure settlers. Next came religious and political tracts. Belles lettres appeared early in the 18th century with Ebenezer Cook's satiric poem "The Sot-Weed Factor" (1708). Its chief character took a jaundiced look at the colony. (Two centuries later he reappeared in a novel of the same name by John Barth, a native Marylander.) Other secular poems appeared throughout the 18th century, pieces imitating formal English works. Though these poems were written in or about Maryland, all but one of the writers in this chapter came from England or Scotland. On this side of the water they planted literary seeds that they brought with them. But the new soil and climate failed to change the crop appreciably.

The crop wasn't without interest, though. As a literary historian, I could boast that an immigrant, Richard Lewis, gave Maryland the best neo-classic poems in all the colonies. I would be forced to add, however, that Lewis was one of the dunces attacked by the English literary dictator Alexander Pope in *The Dunciad.* (Small honor to be a victim of Pope's satire.)

Also worth a boast was the publication in Annapolis of the first belles lettres in the South. In that capital English and Scots immigrants formed one of the outstanding literary coteries in all the colonies, the Tuesday Club. It stood as model for other such clubs, including the Delphian Club in early 19th-century Baltimore. Then, for another boast, add a first for lovers of the novel: *Adventures of Alonso: Containing Some Striking Anecdotes of the Present Prime*

Minister Of Portugal (1775) was the first novel written by an American. The author was identified on the title page simply as a "Native of Maryland Some Years Resident in Lisbon" (it probably was Thomas A. Digges).

Almost as fictional as that novel were Parson Mason Locke Weems's biographies of Washington and other patriots. Fiction or fact, his books brought Maryland literary fortunes to a climax. As author, Weems was the first native-born Marylander to deserve a big patch on the map of early writers. His patch should be even larger because he peddled books up and down the Republic and thus helped keep the light of literacy aglow. Weems aspired "to Enlighten, to Dulcify and Exhalt Human Nature—by GOOD BOOKS."

With these achievements in mind, let us turn to a chronological survey. We begin with an English writer of promotional pieces, George Alsop, who sailed to the Chesapeake and wrote with flair of experiences there. He came in 1658 and published his "Character of the Province of Maryland" eight years later in London. Some readers think that it is as scurrilous a piece of promotional writing as one will find anywhere. Others say that it is almost literature and is close to the crackling wit of the London stages. Here is his elaborate, inventive style in part of a 100-word sentence:

Mary-land is a Province situated upon the large extending bowels of America *under the Government of the Lord* Baltimore, *adjacent northwardly upon the Confines of* New-England, *and neighboring Southwardly upon* Virginia, *swelling pleasantly upon the Bay of Choesapike...being within her own embraces extraordinarily pleasant and fertile. Pleasant, in respect of the multitude of Navigable Rivers and Creeks that conveniently and most profitably lodge within the arms of her green, spreading, and delightful woods; whose natural womb (by her plenty) maintains and preserves the several diversities of Animals that rangingly inhabit her Woods; as she doth otherwise generously fructify this piece of Earth with almost all sorts of Vegetables, as well Flowers with their varieties of Colors and smells, as Herbs and Roots....*[3]

Alsop's book clearly is a serious promotional tract for Englishmen with itchy feet. But much of this *Character* shows the author to have been a London literary wit. In it he combined verse and prose to satirize English society and some Americans—Maryland Quakers, for example, as well as New England Puritans. And the tone throughout is burlesque. In the following lines he made fun of the commonly held unrealistic vision of Maryland as the land of unlimited opportunity:

The Women that go over into this Province as Servants, have the best luck here as in any place of the world besides; for they are no sooner on shoar, but they are courted into a Copulative Matrimony, which some of them (for ought I know) had they not come to such a Market with their Virginity, might have kept it by them untill it had been mouldy, unless they had let it out by a yearly rent to some of the Inhabitants of Lewknors-lane, *or made a Deed of Gift of it to Mother* Coney, *having only a poor stipend out of it, untill the Gallows or Hospital called them away. Men have not altogether so good luck as Women in this kind, or natural performent, without they be good Rhetoricians, and well vers'd in the Art of perswasion, then (probably) they may ryvet themselves in the time of their Servitude into the private and reserved favour of their Mistress, if Age speak their Master deficient.*[4]

Before he wrote this work Alsop had been indentured in 1658 to another Royalist emigré, Thomas Stockett. They settled next to Susquehanna Indians near Havre de Grace, Harford County. He stayed only a little over four years, even though being a servant in the American wilderness beat the life he had endured in England.

Another immigrant, Ebenezer Cook, might well have discouraged Londoners from moving to Maryland when he published his poem "The Sot-Weed Factor." According to the speaker, America is a "shore, where no good sense is found, / But conversation's lost, and manners drown'd."[5]

In making fun of the crudeness of colonial life, this poem also spoofs the false picture promotional writers (not Alsop) gave of the wilderness as a paradise. The author presumably knew what he was satirizing, though we don't have much evidence to go on. What we know a Baltimore librarian dug out. Cook was the son of a London merchant who owned 1,000 acres on Cook's Point, Dorchester County. Probably as agent in Maryland for his father in 1694, Cook collected the evidence which he published in his poem after his return home. In 1717 he returned to settle, first in Cecil County and then in Prince George's. He wrote for *The Maryland Gazette* and in 1731 published "Sotweed Redivivus: or the Planters Looking Glass." Of the two poems, an early literary historian decided, the 1708 version had an abundance of filth and scurrility but had wit too, whereas the later poem lacked only the wit.[6]

The title "The Sot-Weed Factor" was an epithet for Maryland's chief source of income then, tobacco (meaning the weed that makes one drunk), and the hero was exiled by poverty to Maryland, "intending there to open store." There this stranger was swindled by everybody from a Quaker planter to a doctor, who was also a lawyer. Every day was a nightmare of deceit and discomfort. No wonder that he ended with a curse: let cannibals be shipped to Maryland to revenge him, and "May Wrath Divine then lay those Regions waste / Where no Man's faithful, nor a Woman Chaste."

To make his point, Cook chose the fast-paced, awkward rhythm of a verse form used for satire by Samuel Butler in *Hudibras*. It offers plenty of chance for rhyme, and so is suited to humor. For example, Maryland planters are

as tawney as a Moor:
Figures so strange, no God design'd
To be a part of Humane kind:
But wanton Nature, void of Rest,
Moulded the brittle Clay in Jest.

Describing a meal and aftermath, Cook wrote,
Whilst Pone, with Milk and Mush well stor'd,
In Wooden Dishes grac'd the Board,
With Hominy and Sider-pap,
(Which scarce a hungry dog wou'd lap)
Well stuff'd with Fat from Bacon fry'd,
Or with Melasses dulcify'd.
Then out our Landlord pulls a Pouch,
As greasy as the Leather Couch
On which he sat, and streight begun
To load with Weed his Indian Gun,
In length scarce longer than one's Finger
Or that for which the Ladies linger.

Even with sentiments like those, Cook became Poet Laureate of Maryland. How he earned the title is a mystery. Even in a small, new province, it was something to wear the laurels of poetry and lord it over the neglected other poets. Possibly that honor was bestowed by the Assembly, of which his patron Thomas Bordley was Speaker. Maybe it was a joke. But if it was, then why did Cook print "Poet-Laureat, of Maryland" on his "Mors Omnibus Communis. An Elogy on the Death of Thomas Bordley, Esq." (1726 or 1727)? What is important to literary history is that Cook was the first poet laureate in Maryland. That title has been revived and today honors Lucille Clifton. Maryland stands out among states as one that thus officially enwreathes the literary arts.

Cook's rival for the honor, Richard Lewis, late of Eton College, suffered the opposite kind of recognition, ridicule from the giant poet of the English Augustan Age, Alexander Pope. In the satiric *Dunciad* (1728) waspish Pope stung him for cataloguing in verse the plants of the Patapsco region (Lewis settled near the site of Baltimore), and also for being the first poet to mention the hummingbird. Pope wrote:

Yet by some object ev'ry brain is stirr'd;
The dull may waken to a Humming-bird;
The most recluse, discreetly open'd, find
Congenial matter in the Cockle-kind;
The mind, in Metaphysics at a loss,
May wander in a wilderness of Moss . . .[7]

Pope was right in condemning verse so inferior to his own. Lewis may also have lost Pope's favor through overpraising Maryland, where every planter opened his door to entertain strangers and the poor, and where

That good Old-English Hospitality
When ev'ry House to ev'ry Guest was free;
Whose Flight from Britain's Isle, her Bards bemone,
Seems here with Pleasure to have fix'd her Throne.[8]

Today such sentiments echo in the verse of enthusiastic Marylanders. But then our contemporaries have no Pope to criticize them.

Maybe Pope's strictures helped raise standards for other American poets then. In Maryland prospects for literature improved with inauguration of a good printing shop and the first newspaper, *The Maryland Gazette* (1727). It was the first newspaper in the South. For that paper, the printer William Parks solicited local writing, including verse. Soon he published the first belletristic book in the colony and in the whole South, a translation by Lewis of a Latin poem: Edward Holdsworth's *The Mouse Trap* (1728). It was satire, and if it is put next to Cook's "The Sot-Weed Factor" and parts of Alsop's *Character of Maryland,* the conclusion is inviting: satire was the Maryland mode. Later the satiric strain was strong in Poe and Mencken, and today shines in the writings of Karl Shapiro and John Barth.

Truth to tell, not much of that satire or other writing interests us today. Occasionally a curious piece of verse does turn up and is printed. Recently the Maryland State Poetry Society published a page about Mrs. Brasseya Johnson Allen's *Pastorals, Elegies, Odes, Epistles and Other Poems* (1806). She had written these poems before 1785 as "the amusement of my youthful hours and mostly composed while

I was engaged at my needle."[9] But this notice appeared because her book may have been the first collected volume of poems by a woman printed in Maryland. As the first, she was harbinger of numerous 20th-century female poets, most of them better than she was.

Also better were lines I found carved on a memorial plaque affixed to the wall of Midleham Chapel of Ease, Calvert County:
The soul secur'd in her existence smiles
at the drawn dagger and defies its point
The stars shall fade away the sun himself
grow dim with age and Nature sink in years,
but thou shalt flourish in immortal youth
unhurt amidst the war of elements
the wrecks of matter and the crush of worlds.
These lines commemorate the 15-year-old son of the rector, and accompany a heraldic device and the date of the boy's death, 5 January 1759. Who the author was isn't stated, but probably the lines are quoted from a popular poem by Edward Young, English clergyman and poet, well known for *Night Thoughts* (1742-1745).

Lines of this power could not have been written in 18th-century backwoods Calvert County, though English priests here and there were imitating their home poets. For example, over the Bay in Chestertown an Anglican priest, James Sterling, was writing imitations of the English poem "The Seasons." He never matched his model, though he tried to evoke Maryland with lines such as,
Where Susquehanna foams with rock-raised spray,
And swells loved Chesapeake's capacious Bay.[10]

Generally in the mid-18th century literary culture was thin. What there was had to appear in Annapolis, and then only in the season. Literate Marylanders left their isolated plantations for court and legislative sessions, for theatre and horse races. The rest of the time those of them who read simply enjoyed their classics and months-old issues of London's *Gentleman's Magazine* at home.

They savored remnants of their European education along with their toddy. And they went to the theatre. We might be surprised at how often these planters did venture out to see Shakespeare performed in towns around the Chesapeake. For example, in 1751 the Murray, Kean Company came over from a run in Williamsburg. They gave shows not only in Annapolis, but also in Upper Marlborough, Piscataway, Port Tobacco, and Chestertown. Writing on the eve of the American Revolution in Annapolis, the English diarist William Eddis recorded his pleasure in theatre so far from what he called the great

St. John's College, Annapolis, (with McDowell Hall center, topped by cupola) was where Francis Scott Key studied. Just off the left margin of this late 19th-century photograph stands the birthplace of James M. Cain, a house resembling those at far right.

Cook's Point, Dorchester County, Eastern Shore, was a tobacco plantation owned in colonial times by a London sot-weed factor, who was the father of Ebenezer Cook, poet-laureate of Maryland and satirist of colonial crudities. The house pictured was built after Cook's time, but shows the style developed by creators of a Chesapeake culture.

Thomas Jefferson was one of five literary Presidents — Abraham Lincoln, Theodore Roosevelt, Woodrow Wilson, and John F. Kennedy.

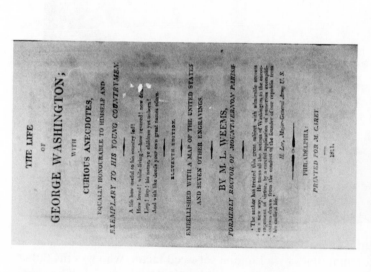

Title page of a major addition to patriotic literature by a Marylander, Parson Mason Locke Weems of Anne Arundel County. Weems wrote and peddled books to encourage literacy as well as patriotism.

For decades Washington was a city in name only and nurtured few writers. How barren it was when freshly carved out of Maryland can be seen in this watercolor sketch (ca. 1803) by Nicholas King, City Surveyor, with the White House in back, left of center.

mart of genius, London.

Far from London in more senses than one, Richard Bard, an amateur writer in Maryland's Piedmont, wrote about frontier cruelty. His manuscript was what literary historians call a captivity narrative, the account of kidnapping of settlers by Indians. These "Indian Captivities" proved popular first as fact and then in fiction. James Fenimore Cooper's *The Last of the Mohicans* and William Faulkner's "Red Leaves" are examples.

The usual ingredients of adventure and personal heroism appeared in Bard's Maryland captivity narrative. But his account is unusual in that it was in verse. The verse is inept, one reason his book isn't read. He wrote it after his escape from captivity and several years after his wife's release for a ransom of 40 pounds.

Here is his story: During the French and Indian War 19 Delaware Indians surrounded the Bards' house at present-day Virginia Mills (then Bard's Mill and part of Frederick County, Maryland, though now in Adams County, Pennsylvania). They captured nine settlers, including six youngsters. The youngest they took from his father's arms, Bard recorded, and "Both head and heart the tomahawk pierced, / In order him to slay." Further along the trail westward over the Alleghenies, they tomahawked another of the party:

O, terrifying 'twas indeed
To hear his dying screams,
And from his head and heart to view
Those red and running streams.
But at his terror they did laugh,
They [the Indians] mock his dying groans:
Most artfully they imitate
His last expiring moans.

Bard escaped and traveled for nine days "In a starving state, / Not having any means of strength, / Except the snake I ate." His conclusion was,

O cruel man in vain you strive,
In vain you follow me:
For since the Lord gainsaith I can
No more your captive be.
God the device can disappoint
Of crafty folk and wise:
So that perform they can't always
Their cruel enterprise.[11]

Even while Bard was led captive over wild mountains, literate planters of Tidewater were busy absorbing the ideas of the European Enlightenment. Marylanders and Virginians were then developing a Chesapeake civilization centered on Annapolis and Williamsburg. Colleges helped. In Annapolis, St. John's College grew out of King William's School, and its graduates like to say it is third in order of founding after William and Mary and Harvard. The Eastern Shore had its college, too, later called Washington College, at Chestertown.

A collegiate sidelight to Maryland history: back before the founding of Maryland a scholar named Edward Palmer of Magdalen College, Oxford University, established a trading post on an island off Cecil County in the Susquehanna River and intended founding a college — Academia Virginiensis et Oxoniensis. Had Palmer succeeded, his college would have predated Harvard. And his Chesapeake scholars could have delighted in Shakespeare's and John Milton's books hot off the press.

But St. John's College did come along early to aid literary culture. It benefited from the light of cultivated neighbors. For example, the intellectual leader of Annapolis was a graduate of the University of Edinburgh. That is not surprising, for the vigorous Scottish Enlightenment sent books and men to educate bright Americans such as Jefferson. And it sent stimulating Dr. Alexander Hamilton to practice medicine in Annapolis. Even though he died relatively young at 42, he managed to raise intellectual and literary levels there.

Hamilton knew firsthand that America could furnish a facsimile of the urbane society of readers that he had known back in Scotland. So in his writings he could venture on new ground. For instance, he wrote the earliest sustained aesthetic criticism of drama in 1755. Doubtless he could do so because Maryland welcomed acting companies, as some other colonial communities did not. For another example of his innovating, his "Quevedo" essay in *The Maryland Gazette* of 1748 was the first criticism anywhere of a number of American authors treated together. This interest in the New World also showed in his appreciation of American nature and scenery. No wonder he also satirized the false ideals of the English. That was partly because he was a Scot and also had married into a leading Maryland political family, the Dulanys.

His major contribution to culture was in the role of Loquacious Scribble, M.D., secretary and orator of the Ancient and Honorable Tuesday Club. In the clubbable age of Dr. Samuel Johnson's London, this Annapolis group modeled itself on the Whin-bush Club of Edinburgh. To its meetings in members' residences came distinguished guests such as Benjamin Franklin in 1754. Since members had fanciful pen names, Franklin was called "Electro Vitrifrico." This club supposedly was model for other clubs in the colonies, all aimed, Hamilton said, to civilize and humanize mankind.

Fortunately for lovers of good reading, Hamilton drew on Tuesday Club meetings for the finest humorous writing in colonial literature (so scholars of 18th-century letters tell us). He clearly profited from reading Rabelais, Cervantes, and Montaigne. His importance as a writer hasn't been fully recognized because his manuscripts are only now being printed. His long *History of the Tuesday Club,* in manuscript at Johns Hopkins University, has the same humor as Henry Fielding's famous novel *The History of Tom Jones, Foundling* (1749). In it he included poems and accounts of the literature of Maryland. He also illustrated his text with humorous sketches of members and meetings. As an example of this book's mock-heroic style, here is Hamilton's description of a fellow member, Jonas Green:

This gentleman is of a middle Stature. Inclinable to fat, round-faced, small lively eyes, from which, as from two oriental portals, incessantly dart the dawning rays of wit and humor, with a considerable mixture of the amorous leer, in his countenance he wears a constant smile, having never been once seen to frown; his body is thick and well-set, and for one of his make and stature he has a good sizeable belly, into which he loves much to convey the best vittles and drink, being a good clean knife and forks man, tho' no Glutton, and his favorite Dish is Roast turkey with oisters, and his darling liquor of late is Grog, he professing himself to be of the modern Sect of Grogorians, and as some think the patron and founder of that sect in Annapolis, which we shall have occasion to describe somewhere in this history, he is a very great admirer, Improver and encourager of wit, humor and drollery, and is fond of that sort of poetry which is called Doggerell, in which he is himself a very great proficient, and confines his genius chiefly to it, tho sometimes he cannot help emitting some flashes of the true sublime, in his club compositions.[12]

Green and other members emitted truly sublime wit in the Battle of Annapolis Wits and Baltimore Bards, as one campaigner called it. It began in a Baltimore County church, we are told, when the eloquent preacher George Whitefield lost the attention of the Rev. Thomas Craddock to a pretty girl in the next pew. The verses Craddock wrote about her came to the eyes of the Tuesday Club: Club members wrote verses in ridicule. Against their satire another

Baltimore County priest, Thomas Chase, joined Craddock to write a long poem praising "The Baltimore Belles."

Such bad verse travels fast. That poem supposedly was found lying on a tavern table and then was circulated in manuscript. An attack on it by an Annapolis Wit appeared in *The Maryland Gazette,* December 17, 1745, as "An Infallible Receipt to cure the Epidemical and Afflecting Distempers of Love and the Poetical Itch."

The battle was joined. Chase lampooned the Wits, calling them dunces, and comparing their writings to different kinds of excrement. At the end of the poetical battle, Dr. Hamilton ran a mock advertisement in the *Gazette* for a runaway servant, "A dapper-witted, *finical Fopling,* known by the Name of Bard, alias, Bavius," whose conversation "turns chiefly on excrementilious subjects." It ended by promising that "any Person who goes upon the *chace*" will be suitably rewarded with "the profit of his poems for one hundred years to come."[13] Annapolis had the victory—or at least the last words.

One of the victors, Tuesday Clubber Jonas Green, was public printer of Maryland and published the poets that we care to recall from the mid-18th century. Among them is his own burlesque of a contemporary genre, the meditative nature poem. Its title misleads the reader into expecting a serious poem: "A Seine Hauling in Severn River, near a delightful Spring at the foot of Constitution Hill." It begins,

Six bottles of wine, right old, good and clear
A dozen, at least, of English strong beer;
Six quarts of good rum, to make punch and grogg
(The latter a drink that's now much in vogue);
Some cyder, if sweet, would not be amiss–
Of butter six pounds, we can't do with less;
A tea-kettle, tea, and all the tea-gear–
To treat the ladies, and also small beer;
Sugar, lemons, a strainer, likewise a spoon–
Two china bowls to drink out of at noon;

This poem runs on to list all the utensils needed for a picnic, and ends with the reminder that "for fear of bad luck at catching of fish" they should carry with them "a ready dress'd dish."[14]

Such mockery attacked the contempt some Englishmen showed for Americans, an attitude Green resented. In those decades before the American Revolution, no Maryland-connected writer was better at expressing that resentment than John Dickinson. He was a native of Talbot County, where Dickinsons had lived for four generations.

He studied law at the Middle Temple, London, practiced in Delaware and Pennsylvania, and served as governor of both states. Besides his prose *Letter from a Farmer in Pennsylvania* (1767), he aided the patriot's cause with the popular "A Song of American Freedom" (1768).

Such writings helped precipitate the American Revolution. Another Marylander, Parson Mason Locke Weems, helped sustain its ideals. Weems's biographies of Washington, Franklin, and Francis Marion made him the most popular of all writers connected with Maryland in his day and for decades afterwards. He ranks at the top, therefore, in this 18th-century chapter, though we don't read his books. Weems's legacy to us, of course, is our image of George Washington. Despite doubts of its truth, that image has come down in the story of Little George and the cherry tree. Supposedly he got the tale from an old lady connected with Washington's family. Weems in fact had married into a family closely related to Washington's mother, Mary Ball.

The story goes that George at age six inadvertently — unluckily, says Weems — "tried the edge of his hatchet on the body of a beautiful young English cherry tree, which he barked so terribly that I don't believe the tree ever got the better of it." When asked if he knew who killed the tree,

George staggered under it for a moment, but quickly recovered himself; and looking at his father with the sweet face of youth brightened with the inexpressible charm of all-conquering truth, he bravely cried out, "I can't tell a lie, Pa; you know I can't tell a lie. I did cut it with my hatchet." — "Run to my arms, you dearest boy," cried his father in transports, "run to my arms; sad as I am, George, that you killed my tree; for you have paid me for it a thousand-fold. Such as act of heroism in my son is worth more than a thousand trees, though blossomed with silver and their fruits of purest gold!"[15]

No cherry trees are reported in Weems's own Maryland childhood. The youngest of 19 children, Weems was born at Marshes Seat, near Herring Bay in Anne Arundel County, 15 miles south of Annapolis. From there he went to Chestertown as a student at the school that became Washington College and then to England as a medical student.

Back in America he decided to become an Episcopal priest. After the American Revolution he again went to England, this time as one of the first two American priests to be ordained. His parish was All Hallows Church at Davidsonville, Anne Arundel County (1784–1792). Then he turned to selling books up and down the coast and to writing books to sell. Why he left off preaching we don't know. From the comments of his bishop we gather that his views were too liberal. For one thing, he preached anywhere, even a ballroom. For another, he permitted Methodists and men of other denominations to preach in his church.

In 1792 he published a medical pamphlet called *Onania*, the text taken from an English book. It sold well, so he left off preaching and took up with Mathew Carey, a Philadelphia publisher, in 1793 as a salesman. After that and for 31 years, he sold books from New York to Savannah, mostly from a Jersey wagon equipped with bookshelves.

In between journeys Weems tried his innovative hand at writing. We know that just six months before Washington's death in 1799, his publisher Carey accepted reluctantly the biography of Washington that was to sell so well even at the then high price of fifty cents. It went through more than 50 editions.

An illustration of Weems's industriousness is his letter to his major source of information about Francis Marion: "I beg you to indulge no fears that Marion will ever die, while I can say or write anything to immortalize him. I hope in three weeks to have it all chiselled out in the rough cast. It will then take me another three weeks to polish and color it in a style that will, I hope, sometimes excite a smile and sometimes call forth the tear."[16]

For years afterwards Weems called forth many a smile and tear. With his books I end the survey of colonial Maryland writing. Looking back over the preceding 175 years, I come again to the question asked at the opening of this chapter: was the Maryland literary landscape only a watery waste? The answer must be no, even though nobody there matched New England's Edward Taylor and Anne Bradstreet, whose religious poems are still read. Remember, though, that those two poets were English Puritans, a group that sanctified writing. The few Puritans who came to Maryland seem to have been fighters, not writers. And though the puritanical sect called Quakers settled in numbers, they always prohibited belles lettres. Only the new national capital Washington boasted brilliant writers, all of them politicians. Of them, the one literary genius in the White House before Lincoln was Thomas Jefferson. His most quoted words as president he wrote in 1809 on leaving office:

The station which we occupy among the nations of the earth is honorable, but awful. Trusted with the destinies of this solitary republic of the world, the only monument of human rights, and the sole depository of the sacred fire of freedom and self-government, from hence it is to be lighted up in other regions of the earth, if other regions of the earth shall ever become susceptible of its benign influence. All mankind ought then, with us, to rejoice in its prosperous, and sympathize in its adverse fortunes, as involving everything dear to man. And to what sacrifices of interest, or convenience, ought not these considerations to animate us? To what compromises of opinion and inclination to maintain harmony and union among ourselves and to preserve from all danger this hallowed ark of human hope and happiness?[17]

Years before Jefferson's presidency and long before Weems completed his printed pantheon of American heroes, Marylanders had set the character of their place and were eager to have writers express it. They weren't disappointed, as we shall see. For with Weems's biographies we have the beginning of the end of the era when authors there could do little but imitate English literature. We wonder how many native geniuses in April 1800 read Baltimore editor John Colvin's invitation "to those who are accustomed to wield the pen, to furnish me with their labors" in belles lettres for *The Baltimore Weekly Magazine*. His invitation opened this way: "In offering this work to the world, I do it with a confidence in public patronage not easily to be shaken; nor will I believe, until actual experiment shall have proven the fact, but that Baltimore will afford a liberal support to one literary establishment, whilst the more northern towns abound with publications of the same nature, and meet with a generous encouragement."[18]

The time was ripe for the growth of native literature in Maryland.

III
Rising Glories of City and Nation

Creation of the national song, "The Star-Spangled Banner," and of the myth of the Old South, as well as of a nursery for Poe's genius.

"I have been feasting my eye for some time on the rich, diversified and boundless future grandeur of this city [Baltimore, 1822] and the rising glories of the nation...."[1]

— William Wirt

"Our literature in the lifetime of the present generation [1850] has grown to a maturity which has given it a distinctive and honorable place in that aggregate which forms national character."[2]

— John Pendleton Kennedy

Francis Scott Key Monument, Baltimore, dramatizes the poet's offering his "Star-Spangled Banner" to Columbia. Altamont Hotel is in back (demolished).

In the 1820s Baltimore was rising to a grandeur — of Baltimore Clipper sails, domes, spires, and landmark books. It was also a place reaching literary maturity. One reason was the coming to Baltimore of America's chief author of the 1800–1820 period, William Wirt. (He wrote the first national biography worth reading.) Another reason was his protégé John Pendleton Kennedy, who raised the level of American fiction.

In this ascent up literary Mount Everest, no writer climbed higher than a newcomer to town, Edgar Allan Poe. He settled there in 1829, full of genius but unknown. In Baltimore this young man of 20 sought one patron, Wirt, and found another, Kennedy. Poe dared the steep ascent to literary heights when these two Baltimoreans were guiding the unusually large number of literati there. If we can imagine them as Poe's literary sherpas (and he did regard them as such), then we can regard Baltimore as training slope for his talents. This chapter examines that city's literary culture of the 1820s as preparation for Poe, the first writer there of international significance.

In 1829 innovation was in the air. Poe's arrival coincided with the opening of the Chesapeake and Delaware Canal, a link with Philadelphia and the North. He was there at the inauguration of the Baltimore and Ohio Railroad, a swift route to the West and the first major track in America. Baltimoreans built the first American steam locomotive just down the street from where Poe's *Al Aaraaf, Tamerlane and Minor Poems* was printed.

No wonder Baltimoreans impressed visitors with their cocksureness. Moreover, their town was second in size only to New York (1830 census), and in hospitality to reform movements they seem to have surpassed more staid towns like New York. Their airy new prison, for example, was admired by Charles Dickens, though some people called it derisively "a palace for felons." As for medical care, townspeople founded the third medical school in the country and the first dental school in the world. Moreover, the city was the capital for free blacks and a center for their organized churches. (Frederick Douglass worshipped in one of them.) Baltimoreans sometimes led the nation in abolition, temperance, and women's rights.

Baltimore also led the nation in wickedness. It was notorious as "Mob Town." In an early mob scene, Poe's grandfather, David Poe, took part in an attack on a newspaper editor for not supporting George Washington. A later mob destroyed the press of another editor whose policies they didn't like, and tore down the printing house. When that editor didn't give in, the crowd again attacked and even pursued him and his supporters into the jail, where they had locked themselves. There several men were killed and others beaten and stabbed. One of the permanently disabled was General "Light Horse Harry" Lee, hero of the American Revolution and father of Robert E. Lee.

On the constructive side, the best young minds of the country came there to make money and to taste the excitements of a boom town. That it was also a world port satisfied these young men's keen zest for enjoyment. (The Hook district of Fells Point, for example, may have provided the epithet "hooker" for prostitute.) But enjoyment wasn't, of course, the only reason ambitious men swarmed to Baltimore. New Englanders, in particular, felt the town's commercial lure. Some of them left disappointed, including Noah Webster, the maker of the first American dictionary. Others came to open businesses, but had more success in literature. John Neal and his partner John Pierpont were examples.

Other New Englanders came to educate the natives, the way they were doing everywhere else. In 1828 a group of them opened the Mount Hope Literary and Scientific Institution, a school touted by Yale's President Jeremiah Day as a builder of character. (The faculty must have been Yale graduates.) To build the town literally came three important architects: Benjamin Latrobe from England, Maximilien Godefroy from France, and Robert Mills from Philadelphia. Their classic restraint created an aesthetic that made Baltimore's rowhouses handsomer than those of other cities. (Classic restraint shaped local writing, too, as we shall see.)

These brick rows filled the Baltimore panorama that impressed the writer William Wirt as he surveyed the town from a hill in 1822 and foretold future grandeur. Like that city, he himself had come a long way through luck and talent. Using one great talent in writing, he had already achieved fame for his pioneering biography of the Revolutionary War patriot Patrick Henry. One stunning feat was his re-creation of the incendiary speech with its famous cry, "Give me liberty or give me death." Since no copy of this speech survived, Wirt had to rely on what people told him. Thus the eloquence that we honor was Wirt's, not Henry's.

Here is the ending of the speech, including Wirt's description of the moment:

"There is no retreat but in submission and slavery! Our chains are forged. Their clanking may be heard on the plains of Boston! The war is inevitable — let it come!! I repeat it, sir, let it come!!!

"It is vain, sir, to extenuate the matter. Gentlemen may cry, peace,

peace — but there is no peace. The war is actually begun! The next gale that sweeps from the north will bring to our ears the clash of resounding arms! Our brethren are already in the field! Why stand we here idle? What is it that gentlemen wish? What would they have? Is life so dear, or peace so sweet, as to be purchased at the price of chains and slavery? Forbid it, Almighty God! — I know not what course others may take; but for me," cried he, with both his arms extended aloft, his brows knit, every feature marked with the resolute purpose of his soul, and his voice swelled to its boldest note of exclamation — "give me liberty, or give me death!"

He took his seat. No murmur of applause was heard. The effect was too deep. After the trance of a moment, several members started from their seats. The cry, "To arms!" seemed to quiver on every lip, and gleam from every eye! Richard H. Lee arose and supported Mr. Henry, with his usual spirit and elegance. But his melody was lost amid the agitations of that ocean, which the master-spirit of the storm had lifted up on high. That supernatural voice still sounded in their ears, and shivered along their arteries. They heard, in every pause, the cry of liberty or death. They became impatient of speech — their souls were on fire for action.[3]

Even as Wirt was prophesying to his daughter the city's bright future, he was creating a more lasting literary work than his *Patrick Henry* or other published books. What he was creating was a series of lively letters to his family. Though these have not been published, except for excerpts, they are well worth inclusion in any literary history of Maryland and the young United States.

This readable treasure of a correspondence grew from Wirt's frequent traveling and his having to use the mails to make his six daughters as literate and generally well-educated as his sons and other men. Such an unorthodox passion gave life to thousands of missives to Laura, Agnes and the rest. In them we find Wirt — a genial gentleman — astonishingly advanced for the 1820s, especially for a Southern place like Baltimore. Other fathers there were training daughters to be ornaments, not competitors.

His advanced notions stemmed partly from his own childhood. He had risen by his own honest efforts — the orphaned son of a Bladensburg innkeeper. His offspring could do the same, he expected, regardless of sex. He wrote one daughter, "Never beg while you can help yourself." As educated women, they were as vital as men to the success of the republican experiment: America required a "highly literate and politically sophisticated constituency." Always they were urged to write well, and they did.

In thus advancing women, Wirt seems true to his character as an innovator. As advocate he had argued landmark cases before the Supreme Court. So famous was he that when Jefferson offered him the professorship of law and the presidency of the University of Virginia, Wirt chose lawyering instead.

His second claim to fame came from his published belles lettres. At 20, as a member of a literary coterie in Richmond, he had contributed to books of essays called *The Rainbow* and *The Old Bachelor.* Most of these were gently satirical and imitative of the English *Spectator.* Then great success came with his novel *Letters of a British Spy* (1803). Success came not just because readers wanted to read about the American Revolution: they were proud that an American had written it. In 1817 he published the pioneering biography of Patrick Henry.

In family letters Wirt covered topics much more humble than America's freedom.[4] He supervised daily life: his daughters should ply the toothbrush assiduously in order to have "a blooming winter," and they should take cold showers. They should walk daily, also, even when they lived in Washington where they ran the danger of encountering crowds of Congressmen. His advice: walk on the opposite side of the street or stick to the side streets. Congressmen in bunches evidently were not to be trusted then.

All this epistolary advice flooded in to Baltimore and Washington for their mother, Elizabeth Washington Wirt, to oversee. She already had to look after what she called the petty details of a large household (five servants besides the ten children). She read a lot, mostly fiction, though she exercised her mind in natural philosophy. Such study relieved ennui, she said. Then in 1829 she enjoyed an intellectual triumph by publishing the first flower dictionary in the country, *Flora's Dictionary.* That popular book showed her literary talent as well as her success in research.

Just before its publication she wrote her husband on vacation at Cape May that the very hot Baltimore weather had prevented operations of the press. She added that she was afraid that the publisher, Fielding Lucas, Jr., would find the notes too voluminous. Lucas printed them all, though he had not taken the trouble to read them. He trusted her judgment.

Of more importance to literary history was her husband's creating the legendary Old South that has since added glamor to *Gone With the Wind* and other novels, plays, and movies. He did this myth-making through his biography of Patrick Henry. It presaged the "Virginia novel," a sub-genre that Wirt's protégé John Pendleton Kennedy also promoted. To create this genre Wirt portrayed the Revolutionary era in Virginia as a golden age of heroic men. Kennedy's four novels made readers admire his imagined Southern Cavalier aristocracy.

It is one of the ironies of literary history that these Baltimore authors, these two city dwellers, dreamed up a paradise of plantations, of delicate ladies in crinoline, and of knights without armor. Why did they do it? The answer seems to be that both Wirt and Kennedy had held political office in an era of democratic leveling, and so they embraced the Cavalier ideal of aristocracy. They liked the old-fashioned conservative gentry with Southern manners. But they disliked the rootless mercenary world coming in with its middle-class values.[5]

Through his mother, an aristocratic Pendleton of Virginia, Kennedy knew Piedmont farms across the Potomac from Maryland. There he often summered. There too he knew his cousins, the writers Philip Pendleton Cooke and John Esten Cooke. All three cousins wrote historical romances. The Cookes relished re-creating medieval times, and Kennedy's *Horse-shoe Robinson* re-created the American Revolution, and his *Rob of the Bowl*, early Maryland. Next to these novels we should put another local historical romance, *Nick of the Woods,* by a sometime Marylander Robert Montgomery Bird. (He lived at Bohemia Neck near Elkton, Cecil County.) In such books historians find reflected the Southern mind moving towards a certain unreality that all but invited the shock of the Civil War.

Kennedy reflected his city and state, in dividing his sympathies during the prelude to the Civil War. He was a Unionist in deed but a Southerner in spirit. As an urbane Baltimore lawyer, he served in Congress and in the national cabinet. Yet he was a planter in imagination. As a forward-looking American leader, he sent Perry to open Japan to trade, and he persuaded Congress to back Morse's telegraph. Yet the mythical Virginia of plantations looked ideal. It is too bad that he failed to portray this conflict directly.

Instead, Kennedy became the town's civic monument, a charming, urbane gentleman. He called himself a quasi-lion. As such, he took charge of creating the Peabody Institute, and he also became chancellor of the University of Maryland. His devotion to his native town was complete, though he substituted summering at Saratoga and Newport for Marylanders' usual retreat at Virginia's White Sulphur Springs. At 72 he returned from two years abroad, glad to be back at 90 Madison Street once more. He had been afraid that he would die abroad. Though he did die out of town, at Newport, he was buried at Green Mount Cemetery, final haven of all genteel Baltimoreans then.

Looking back over his long life in Baltimore, he could see his achievements, both literary and political. Though he had always had an eye to the main chance, no doubt he was propelled forward by his good looks and charm. His portrait still makes grown women fall in love with him. Back in 1820 he dressed dashingly. He even had a red lining in his overcoat of somewhat exaggerated fashion. A Baltimore dandy!

Like Beau Brummel, he courted society and won. He married into the rich merchant class that had social standing as well as money. By age 25 he had entered the inner circle of Maryland politicians. Then, by applying himself to writing fiction, he stood at age 35 as the major Southern writer. In all this he followed the pattern of his mentor William Wirt, whose biography he wrote. He followed Wirt also in giving up literature at a relatively young age to make money and to promote the civic good.

If he had stuck to writing, who knows how much of Baltimore would have been caught in his prose? Just as one of his friends, Washington Irving, captured Old New York in books, Kennedy might have saved Old Baltimore. Back in 1819–20 he did in fact begin such a record in the anonymously published *The Red Book,* a fortnightly periodical offering satirical sketches of Baltimoreans. Here is his satiric touch in a later fictional characterization of William Wirt:

...a close acquaintance with a great many persons...has rendered Philly Wart — as he is universally called, — a kind of cabinet counsellor and private advisor with most of those who are likely to be perplexed with their affairs. He has a singularly retentive memory as to facts, dates, and names; and by his intimate knowledge of land titles, courses and distances, patents, surveys and locations, he has become a formidable champion of all ejectment cases. In addition to this, Philly has such a brotherly and companionable relation to the greater number of the freeholders who serve upon the juries, and has such a confiding, friendly way of talking to them when he tries a cause, that it is generally supposed he can persuade them to believe anything he chooses.[6]

Some of his fiction is still worth reading, though it is of most interest to students of American literature. Of the four novels, *Swallow Barn, Rob of the Bowl, Quodlibet,* and *Horse-shoe Robinson*, the first is

Terra Rubra, named for the red soil of that part of Carroll County, was birth-place of Francis Scott Key, whose monument is at left. Key lived 20 years on M Street, Georgetown, and died on Mount Vernon Place, Baltimore.

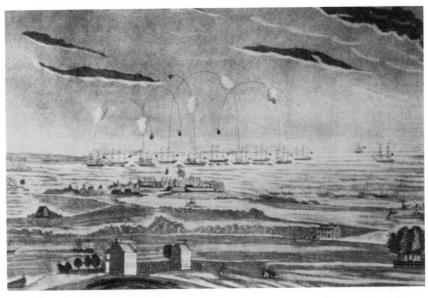

Contemporary print of Fort McHenry (flying the flag) defending Baltimore from British attack in the War of 1812 shows why Key, an eyewitness, wrote about bombs bursting in air in his "Star-Spangled Banner."

This engraving of William Wirt in Baltimore suggests the eminence in literature and public life that led Poe to ask his patronage.

Silhouette of Francis Scott Key, said to have been cut by himself. A lawyer, he belonged to a class of gentlemen who wrote for pleasure and practiced other arts as well.

When Baltimore was a boom town and Poe settled there, many children's books came from Lucas and other publishers. This one was perhaps written and illustrated by John H. B. Latrobe, when he was studying law, though most stories were pirated from England to satisfy sentimental tastes — as the graveside scene here must have done.

Tusculum, Wilkes Lane, Baltimore, was residence of William Gwynn, an editor, and meeting place of the Delphian Club of literati. This sober façade contrasted with members' racy writings and bibulous sessions. The Delphian inspired Poe's fictional Folio Club, created in Baltimore. The photograph was taken at the end of the 19th century.

12 West Madison Street, just off Washington Place, Baltimore, residence of John Pendleton Kennedy, projects the solid worth of its owner in its ample scale and dignity. Besides wealth, Kennedy had the perception to become Poe's first patron.

In this portrait, charming John Pendleton Kennedy looks like a hero of the Old South, a myth that he and William Wirt created in literature.

most readable now. Its hero gives us the simple homespun life of rural Virginia. He was a hearty gentleman-farmer, unpretentious and simple-hearted. His old-fashioned ways delight us, and so does Kennedy's gentle satire. Like the first readers, we enjoy knowing the open-handed hospitality, the fried chicken and ham feasts, the whisky toddies, and the whist games.

Though the charm of rural life comes through, Kennedy saw the people critically because their culture was doomed from conflicts within, particularly the clinging to old ways. Remember, Kennedy wrote from the perspective of Baltimore. In that perspective, urban industrial chaos was replacing the old agricultural order and hierarchy. And that was too bad.

We see his prejudices when, as a literary man, he chose between his contemporary English novelists, Charles Dickens and William Makepeace Thackeray. He met both when they lectured in Baltimore. Dickens he rejected as being personally vulgar, "a blasé'd hero of the green room." Thackeray he took to immediately. At their second meeting in September 1858, he agreed to add a chapter to the Englishman's novel *The Virginians*, a chapter that brought the hero through the Virginia that Kennedy knew well from Fort Duquesne to the coast. Although we don't know if the fourth chapter of volume two is in fact all Kennedy's, we know that he at least provided an outline and a rough map.

Kennedy's rejection of Dickens went along with his resentment of New England's commercialism as sad portent of things to come. When Boston critics failed to praise his biography of William Wirt, he wrote his publishers in Philadelphia, "What in the devil is the reason those Yankees will not say a good word for anything out of Yankeedom?"[7] (He here sounds like Poe and other Southern writers.)

Kennedy, of course, had known Yankees when he lived in Washington as Congressman and Secretary of the Navy and had lorded over them as chief resident writer. The high point of Washington literary life in the first half of the 19th century was this Baltimorean's taking over the old Tobias Lear house on G Street, east of 18th Street, William Wirt's residence earlier.

Second to Kennedy's was the literary distinction brought to the capital by the historian George Bancroft. This old Bostonian had served in President Polk's cabinet as Secretary of the Navy for eighteen months in 1845-1846. Then in 1874 he returned to a house on H Street between Connecticut Avenue and 17th Street. There he revised his *History of the United States*, the latest edition of which pleased him, he said, because "I want my history to be correct in every statement and in every particular." Of course it wasn't: every page cast a vote for Andrew Jackson. Despite his democratic theme, Bancroft lived the life aristocratic. As seen by a journalist, "On horseback, the old historian wears a short black velvet coat, about which his long white beard falls like silk lace.... His groom is dressed in as fancy a livery as the servants of any of the rich in Washington."[8] Writers of that city always appear to be better dressed than their Baltimore colleagues.

Two other immigrant writers contributed to whatever literary culture the District had before the Civil War: James Kirke Paulding came from Washington Irving's literary circle of the Salmagundi Club in New York to live on Lawrence Square. He too served as Secretary of the Navy (certainly the post for writers). His historical novels of colonial New York life found an audience, as did his essays and poems – all now forgotten. (Even his authorship of the Peter-Piper jingle is forgotten.)

Also forgotten is Joel Barlow, another immigrant-writer, who built Kalorama, a big house on the bank of Rock Creek north of the city. There between 1807 and 1811 this poet from Connecticut nurtured the capital's first literary circle. There too he published *The Columbiad*, 3,675 rhymed couplets in ten books. That poem was condemned by Nathaniel Hawthorne for its ponderosity of leaden verses. Appropriately a Washington ordinance expert named his newly invented bomb-cannon in honor of this epic poem, Columbiad.

We can easily pass quickly over these two immigrants in Washington, but not over Wirt and Kennedy. Though these last did live for a time in Washington, we must see them as part of Baltimore, a city abuzz with literary talk and publishing. There they joined men who came from all over to work; a surprising number of them were dabblers in literature. In the writings of these newcomers – letters, satires, poems – we find the usual imitation of English works. We also find occasional perceptions of what their young country was all about. There literati revealed the power of a city to make writers aware of the changes going on in society.

Like fellow writers up and down the coast, they also were part of the search for a national literature: for example, William Gilmore Simms was searching in Charleston, South Carolina; Charles Brockden Brown, in Philadelphia; and James Fenimore Cooper, in New York. Soon Nathaniel Hawthorne and the Transcendentalists were to bring an indigenous literature to flower in New England.

There in the North the Transcendentalist Club of Ralph Waldo

Emerson and Margaret Fuller made a contrast with the major Baltimore literary circle, the Delphian Club. Those New England writers dealt with philosophic questions; the Maryland crowd wrote satire and light verse, works closer in spirit to those of Washington Irving's Salmagundi Club in New York. Curiously, neither Wirt nor Kennedy belonged to the Delphian that was founded in 1816 and lasted up to the time of Poe's residence. Maybe Wirt was too distinguished a writer already when he moved to town from Virginia. A more probable reason was that he was too old. And Kennedy founded his own Belles Lettres Society that ranged beyond the literary into law.

The literary bent of the Delphians must have caught Poe's fancy because he created a fictional Folio Club as a linking modus for the short stories he wrote while he was living in Baltimore. In both clubs, the model and the fiction, members met to listen to readings of their own manuscripts and to drink champagne. Members adopted fanciful noms des plumes in the tradition of the Annapolitan Tuesday Club of the 18th century. (The Tuesday Club records had passed to the Delphians by 1812 deposit in the Baltimore Library.)

One of the prominent members, J. H. B. Latrobe, son of the famous architect, rejoiced in the name of Sir Joselyn Mittimus of Mittimus Hall. At the time he was reading law and earning a living doing hack writing. What he wrote for children in the 1820s shows us a demand for cheap children's books. He recalled what he had written for the bookseller Fielding Lucas, Jr., before he was 21: "I revised Jack the Giant Killer, wrote in rhyme and illustrated the Juvenile National Calendar. Invented Tray's Travels and showed the good dog upon them. Cinderella did not escape me in those days, and the boys and girls of Baltimore, now elderly people, may some of them, perhaps, remember the small octavo, sixteen paged books, on each page of which was a gaudily colored print, explained by eight lines of doggerel below it."[9]

In that same memoir, Latrobe noted that the slight touch of Bohemianism about him could be traced back to members of the Delphians. Their tone was light and satire was rampant in their writings. Their evenings evidently were lively with male humor. Though much of what they wrote was published in the periodical *The Portico*, some was too bawdy for publication. For example, in their manuscript minutes, appropriate verses accompany the watercolor sketch of two club members on an outing drawing in the sand a picture of a whale-size male generative member. We are not surprised to hear that the Delphians even elected Lord Byron an honorary club member, notorious womanizer and nonconformist though he was. Another member from New England, John Neal, later reminisced that the Delphians had given "a large portion of the happiness I enjoyed in the South. High-minded, generous, unselfish men, they were both intellectual and companionable, indulgent, and with all their whims and freaks, congenial."[10]

Neal must be singled out here because of his connection with Poe's emergence as a major writer. Though he had left town before Poe published *Al Aaraaf*, he praised Poe's verse in his journal, *The Yankee and Boston Literary Gazette*, September, 1829. Because Poe had dedicated "Tamerlane" to him, Poe's envious cousin Neilson Poe suspected the existence of a mutual admiration pact, though there was none.

"Crazy Neal," as some called him, had been born in Maine, had lived seven years in Baltimore and several years afterwards in England, and ended his career back in New England. His nom de plume in the Delphian, Jehu O'Cataract, suggests the torrent of words his pen produced. In Baltimore he wrote five novels, a tragedy in verse, two long narrative poems; he helped compile Paul Allen's *History of the American Revolution*; he prepared the index of *Niles' Register*, a national weekly chronicling news; he worked for magazines and newspapers; he also studied law. He put in a 16-hour day. His success as a writer we can see in the recollection of Nathaniel Hawthorne: that wild fellow John Neal almost turned his youthful brain with his romances. James Russell Lowell in a survey of American literature portrayed Neal as a precipitate swaggerer: "In letters, too soon is as bad as too late; / Could he only have waited he might have been great."[11]

Though a Quaker, Neal lacked that sect's restraint. Two of his *romans à clefs* recounted a Baltimore love affair. It is hard to believe that, as reported, he left town under the cloud of that scandal. He did leave in 1823 for England, where his enthusiastic nationalism led to a series in *Blackwood's* about American writers — a first.

Before Neal left he was challenged to a duel by another local writer, Edward Coote Pinkney, who was notorious for his thin skin and habit of challenging to duels. Neal recorded the whole to-do in yet another novel. The cause was a satirical portrait of an eminent Marylander, William Pinkney, Edward's father, in Neal's fiction *Randolph*. The father was presented as being too much impressed with his position as ambassador to England and as an attorney to rival William Wirt. To make matters worse for Neal, just when the novel came out the father died. The challenge to duel then arrived. When Neal refused to fight, young Pinkney published an insulting note committing "this Craven to his infamy" as a man "unpossessed of courage to make satisfaction for the insolence of his folly."[12]

Since Poe admired Pinkney's verse, it's a pity that writing challenges and insults substituted for lyrics. Pinkney himself made excuses for the paucity and weakness of his poems. He noted that he had first made the mistake as a youngster of joining the U.S. Navy, "a profession very unfavorable to literary pursuits." And then he had become too busy as an editor in Maryland and had no leisure to devote to poetry. He was a Herman Melville without a Moby Dick to inspire him — a Richard Henry Dana who failed to exploit his voyages in books.

As it was, he wrote lyric love songs that some critics find reminiscent of 17th-century English Cavalier verses such as Robert Herrick's. Poe quoted Pinkney's "Health" as being full of brilliancy and spirit. It begins:

I fill this cup to one made up
Of loveliness alone,
A woman, of her gentle sex
The seeming paragon;
To whom the better elements
And kindly stars have given
A form so fair, that, like the air
'Tis less of earth than heaven.

Pinkney's lyric gift reminds us that song was an important literary tradition in Maryland. (It was one of the three literary forms characteristic of the South generally. The other two were oratory and the historical novel.) English immigrants had brought their songs along with them, and African slaves brought theirs. Men of the educated class often could compose or set words to music just as easily as they could learn a new dance. A case in point: I have a sheet music copy of the French national anthem "La Marseillaise," with English words by "A Gentleman of Baltimore."

The traditional Scottish and English ballad also entered the Maryland song book. How Americanized that tragic genre became is evidenced by a ballad about Captain Miller's murder. This foul deed happened on the Chesapeake and Ohio Canal that paralleled that Potomac River from Georgetown, D.C., northwest into the upland mountains of Western Maryland. The characters sailed the canal together — Captain Miller, Johnny Howard, and the black boatman. The murderer:

Himself a gay young fellow, as you can plainly see,

His name was Johnny Howard, and a noble lad was he.
He boated on the waters for many a night and day,
Until he met a Negro, who swore his life away.
The Captain precipitated the murder himself:
The Captain he got rageous and in an angry passion flew,
The hatchet in his hand young Howard for to slew,
Johnny being informed of this, and in no way slow,
Quickly picked up the spreaders stick and laid the Captain low.
Then the trial in the Cumberland courthouse, Allegany County, comes into the story, followed by conviction on evidence given by the boatman. The end tells of the arrival of Howard's sister from Jersey "heart grieving for to see" and to "take farewell of me."[13]

Back in the 18th century, members of the Annapolitan Tuesday Club also devoted a lot of time to music, and the Delphians sponsored publication of songs. At that time members of the Thespian Club, to which Poe's father belonged, sang the old Cavalier songs of 200 years earlier, pieces by Sir John Suckling and that whole melodious nest of singing birds. Many professional men — lawyers such as Francis Scott Key, for example — turned out songs. Key wrote hymns and songs, including one for his fellow Delphians addressed to a young lady taking a shower bath.

His "The Star-Spangled Banner" stands out as the most familiar Maryland writing of all. The story of its composition has entered American memory the way Paul Revere's ride has. Key, a resident of Georgetown, had witnessed the British troops' burning of the Capitol and White House in Washington in 1814, and then had watched the bombardment of Baltimore when held on a British ship in the harbor.[14] Released after the failure of that attack, he wrote his poem in a Baltimore tavern. It was set to a popular tune, printed immediately, and sung first by jubilant Baltimoreans from a nearby stage. It caught on. I quote from the most controversial stanza:
Bless'd with victory and peace, may our Heaven-rescued land
Praise the Power that hath made and preserved us a nation.
Then conquer we must, for our cause it is just —
And this be our motto —"In God is our trust!"[15]

By chance, two guests of Key's Delphians added to the nation's famous songs. Samuel Woodworth wrote "The Old Oaken Bucket" (1817), and John Howard Payne, "Home Sweet Home" (1823). Payne's was written abroad a decade after he had been rescued from bankruptcy in Baltimore. The story goes that he walked into Coale's Bookshop on Baltimore Street and by chance caught the interest of two browsers, Jonathan Meredith, William Wirt's law partner, and Alexander Hanson, newspaper publisher. They found jobs for him and later sent him abroad to pursue his career in theatre. For him Baltimore provided a very sweet home, and Washington, a final home when he was buried there in Oak Hill Cemetery.[16]

Fortunately for other Maryland writers of songs, Baltimore was a center of music publishing. Evidently poets there liked to publish their lyrics set to music: for example, I have "The Withered Geranium" in sheet music and also as a poem in a local periodical. Foremost among music publishers were the influential Carrs, father and sons, who had opened a shop in 1794, having come directly from publishing music at Middle Row, Holborn, London. F. D. Benteen, another house, published Stephen Foster's songs quite early, including "Jim Crackcorn" (1846), Lincoln's favorite minstrel song. A third publisher, Dielman, got out a humorous glee called "Bees' Wings and Fish," composed while people were enjoying the drink of that name.

One of the most popular American songs was written by a Delphian Clubber, John Pierpont. He published in Baltimore the first edition of his poem "Airs of Palestine" — 800 lines of praise for sacred music. A public recital at Baltimore College paid for his trip to Boston to sell the copyright for $100. The poem ran through two more editions that same year, and made him famous. In the Morgan Library on Madison Avenue, New York, are preserved all three editions and many manuscripts, saved by his grandson J. Pierpont Morgan.

Poe would have liked such fame — and the money — at any time in his career. He even declared that he would rather have written the best song of a nation than its noblest epic. He did, of course, write the best examples of many other types of literature before he was through. But at that moment in literary history, the neophyte Poe was just making his entrance.

We can imagine the slight dark 20-year-old newly arrived in town and eager to begin. He first sought a guide on his ascent of literary heights. To that end he very soon marched up to the big front door of the Paradise Row mansion on West Baltimore Street of the chief of the literati, William Wirt. That gentleman, looking every inch a Roman Senator, received him kindly. Poe's brashness had purpose: he wanted Wirt's aid in getting his poem "Al Aaraaf" published. What he got instead were some kind words. Wirt read the poem, but said that he was too old-fashioned to judge the merit of the piece. It was much too modern: so Attorney Wirt shut the door.

IV
Irrecoverably a Poet

Wizard writer of wonder songs, Edgar Allan Poe: how in Baltimore he found himself—and was found—as a professional author.

"Baltimoreans are reminded from the cradle that Edgar Allan Poe was one of them, and that, whatever Europeans may think about his genius for poetry, he was pretty much a washout at everything else, from West Point to the saloon bar.

"When I first came to Baltimore at seventh-grade age, I attended a school named for Poe because his bones rested in a cemetery across the street, and my earliest instruction there was in the history of Baltimore politics. The great poet, went the story, spent his final day on this earth being hustled from polling place to polling place in East Baltimore; the more often he voted, the more drinks he earned. The story may be apocryphal—I don't know—but it was the kind of political lore one grew up with in Baltimore."[1]
— Russell Baker

"If the poem is published, succeed or not, I am 'irrecoverably a poet.' . . . I should add a circumstance which, tho' no justification of a failure, is yet a boast in success—the poem is by a minor & truly written under extraordinary disadvantages."[2]
— Edgar Allan Poe

"It was my choice or chance or curse
To adopt the cause for better or worse
And with my worldly goods and wit
And soul and body worship it."[3]
— Edgar Allan Poe

Edgar A. Poe.

This engraving shows Edgar Allan Poe as a young man on the rise after he left Baltimore at 26. He said that the picture did not look like him; readers will agree since they know him as a tragic-looking man with a mustache — and so he was later.

With this vow, "for better or worse" Poe married literature in Baltimore. This chapter centers on his honeymoon, a five-year apprenticeship. During it he settled into his writing career, and he also was recognized as a writer. There he revealed what H. L. Mencken later called his prodigal and arresting originality.

Although Poe was 18 before he came to Baltimore, he had roots there. His father David Poe, Jr., a third generation Baltimorean, had married a gifted English actress, Elizabeth Arnold, and acted with her in East Coast theatres. But, hot-tempered, untalented, and often drunk, he quit the stage in 1809, soon deserted his young family, and died in 1810, soon after his wife. Then the oldest son Henry went to live with Poe grandparents in Baltimore. Edger and Rosalie were taken in by wealthy Richmond families. Edgar's foster family, the John Allans, never adopted him, although they brought him up as a privileged son. Edgar at six was taken to England and five years of schooling. He continued his education in Richmond where he began to write. As the Allans were childless, and as John Allan had inherited a fortune, this foster son might well have inherited that fortune, in his turn.

But things had a way of turning out badly for Poe. In his adolescence he did not get along with Allan, a rather difficult and dour Scot. So when Poe matriculated at the University of Virginia and ran into heavy debt, Allan cut off funds and Poe had to leave college. The death of Mrs. Allan and remarriage of Allan ended Poe's dependence on that family.

His coming to Baltimore was both natural and right. Though in Richmond he had gone to school with scions of Virginia's First Families, he was always marked as the son of actors, a breed stigmatized as low and immoral. By contrast, in Baltimore the young man was a Poe. What that meant was membership in a clan of some standing. After all, his great-great grandfather had settled there when there were only 25 houses and had died there in 1756. In a town where such things mattered (and still do) Poe rehearsed his genealogy. He did it for money. One time he begged from a relative in Georgia, a man he had never met, and genealogy was his plea. Another time he tried to collect repayment of loans advanced during the American Revolution by his grandfather, David Poe. Among the family vouchers filed in proper form in Annapolis, Poe wrote, were letters from Washington, Lafayette, and many others speaking in high terms of the services and patriotism of "General" Poe.[4]

That repayment never came. The widow did draw a pension on which she, her daughter Maria Clemm (sister of Poe's father), and two Clemm children lived. The addition of Poe and his older brother Henry increased the need for money. To get some became the business of Mrs. Clemm, with Poe's help. Of Mrs. Clemm a kind observer said she was a sort of universal Providence for her strange children (Poe included). Less kind, a modern judgment held that she pursued mendacity with a zeal and a technical sufficiency that left her victims breathless.

In that strange household, Poe's older brother Henry exerted direct influence on Poe toward a literary career. Two years before Poe moved in, Henry had introduced him during a visit to literary friends. Lambert Wilmer was possibly one, because he and Henry both published literary versions of Poe's frustrated romance with a Richmond girl, Elmira Royster. Poe himself used that experience in "Tamerlane," a poem in his 1829 Baltimore volume. Since Baltimore readers digested these three retellings, they must have grown tired of Poe's broken heart.

Certainly Henry Poe aspired to a literary career, too. Both he and Edgar joined in the charming custom of writing verses in the friendship albums of young unmarried ladies. They also mingled with a young set of writers and bon vivants. Before Edgar came to town, Henry had published poetry in the weekly newspaper *The North American*. Among his poems there, one interests us as biography. Henry implied that his and Edgar's sister Rosalie was illegitimate, but doesn't say whether she was his father's or his mother's child. This poem also demonstrates the poor quality of verse by less gifted writers when compared to his brother Edgar's:

FOR THE NORTH AMERICAN

> *In a pocket book I lately found three locks of hair, from which*
> *originated the following lines: —*
> *My Father's! — I will bless it yet —*
> *For thou has given life to me:*
> *Tho' poor the boon — I'll ne'er forget*
> *The filial love I owe to thee.*
> *My Mother's, too! — then let me press*
> *This gift of her I loved so well, —*
> *For I have had thy last caress,*
> *And heard thy long, thy last farewell.*
>
> *My Rosa's! pain doth dim my eye,*
> *When gazing on this pledge of thine —*
> *Thou wer't a dream — a falsity —*

Alas! — 'tis wrong to call thee mine!
A Father! he hath loved indeed!
A mother! she hath blessed her son, —
But LOVE is like the pois'ning weed,
That taints the air it lives upon.[5]

Though the Poe brothers seem not to have faced their writing careers under ideal conditions, they did meet the standards set for gentlemen by Proper Baltimoreans. Together they must have appeared to be gay young blades about town. They looked alike and were called handsome. One of their literary crowd later described Poe as having a broad forehead, large magnificent gray eyes, and rather curly brown hair. He was five feet seven in height — Henry was a little taller. Edgar struck some people as playing the stage Virginia gentleman. He dressed neatly, wore Byron collars and a black neckerchief, and, people said, looked the poet all over.

With this picture in front of us, let us move through a chronology of Poe's years in Baltimore. They begin in March 1827 when Poe quarreled with his guardian Allan and sailed to Baltimore on his way to Boston. He was then just 18. He returned in spring 1829 after a stint in the U.S. Army. He called upon William Wirt then and, without Wirt's hoped-for aid, arranged to have *Al Aaraaf, Tamerlane, and Minor Poems* printed by Hatch and Dunning on Baltimore Street. Before the book came out he sent off one of his poignant letters, most of them in the vein of this quotation: "I was in a most uncomfortable situation — without one cent of money — in a strange place & so quickly engaged in difficulties after the serious misfortunes which I have just escaped — my grandmother is extremely poor & ill (paralytic)[.] My aunt Maria if possible still worse & Henry given up to drink & unable to help himself, much less me — ."[6]

The publication of his poems in December brought mixed reviews. But they were blessed with enthusiastic notice from John Neal, an ex-Delphian Clubber, then an editor in New England. Neal said, "If the young author now before us should fulfill his destiny. . .he will be *foremost* in the rank of *real* poets."[7]

In 1830 Poe may have published an anonymous satiric poem in Baltimore called "The Musiad or Ninead, a Poem by Diabolus, Edited by ME." Possibly the author was Poe — or his brother. Whoever wrote it, the piece is flattering to Poe and critical of everyone else. He opened with a slap at one of the immigrant writers from New England, Rufus Dawes:

Why not a Muse will deign to dwell with us —

Why Moore shall make a poem — and Dawes a fuss
I sing: or will, if God will grant the power
To Rufus Dawes to hold his tongue one hour.

He even dared put in a crack at the most distinguished writer in Baltimore:

While Patrick Henry, Wirt, is thinking now
Calliope a lighter load than thou!
He would have died to set the country free —
But oh! to die so damned a death in thee!

The section about Poe concerns us here because it is both apt and complimentary:

Next Poe who smil'd at reason, laugh'd at law,
And played a tune who should have play'd at taw,
Now strain'd a license, and now crack'd a string,
But sang as older children dared not sing.
Said Clio "By all the wise, who can admit
Beardless no goat a goat — no wit a wit,
Say! did not Billy Gwynn, the great, combine
With little Lucas to put down thy line?
And thou! thy very heart is on thy toy!
Thy red-hot lyre will burn thee — drop it, boy!"[8]

A note about William Gwynn is in order because Poe had applied to him for a job on his newspaper *The Baltimore Gazette* and failed to get it. Calling him "the great" called attention to his obesity as well as his importance. Fielding Lucas, Jr., the publisher, is "little" because he was very large and possibly had made some little-minded comment on Poe's verse.

Having failed to find work with the great Gwynn or anyone else in Washington or Baltimore, Poe entered West Point as a cadet in late June 1830. He left the military academy in the winter, arranged for publication of some poems in New York, and was back in Baltimore in time to receive reviews of that volume in the spring of 1831. That book didn't make the sensation merited by such poems as "To Helen" and "To One in Paradise." Beginning in March he shared a room with his brother Henry at the Poe-Clemm house in Mechanic's Row, Old Town. Five months later Poe accompanied his brother's body to be buried in the Poe lot of Western Burying Ground.

Poe was writing stories in quantity; by July he had written enough to enter a contest sponsored by a Philadelphia newspaper. Though he didn't win, he was evidently a runner-up because soon five of his stories appeared in print — but anonymously. During the next four years Poe lived with his relatives and wrote. We don't know just where and when specific poems and stories got put down on paper. We do know of an outpouring of poetry high in quality and of tales that promised greatness ahead.

We can't say just how much living in Maryland affected his work. Writers themselves often don't know, and critics can only speculate. The genesis of a Poe story may have come from a local incident. Or it could have evolved from his individual psyche and the power of his imagination. As another possibility, a story of his could well have been inspired by a certain piece in *Blackwood's*. He probably had access to magazines and books of the Library Company of Baltimore (founded 1796) housed in the Assembly Room and Library Building or in the Atheneum, which in 1825 contained 8,000 volumes. In one place or the other Poe found the current magazines that led him to become a magazinist himself, and one of the first water. At that time he surveyed the whole range of topics and styles in English and American magazines. Then he contributed his own writings to magazines and newspapers up and down the coast.

Besides reading matter, Baltimoreans provided Poe with events. For example, one of his best known stories, "Berenice," probably began with the scandal of enterprising people in town robbing graves to obtain human teeth for dentists. Also on the unpleasant side, the cholera epidemic of 1831 gave him firsthand the terrors of a plague. Soon after, he wrote his tale "King Pest" and later "The Masque of the Red Death," both stories of plague. Another newsworthy event then was an early morning rain of meteors. That shower lighted the skies and terrified residents. Echoes went into Poe's "Eiros and Charmion" and "Shadow."

In 1832 Poe moved with the Clemms to an Amity Street rowhouse, today the Poe House museum. That year he finished eleven tales that he wanted to put out as a book. Though frustrated in that scheme, he did publish them separately in newspapers and magazines. His original plan had been to connect these tales on the model of Chaucer's *Canterbury Tales*. For this binding narrative, he invented the Folio Club, on the model of the Delphian Club. Like the Delphians, members met monthly to read and discuss each others' writings. In Poe's imaginary club, each member became a caricature and bore a silly name on the order of the Delphians'. He even invented a Mr. Bibulous O'Bumper, perhaps in mockery of his own satan Demon Rum. And Satan was there at meetings too, disguised as De Rerum Natura. In the tales members told, Poe sketched out fantasy, horror, mystery, science fiction, and the grotesque, all the types of stories he later perfected. He enriched Maryland and world literary history by imagining so varied and innovative a set of stories.

In October 1833 in a rowhouse opposite the old Cathedral, Poe began his career as a local literary light, and then a national one. There he received first prize in a contest sponsored by a Baltimore newspaper *The Saturday Visiter* [sic] for his story "Ms. Found in a Bottle." How it all happened can be approached through a journal entry of John H. B. Latrobe, one of the judges: "Monday, October 7, 1833: After dinner Kennedy and Dr. Miller met at my house to decide the merits of certain compositions offered for premiums for the 'Saturday Visiter,' and made our selection of prose and poetry, and had altogether quite a pleasant afternoon and evening."[9]

The judges had chosen his poem "The Coliseum" as winner, too, but gave him second prize because they didn't want to give both prose and poetry prizes to the same writer. Poe was furious when he heard that. Why he was we can see when we compare his entry with the winner, John Hewitt's. I print the opening stanzas of both poems here:

THE COLISEUM
by Edgar Allan Poe

Type of the antique Rome! Rich reliquary
Of lofty contemplation left to Time
By buried centuries of pomp and power!
At length — at length — after so many days
Of weary pilgrimage and burning thirst,
(Thirst for the springs of lore that in thee lie,)
I kneel, an altered and an humble man,
Amid the shadows, and so drink within
My very soul thy grandeur, gloom and glory!

THE SONG OF THE WIND
by John Hewitt

Whence come ye with your odor-laden wings
Oh, unseen wanderer of the summer night?
Why, sportive, kiss my lyre's trembling strings,
Fashioning wild music, which the light
Of listening orbs doth seem in joy to drink?
Ye wanton 'round my form and fan my brow,
While I hold converse with the stars that wink
And laugh upon the mirror stream below....

Latrobe later recorded an anecdote that portrays Poe at the time of winning. It shows Poe's creating a new kind of romance, the quasi-scientific hoax telling about a journey into space. (He published it as "The Unparalleled Adventures of Hans Pfaal.") He was recounting a balloon trip to the moon, in fact his first sketch of the fantasy fiction that he went on to develop and that so many other writers have also developed.

When he warmed up, he was most eloquent. He spoke, at that time, with eager action; and, although, to judge from his outward mien, the world was then going hard with him, and his look was blasé, yet his appearance was forgotten, as he seemed to forget the world around him, as wild fancy, logical truth, mathematical analysis and wonderful combination of facts flowed, in strange commingling, from his lips, in words choice and appropriate, as though the results of the closest study. I remember being particularly struck with the power that he seemed to possess of identifying himself with whatever he was describing. He related to me all the facts of a voyage to the moon, I think (which he proposed to put on paper), with an accuracy of minute detail, and a truthfulness as regards philosophical phenomena, which impressed you with the idea that he had himself just returned.[10]

Though the narrator of this anecdote appreciated Poe, he didn't become the patron Poe needed. Another of the judges did — John Pendleton Kennedy. Later when Poe said that Kennedy had saved his life, he may have meant literally — saved him from suicide. But he might well have meant that Kennedy's patronage proved the turning point in his career: with it Poe secured his high place among American writers.

The first chance to help came after the death of Poe's guardian, Allan, confirmed Poe's disinheritance. Just before that, Poe had sold "The Visionary" to *Godey's Lady's Book* and it was published unsigned, his first prose in a national magazine of wide circulation. He then asked help from Kennedy to persuade the Philadelphia publishers Carey & Lea to publish the Folio Club tales. (That firm had published Kennedy's first novel shortly before.) With that request Poe said that he was penniless and needed help. Kennedy acceded to this and to other requests for money, though he failed to get the tales published.

By the following March, Poe wrote that he was even worse off than in November. He said that Kennedy's invitation to dinner had wounded him to the quick because he had no decent clothes to wear. Kennedy sent clothes, and, he later recalled, "gave him clothing, free access to my table and the use of a horse for exercise whenever he chose—in fact, brought him up from the very verge of despair."[11]

Would that we had more such anecdotes of his Baltimore days. As it is, we know little about his daily life. He must have read and written a great deal of the time. The 20 months between May 4, 1833, and January 21, 1835, are blank of letters, except for two to John Pendleton Kennedy in November and December 1834. That makes quite a gap.

Poe's friend Lambert Wilmer helped fill that gap with recollections of months just before then. Wilmer first knew Poe in Baltimore during the first three quarters of 1832. His intercourse with Poe, he wrote, had been almost continuous for weeks together. They had taken long daily walks outside town, and most important, "had long conversations on a great variety of subjects." Wilmer added, "His, Poe's, time appeared to be constantly occupied by his literary labors; he had already published a volume of poems, and written several of those minor romances which afterwards appeared in the collection called *Tales of the Grotesque and Arabesque*. He lived in a very retired way with his aunt, Mrs. Clemm, and his moral deportment, as far as my observation extended, was altogether correct.

"In his youthful days, Poe's personal appearance was delicate and effeminate, but never sickly or ghastly, and I never saw him in any dress which was not fashionably neat and with some approximation to elegance. Indeed, I often wondered how he could contrive to equip himself as handsomely, considering that his pecuniary resources were generally scanty and precarious enough."

Since we have so few anecdotes of Poe's Baltimore days, this one of Wilmer's is especially important:

I have seen an article in a British review in which a comparison was made between Poe and Swift, Savage, DeQuincey, Coleridge and other celebrated delinquents of English literature. All the latter were admitted to have had some "redeeming qualities," but Poe, said the reviewer, had none, he had no human sympathies, no amiable weaknesses, no vices of a specially human consistency, "in short, he was a demon and not a man."

A trifling incident, which just now occurs to my remembrance, may properly be placed in juxtaposition with this Englishman's Phillipic. One day, Poe, his cousin Virginia, who afterwards became his wife, and I were walking in the neighborhood of Baltimore when we happened to approach a graveyard, where a funeral was then in progress. Curiosity attracted us to the side of the grave, where we stood among a crowd of spectators who had accompanied the corpse to the place of interment. I do not remember that there was anything particularly touching in these obsequies, but Virginia became affected and shed more tears than the chief mourner. Her emotion communicated itself to Poe; and if an English reviewer could have seen him at that moment, weeping at the grave of a stranger, he might have given him credit for some "human sympathy."

Other pictures of Poe in those days came out in Wilmer's proof that Poe was not "at every period of his life, an habitual drunkard." Although writing after Poe's death to defend him, Wilmer here helped confirm the industriousness of those Baltimore years:

And however dry might be the subject of our discourse, and however dusty the road we traveled, we never stopped at any hotel for liquid refreshment, and I never observed any disposition on the part of my companion to avail himself of the liberal supplies of alcoholic beverage which were always to be had in the vicinity of Baltimore. In short, his general habits at that time were strictly temperate; and but for one or two incidents, I might have supposed him to be a member of the cold water army. On one occasion, when I visited him at his lodgings, he produced a decanter of Jamaica spirits, in conformity with a practice which was very common in those days, especially in the Southern and Middle States, where one gentleman could scarcely visit another without being invited to drink. On the occasion just referred to, Poe made a moderate use of the liquor; and this is the only time that ever I saw him drink ardent spirits. On another occasion I was present, when his aunt, Mrs. Clemm, scolded him with some severity for coming home intoxicated on the preceding evening. He excused himself by saying that he had met with some friends, who had persuaded him to take dinner with them at a tavern, where the whole party had become inebriated — a circumstance for which many a poetical gentleman's experience might furnish a parallel. I judged from the conversation between Mrs. Clemm and Poe, that the fault for which she reproved him was of rare occurrence, and I never afterwards heard him charged with a repetition of the offense.[12]

In Wilmer's words we glimpse Poe in his early 20s and before he left town in 1835. Poe began writing the never-completed blank verse tragedy *Politian* in that year. He also sent the *Southern Literary Messenger* in Richmond book reviews and stories, including "Hans Pfaal," "Morella," and "King Pest." Then, through his patron Kennedy's influence, he got the job of assistant editor of the *Messenger.* In mid-summer he moved to Richmond. From there he wrote that he was preparing for his aunt Maria Clemm and her daughter Virginia to join him. At that point his Baltimore cousin Neilson Poe offered to take 12-year-old Virginia to live with him and his wife, who was her cousin. That offer provoked one of Poe's most moving letters, part of which must be quoted here:

My dearest Aunty,

I am blinded with tears while writing this letter — I have no wish to live another hour. Amid sorrow, and the deepest anxiety your letter reached — and you well know how little I am able to bear up under the pressure of grief — My bitterest enemy would pity me could he now read my heart — My last my last my only hold on life is cruelly torn away — I have no desire to live and will not *But let my duty be done. I love, you know I love Virginia passionately devotedly. I cannot express in words the fervent devotion I feel towards my dear little cousin — my own darling. But what can [I] say. Oh think for me for I am incapable of thinking. Al[l my] thoughts are occupied with the supposition that both you and she will prefer to go with N. Poe; I do sincerely believe that your comforts will for the present be secured — I cannot speak as regards your peace — your happiness. You have both tender hearts — and you will always have the reflection that my agony is more than I can bear — that you have driven me to the grave — for love like mine can never be gotten over.*[13]

The upshot of all the feeling conveyed here was a wedding. On September 22, 1835, Poe took out a marriage license in Baltimore and was secretly married to Virginia. Though we have no proof that the marriage actually took place then, several leading Poe scholars now believe it did. The couple were publicly married in Richmond the following May. They never returned to live in Maryland, though he sometimes tried to come back.

Poe also visited Baltimore fairly frequently. About those visits we fortunately have recollections by Dr. R. D. Unger, a man 15 years younger than Poe. Though written down many years after first meeting Poe in 1846, these memories complete our picture of Poe up to the time of his final visit.

[During the late 1840s] he was missed a great deal, being a sort of "hanger on" around the newspaper offices and saloons. John Boyd, Coffee House, afterwards known as Reilly's on South Street, near Baltimore Street — a "cellar" restaurant — was one of his favorite resorts. In this place was a small room, the walls of which were covered with portraits of actors and actresses, old theatre bills, &c. Poe would spend a happy hour or two in this room if he had "a chum" with

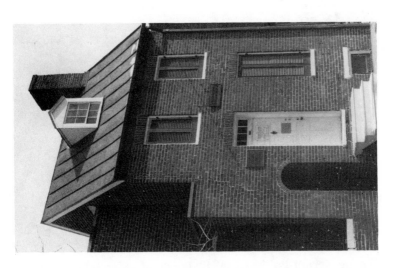

The Poe House, 203 Amity Street, was Poe's second Baltimore home during his apprenticeship. He shared the attic room, lighted by the gable window, with his dying brother Henry. The raven reminds modern visitors that here Poe wrote poems (though not "The Raven").

On this bird's-eye view of Baltimore, 1859, are numbered sites associated with Poe: 1. Residence on Wilkes Lane, between High and Exeter Streets; 2. Second residence with the Clemms, 203 Amity Street; 3. City Assembly Room and Library; 4. Barnum's Hotel, Monument Square; 5. Hatch & Dun-

ning, publishers of *Al Aaraaf;* 6. J. H. B. Latrobe's house, 11 West Mulberry
Street, where Poe received the *Saturday Visiter* prize; 7. Odd Fellows Hall;
8. Washington Hospital, where he died; 9. Western Burying Ground, where
he was buried.

86

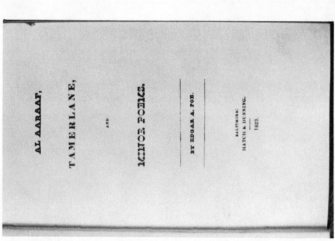

William Hand Browne, a literary ex-Confederate from Virginia, gravitated to the big city of Baltimore and to major tasks, including resuscitating Poe's reputation. He also discovered the talent of Lizette Woodworth Reese when he was writing and editing in Baltimore.

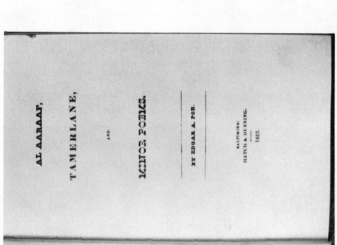

The starkness of this title page in the only book Poe published in Baltimore belies the riches within and also in the stack of manuscript poems and stories that he wrote during the succeeding six years in town.

Here is the elegant back parlor of J. H. B. Latrobe's house, West Mulberry Street, Baltimore, where Poe received a prize from a local newspaper, the *Saturday Visiter*, for his story "Ms. Found in a Bottle." Today the room displays wares of a dealer in traditional house furnishings, including table lamps.

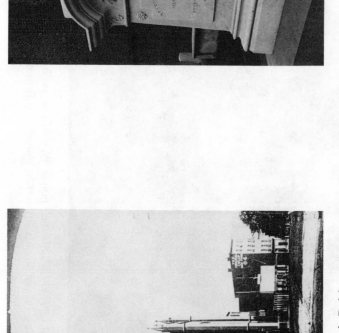

Some of the atmosphere of Poe's Baltimore comes through in this late 19th-century photograph of the towered Odd Fellows Hall, Gay Street, Baltimore (demolished), where Poe lectured on American poetry in 1844, five years before his death. The Odd Fellows American lodge had its origin in Baltimore, a fact that may explain the large size of its building.

At the corner of Fayette and Greene Streets, just behind a brick wall, stands this stone covering the bones of Edgar Allan Poe, of his wife, Virginia, and of his mother-in-law, Maria Poe Clemm. Recently the cemetery has been tidied up for visitors from around the world.

him provided he could get a glass or two of ale or brown stout whilst there. He often alluded to the circumstance that his mother, (who died when he was quite young), was an actress; but I never heard him refer to his father. After a visit to Boyd's, he was the "moodiest of the moody." Poe never was a brilliant talker, but he was a hard worker (and a hard drinker) when he had work to do. His mentality was of a peculiar quality and, on some occasions, especially after a drinking "bout," his talk would run on the supernatural . . . .

Now, to conclude I will give you a story told me by an infamous woman, named Mary Nelson, who kept an improper house in what was then known as Tripolet's Alley. As an alley it no longer exists. Edgar Allan Poe was not a profane man, by any means, nor was he mentally debased; but (so this woman said) he came to her house once, "half seas over," with a man named William Smith. Smith bought a bottle of Champagne and two of the female inmates of the place were called into the "Parlor" to help drink the wine. One of these girls was quite young a mere child of 16 — and very beautiful. Poe got into a conversation with her and became terribly smitten. Her name was Leonora Bouldin, *and they called her "Lenore." The woman Nelson said that, after talking a while with this girl, Poe gave her good advice, spoke of her parents, and finally got her crying. After her sobbing was over Poe pressed her to his heart and promised to see her again, but he never came back to the place.*[14]

Poe's visits continued after his wife Virginia died on January 30, 1847. Unger said that her death left her husband not caring whether he lived an hour, a day, a week or a year — she was his all. While she was still alive he published a story "Eleanora" that celebrated a love such as he had for Virginia. This story told of the romance of an older man for his 15-year-old cousin. Through the story Poe conveyed the discovery of love and a home, just his experience in Baltimore. He wrote other pieces in her memory, such as his famous poem "Annabel Lee." One of his tenderest poems was addressed to Mrs. Clemm and is called "To My Mother." It honors a relationship begun in Baltimore, a relationship that sustained this troubled writer to the end:

Because I feel that, in the Heavens above,
The angels, whispering to one another,
Can find, among their burning terms of love,
None so devotional as that of "Mother,"
Therefore by that dear name I long have called you —
You who are more than mother unto me.
And fill my heart of hearts, where Death installed you

In setting my Virginia's spirit free.
My mother—my own mother, who died early,
Was but the mother of myself; but you
Are mother to the one I loved so dearly,
And thus are dearer than the mother I knew
By that infinity with which my wife
Was dearer to my soul than its soul-life.

This sonnet reflects Poe's last sad years. For happy contrast let us pick his last year in Baltimore, 1835, as a landmark. That year he was publishing remarkable stories and criticism for a national audience. He clearly was becoming a force in American literature. For the South generally, that year was *annus mirabilis.* For instance, John Pendleton Kennedy crowned his novel-writing with *Horse-shoe Robinson* then. Also, William Gilmore Simms published two novels, and Augustus Baldwin Longstreet wrote *Georgia Scenes.*

That year was important to this literary history because then Poe completed his apprenticeship. He had worked for one-fifth of his career in Baltimore. It was the rising 20 per cent. At age 20 he had published there his first solid volume of poems. Of his finest poems, a half dozen can be connected with Maryland, including "To One in Paradise" and "The City in the Sea." At the same time he launched his major types of fiction and won notice with winning the *Baltimore Saturday Visiter* contest. And in literary criticism he cleared the ground.

So we can conclude that in Maryland Poe gave the measure of his genius. He explored the full range of literary genres that was to be his—haunting poetry, acerb criticism of literature, and tales of mystery and imagination. He became the first complete man of letters in the history of the United States. And he emerged in Baltimore, as Mencken recognized, as the most potent and original of Americans.

Even so, local watchdogs of culture, including editors, failed to see Poe's significance. One Baltimore editor, for example, turned down his story "The Mystery of Marie Roget—A Sequel to the Murders in the Rue Morgue." Poe had even cut the price from $100 to $40. For another example of blindness to Poe's worth, consider this Baltimore commencement message, delivered at St. Mary's College, July 15, 1846:

But when our lands become more settled and cultivated, when our people throw aside their insatiable thirst for lucre, when the sciences are properly studied, and the labors of genius are well rewarded, then shall our literary taste be on a level with our national importance.

A valuable literature will displace the light, the dangerous, and the false literature of our own day and the American mind and pen will be admired and valued, wherever the American name is known.[15]

Isn't it ironical that at that very time, Poe was writing "The Raven" and other valuable literature? He even lectured on advances in American poetry in Washington (March 1843) and in the Baltimore Odd Fellows Egyptian Salon on Gay Street, January 31, 1844.

If he had found a capitalist, he would have ended his days in Baltimore, but in less dramatic circumstances than he did six years later. He might even have lived longer. As it was, he worked in other cities. First, after leaving Baltimore in 1835, he edited in Richmond. Early in 1837 he moved to New York, and the middle of the next year to Philadelphia. In that literary capital he enjoyed great success. Then he went back to New York in 1844 for a disastrous stay—New York was never good for him. There he got into silly quarrels with other writers. There too he finally found his magazine, but lacked funds and energy to make it first-rate. Then in 1847 the death of his beloved wife from tuberculosis all but destroyed him. From that time on he suffered from bad health, from erratic behavior (including one attempt at suicide), and from drinking bouts that led to delirium tremens. He died within three years of his wife from what was then diagnosed as "congestion of the brain."

Though Poe never had the chance to live and work in Baltimore after 1835, he came "home" to die. His return was fitting because his father's family had been part of Baltimore history for so long and were buried there. The second reason was that there his posthumous reputation found its best defenders. How much he needed their help we discover from this statement by Poe's friend from Baltimore days, Lambert Wilmer: ". . . by continued and well-directed efforts, the newspapers of our country have succeeded in giving Poe a character 'as black as Vulcan's smithy' and in this hideous drapery, woven by demoniac malice, the unrivalled poet of America is now presented to the world."[16]

Since that black character persists in the popular image of Poe, we must give the facts here about his death in Baltimore. Not to do so would be a disservice to literary history.

Facts about Poe's last days in Baltimore and his death are hard to prove. What we do know for certain is that a compositor on the Baltimore *Sun* named Joseph W. Walker found Poe semi-conscious in a public house, Gunner's Hall, at 44 East Lombard Street, just several doors east of High Street. The pub was serving as Ryan's

Fourth Ward polls that day, October 3, 1849. Much speculation centers on whether or not Poe had been drugged by politicians and taken from one polling place to another to vote as a "repeater." (Such practices were common then.) But a leading Poe scholar in 1969 called that rumor twaddle![7]

What we know for sure is that Walker summoned Poe's uncle by marriage, Henry Herring, and a doctor, Dr. Joseph Snodgrass, one of Poe's Baltimore literary group. They took him by carriage to Washington Hospital, located on a hill about eight blocks northeast of Gunner's. (That building is now part of Church Home and Hospital.) Poe was taken to a second floor room in the tower facing the court. When he roused from unconsciousness the next morning, he couldn't tell Doctor John J. Moran what had happened.

Moran and his wife, who nursed Poe, were the sole witnesses of Poe's final hours, hours of deliriousness interrupted by lucid periods. Dr. Moran reported words of despair and self-reproach. Moran's wife read him the fourteenth chapter of St. John when Poe questioned whether there was hope for him in the next world. At one point Poe called loudly for "Reynolds!" About three in the morning of Sunday, October 7, Poe seemed to rest. About five he said, "God help my poor soul" and died.

Neilson Poe arranged for the funeral to take place the very next day. That Monday afternoon, October 9, 1849, was gloomy — not raining but threatening and cold. The service was conducted by the Rev. W. T. D. Clemm, a son of James L. Clemm, a relative of Maria Clemm. He was pastor of Caroline Street Methodist Church. After the service in the hospital rotunda, the mourners accompanied the hearse across town to Western Burying Ground at Fayette and Greene Streets. They included Henry Herring, Dr. Snodgrass, and Z. Collins Lee, a classmate of Poe's at the University of Virginia who lived in Baltimore. Neilson wrote Maria that "he lies alongside his ancestors in the Presbyterian burying ground on Green[e] Street."[18]

Poe's death got little notice in Baltimore newspapers, though Richmond papers gave it a lot of space. The one obituary that was reprinted everywhere was by Poe's literary executor, Rufus W. Griswold, and published in the evening edition of the *New-York Tribune* on October 9: "Edgar Allan Poe is dead. He died in Baltimore the day before yesterday. This announcement will startle many, but few will be grieved by it."

Thus began a villainous course of defaming Poe. Griswold's biography of Poe took the same tack, and through distortion — and even invention — attacked the man. His motivation we can't know, though we sense revenge and envy. We can even say how like Poe it was to have chosen an enemy as his literary executor: who else could keep controversies going and an author's memory alive? (To be fair, Griswold did put out a useful edition of Poe's writings.)

Certainly Poe's fans could not have done so alone. With an opponent like Griswold ruining the reputation of their idol, the Poemaniacs, as Mencken called them, had their inspiration. They went too far, of course, and Mencken blamed them for whatever coldness he displayed towards Poe. He said that they "haunted my school-days in Poe-ridden Baltimore, mixing pifflish local pride with more pifflish literary criticism."

That Poe-ridden place, however, yielded defenses that held up under later scrutiny. The defenders' strength came from digging for facts. These they collected in letters and interviews. Then this so-called Poe Cult published what they had found. What's more they supported in every way the attempt to write a truthful biography of Poe by John Ingram, an Englishman. When it came out in 1875, one of the Baltimore contingent wrote the author that not only did he welcome the correction of Griswold's lies and the vindication of Poe, but also he admired "the stranger whose generous enthusiasm had led him to take so much pains, under great disadvantages, in doing what none of Poe's countrymen and even kindred, had ever done."[19]

We must immediately record what Poe's fellow Maryland writers did do because their work makes a proud chapter in this literary history. They helped resuscitate Poe's reputation and unearthed the truth about his life and character. They also ferreted out fugitive writings from local papers. The result we all know: Poe's works spread and spread; also, the man Poe emerged — not as an irresponsible, drunken bohemian but as a tragic man facing what he called the unmerciful disaster that overtook him faster and faster.

The list of local defenders of Poe is long. At the end of this survey of them will come the literary classic that their efforts called into existence. These efforts included publishing important Poe letters. For example, Edward Spencer, playwright and editor of the Baltimore *Sun,* edited correspondence between Poe and Dr. Joseph Snodgrass, the Baltimore friend who had assisted when Poe collapsed that Election Day.

Another defender, Father John Banister Tabb, gathered recollections about Poe from people in town. He also wrote poems about his fellow poet. One of the most poignant he created when Poe was excluded by the committee choosing Americans to be included in the Hall of Fame in New York. He called it "Poe's Critics."

A certain tyrant, to disgrace
The more a rebel's resting-place,
Compelled his people, every one,
To hurl in passing there a stone;
Which done, behold the pile became
A monument to keep his name.

And thus it is with Edgar Poe:
Each passing critic has his throw,
Nor sees, defeating his intent,
How lofty grows the monument.[20]

A third defender of Poe, William Hand Browne was, like Tabb, both a teacher and a Virginian. He liked to give the defense a sectional turn. Writing in 1880, when he was librarian of the then new Johns Hopkins University, he revealed that some of the old vindictiveness against Poe occasionally cropped up in Northern newspapers "partly because they hate the South and everything Southern, and partly because some of the old 'mutual admiration' set still survive, and have never yet forgiven the man who told them the truth about themselves."[21]

Later Browne helped his colleague in the English Department, John C. French, find lost poems by Poe. One day after French's telling his class that no file existed of the 1833 newspaper *The Saturday Visiter* containing Poe's prize-winning entry, a student surprised him by saying she knew of one. It was owned by a granddaughter of the original editor. That old lady didn't welcome his inquiry. When she didn't answer his letter asking to see the *Visiter,* he put literary interest above good manners and went to her house. There, he said, her native politeness forced her to let him see the bound volume. In it he discovered that published accounts of the contest were inaccurate. More important, he found lost poems of Poe.

As footnote to local Poemania: readers won't be surprised to learn that a preeminent Poe collector in the 20th century, William H. Koester, was a native and resident of Baltimore, that most Poe-conscious of American cities. He was the son of a German immigrant baker in West Baltimore. (For decades Koester's Bread was a fixture on tables in town.) People who knew him as collector between the 1930s and his death in 1964 say he engagingly combined shrewdness and openhandedness. His collection now rests among other riches of the University of Texas at Austin, not at Johns Hopkins or another

Maryland archive.

No doubt French's turning up "Serenade," "Fanny," and the poem beginning "Sleep on..." deserves our praise. And so does Koester's useful collection. But the work of an English woman teaching in Baltimore, Sara Sigourney Rice, brought forth a world masterpiece, the sonnet by Stéphane Mallarmé called "Le Tombeau D'Edgar Poe." How she did it is part of a larger story. But first I print the poem here with a modern English translation by a current Johns Hopkins professor, Richard Macksey:

Tel qu'en Lui-même enfin l'éternité le change,
Le Poete suscite avec un glaive nu
Son siècle épouvanté de n'avoir pas connu
Que la mort triomphant dans cette voix étrange!

Eux, comme un vil sursaut d'hydre oyant jadis l'ange
Donner un sens plus pur aux mots de la tribu
Proclamèrent très haute le sortilège bu
Dans le flot sans honneur de quelque noir mélange.

Du sol et de la nue hostiles, ô grief!
Si notre idée avec ne sculpte un bas-relief
Dont la tombe de Poe éblouissante s'orne

Calme bloc ici-bas chu d'un désastre obscur
Que ce granit du moins montre à jamais sa borne
Aux noirs vols de Blasphème épars dans le futur.

* * *

Such as to at last into Himself eternity
Transforms him, the Poet rouses with a naked sword
His age now terror-struck to have ignored
In that strange voice the triumph of fatality!

They, like Hydra's vile spasm, at hearing then
The angel give purer meaning to the words of the tribe,
Loudly bruited the slander of a witchcraft that imbibed
In the honorless flood of some black drunken fen.

From the warring earth and hostile sky, Antitheses!
If our imagination does not carve a frieze
That we may adorn Poe's dazzling tomb with it,

Calm block fallen from some obscure disaster
At least let this granite clearly mark the limit
To dark flights of struggling Blasphemy, ever after.

This sonnet is a classic that no Marylander could have written, but should have. That a French poet created it is entirely appropriate, however. French writers at mid-century had discovered Poe's poetry and prose and had adopted him as their own. Mallarmé had translated the poems into French, and Baudelaire had translated tales. Through Valéry and others, Poe's influence spread abroad and his fame continues to grow there. A local anecdote will illustrate the attitude of foreigners today. One afternoon when a friend of mine was driving French relatives to the Baltimore-Washington International Airport, he casually remarked that they were then passing Poe's grave. The relatives almost fell out of the car in their excitement: they had no idea of Poe's close ties with Baltimore—much less that his sacred bones rested there.

The story of how this honored and complex French poem came to join those bones in Baltimore is simple. A local school teacher, Sara Sigourney Rice, wrote Mallarmé for a tribute to Poe's memory and he gave her one. She printed it with other tributes by prominent American and English writers in a memorial volume. Publication coincided with reinterment of Poe's bones under a new stone monument. Raising the $1,000 for the monument proved more difficult than collecting tributes, however. Ten years and the coins of schoolgirls and boys (among other gifts) went into its erection. With the money, Rice commissioned a tombstone that Mencken later called cheap and hideous, one quite as bad, he said, as the worst in Père Lachaise Cemetery in Paris. Under it, Poe's body was reinterred, together with that of Mrs. Clemm and, later, his wife.

To the unveiling of this monument, Rice invited people who had known Poe. Certain ones were asked to speak. The poet Walt Whitman refused to make a speech, though he did attend. Out of the occasion he set down in his journal one of the most memorable images of Poe that we have:

. . . In a dream I once had, I saw a vessel on the sea, at midnight, in a storm. It was no great full-rigg'd ship, nor majestic steamer, steering firmly through the gale, but seem'd one of those superb little schooner yachts I had often seen lying anchor'd, rocking so jauntily, in the waters around New York, or up Long Island Sound—now flying uncontroll'd with torn sails and broken spars through the wild sleet and winds and waves of the night. On the deck was a slender, slight,

beautiful figure, a dim man, apparently enjoying all the terror, the murk, and the dislocation of which he was the centre and the victim. That figure of my lurid dream might stand for Edgar Poe, his spirit, his fortunes, and his poems — themselves all lurid dreams.[22]

Thirty years before Whitman attended that unveiling, he had met Poe in New York and had an interview about a piece of his that Poe had published about 1845 in *The Broadway Journal:* "Poe was very cordial, in a quiet way, appear'd well in person, dress, &c. I have a distinct and pleasing remembrance of his looks, voice, manner and matter; very kindly and human, but subdued, perhaps a little jaded."[23]

At the time of honoring Poe's memory in Baltimore, Whitman set down his critical judgment of Poe's poetry, a judgment that has since become part of American literary history. Whitman wrote:

Almost without the first sign of moral principle, or of the concrete or its heroisms, or the simpler affections of the heart, Poe's verses illustrate an intense faculty for technical and abstract beauty, with the rhyming to excess, an incorrigible propensity toward nocturnal themes, a demoniac undertone behind every page — and, by final judgment, probably belong among the electric lights of imaginative literature, brilliant and dazzling, but with no heat. There is an indescribable magnetism about the poet's life and reminiscences, as well as the poems.[24]

In modern times Thornton Wilder, a prominent novelist and playwright, wrote a useful summing up in a letter of January 23, 1952 to Professor Henri Peyre at Yale:

Very amused that you had seen somewhere my presumptuous commendation of Poe, — presumptuous but none the less opportune. His reputation has fallen unbelievably low in this country; even our Southern mandarins dismiss him as a "magazinist," And why did [T. S.] Eliot accept the official invitation to furnish the anniversary éloge *at the Library of Congress, if he had no more to say than that Poe was an adolescent writing for adolescents and that three great French poets admired him because of their inability to see how vulgar his English style was? . . .*

I called my lecture "Poe — Criminal, Victim, and Detective." Nightly he murdered Mr. Allan and nightly he buried his tubercular brides in subterranean vaults; and day and night he was himself hunted and stifled; but he called on the Mind to save him, to bring control and order and to explain the procedures of evil, — and not only evil, but all magic and spell of the irrational including poetry itself, the mystery of being, itself. Astronomical physicists find that much of Eureka *is misguided (at Harvard I persuaded two of them to read it); but they acknowledge its fascination, and its fascination is its courage. If Mind operated in the Universe, Mind might operate that way.*

No wonder that some great Frenchmen recognized an insatiable and audacious curiosité; *and no wonder that a fastidious and* frileux *ex-American was rendered uncomfortable by a writer who did not ask refuge of any dogma or system* . . . . [25]

Let Washington then be the scene for the end of this chapter: first, with T. S. Eliot belittling Poe to an audience at the Library of Congress, and second, in an anecdote from Mary E. Phillips's biography of Poe (1926): "A Washington, D.C. dealer in old books some years ago was called by two ladies, the Misses Wolfe, to look over their little library of small value. When leaving he noticed a card-bound book serving as a bureau caster and asked about it. The ladies said: 'That's nothing. It's by Mr. Poe: he used to call in Baltimore. It was his gift. It fell very flat when published.'"[26]

So much for *Al Aaraaf, Tamerlane, and Minor Poems* (1829)! (Or was it the even richer volume of 1831?) And so much for the early marriage of Poe to poetry, of which those Baltimore books were first fruits. A copy of *Al Aaraaf* would sell today — if you could find one — for between $40,000 and $50,000.[27]

V
Dawn of a Fine Literary Day?

A gap separating the ridiculous *Ten Nights in a Bar-Room,* by T. S. Arthur, from the sublime slave narrative *The Life and Times of Frederick Douglass,* with notes on what Poe called the "spleen of the little fish" (fellow writers in Baltimore).

"I look anxiously for the first number [of a new Baltimore magazine called *American Museum of Literature and the Arts*] from which I date the dawn of a fine literary day in Baltimore."[1]

— Edgar Allan Poe, an exile from Baltimore

"Charles Carroll the Signer is dead and Archbishop Carroll is dead and there is no vision in the land."[2]

— Ralph Waldo Emerson, a visitor to Baltimore

"[When a slave boy in Baltimore] fortunately or unfortunately, I had, by blacking boots for some gentleman, earned a little money with which I purchased of Mr. Knight, on Thames Street, what was then a very popular school book, viz., *The Columbian Orator,* for which I paid fifty cents.... I met there one of Sheridan's mighty speeches on the subject of Catholic Emancipation, Lord Chatham's speech on the American War, and speeches by the great William Pitt, and by Fox.... Here was indeed a noble acquisition. If I had ever wavered under the consideration that the Almighty, in some way, had ordained slavery and willed my enslavement for His own glory, I wavered no longer. I had now penetrated to the secret of all slavery and all oppression, and had ascertained their true foundation to be in the pride, the power, and the avarice of man."[3]

— Frederick Douglass

Young Frederick Douglass was painted (probably by Elisha N. Hammond) after his escape from slavery in Baltimore and about the time of writing his first memoir.

Poe might well have fared well in Baltimore had he been given a magazine to edit there. If he had come back, the fine literary day that he predicted would have dawned there. But that dawn proved false, though other writers did try to keep the promise. Luckily for the reader, this chapter turns up a surprise. It also introduces Poe's rivals, some of them colorful men and women. And its climax is one great book.

We begin with just how Maryland's literary life looked to an outsider in 1843, after Poe and the writers in his group had gone to other places or into other lines. We find out from the prominent New England essayist Ralph Waldo Emerson's letter to his wife from Baltimore:

Concerned like all New Englanders for cultural life, Emerson asked a native,

Q: "Have you any libraries here?"
A: "None."
Q: "Have you any poet?"
A: "Yes, Mr. McJilton."
Q: "Who?"
A: "Mr. McJilton."
Q: "Any scholar?"
A: "None."

To this exchange the author of "The American Scholar" (1837) added: "Charles Carroll the Signer is dead and Archbishop Carroll is dead, and there is no vision in the land."[4]

At about the same time Poe wrote to the editors of a new Baltimore magazine called the *American Museum of Literature and the Arts*: "I look anxiously for the first number from which I date the dawn of a fine literary day in Baltimore." (September 4, 1838)[5]

Later Poe wrote, again to a Baltimore editor: "How is it...that a *Magazine* of the highest class has never yet succeeded in Baltimore?" He added the sour note, "I have often thought, of late, how much better it would have been had you joined me in a Magazine project in the Monumental City, rather than engage with the 'Visiter'—a journal which has never yet been able to recover from the *mauvais odeur* imparted to it by Hewitt." Poe's conclusion, though, was, "Notwithstanding the many failures in Baltimore, I still am firmly convinced that your city is the best adapted for such a Magazine as I propose, of any in the Union."[6]

The ex-resident Poe's optimism here contrasts with Emerson's lamenting. True, a certain vision *had* gone from the land with the last of the Signers, Charles Carroll. Two other reasons for pessimism about Maryland writing were, first, Poe's failure to find a capitalist to back his proposed magazine there, and, second, the sidetracking of energies to the politics of slavery and secession. But this chapter springs a surprise. Unexpected turns of literary fortunes in the pre-Civil War era have left us many dull pieces and, wonder of wonders, one classic.

Whether writing trash or classic, no author had an easy time in Maryland then. Poe's struggle to make a living by writing in the 1830s would today be like suffering as a gifted writer in a Third World country. The parallel is striking. Back in 1835 Baltimore, Poe found a literary circle but no reading public big enough to support him. Both he and today's Third World writer make us curious about how to overcome such an obstacle.

In Poe's case the way was his lucky landing in a city that, like him, was just entering into greatness. He became part of its dash forward. And there he met other writers, men attracted by Baltimore's numerous publications and literary pretensions. Along with Poe they cultivated literary fields as promising as the virgin land other American pioneers were bringing to cultivation then in the West. Poe, of course, garnered the bumper crop. The others — harvesting little — enter this literary history for two reasons. One reason was their usefulness to him. They encouraged him to write and to reach for highest standards. Besides that, they joined him in creating a lively literary center.

What stimulated them and Poe to do so was the energy generated in that boomtown. That electricity came from the clash of cultures: side by side were men who staffed the port, European immigrants, planter aristocrats, black slaves, free blacks, and young, talented men from older cities such as Boston and from rural Pennsylvania and Virginia. Besides this clash of cultures, another reason for Baltimore's literary ferment came from its being a place of disequilibrium. There the old was being speeded out of the way. In its place came what one historian has called "new coalescences in thought, imagination, feeling and creative form."[7] It was the kind of place where the creation of literature was most likely.

Better than his fellow writers in town, Poe caught that new spirit. One result was his new idea of making things short: he promoted the short story, the short poem, and the single effect. Such innovations proved that he cleared the ground and erected brand new structures very much the way his contemporary frontiersmen were doing in the West. Therefore, Mencken insisted that Poe reflected Jacksonian America almost as brilliantly as Davy Crockett.[8]

Still, Baltimore was not wild Tennessee. And as a literary historian, I must tell more here about what manner of place Poe and those other young literati flocked to in the 1830s. Though Baltimore ranked second after New York in size, physically the town was compact and built in red brick rows lining an irregular street pattern. Workers there walked to their jobs from small rowhouses like those of Poe and his fellow writers. Businessmen lived above their shops and offices.

Everybody crowded around the harbor. (Poe first lived only three blocks from City Dock.) Baltimoreans depended on the port for livelihoods, though the nation's first industrial park was developing at Canton, a district next to Fells Point. From the South came raw cotton for mills like the ones John Pendleton Kennedy owned on Gwynns Falls. The cotton duck manufactured there soon after was made into Union Army tents. Spanish America sent up sugar, copper, hides, and coffee, and took back wheat and flour. Chesapeake Bay tobacco was made into cigars and exported to Europe by Mencken's grandfather and other German immigrants.

Familiar sights to Poe and other writers were sails of clipper ships. The famous *Ann McKim* shone white against the smoke of the *Chesapeake* and other steamboats. Emigré New England writers as well as passengers from abroad liked this busy port. Their comments make boring reading because they all praised the same two local products: 1) beautiful women such as Betsy Patterson, who angered Napoleon by marrying his brother, and 2) succulent food, gathered from that vast protein factory of Chesapeake Bay (Mencken's phrase). Anthony Trollope, the English author of the Palliser novels, reported that the greatest gift of nature to Maryland was the sending of canvas-backed ducks, "web-footed birds of Paradise."[9]

Even the mint juleps of Barnum's Hotel on Monument Square lived in legend, fixed there when the English novelist William Makepeace Thackeray sipped them with the American essayist Washington Irving. Charles Dickens stopped at that hotel also, but he praised the comforts — hot water, not juleps.

By contrast, few visitors or residents liked Washington. One negative summation came from Charles Francis Adams who had known the capital practically from its beginning, when his grandfather John Adams was the first President to occupy the White House. His observation about that city when he was there on the eve of the Civil War was "the same rude colony camped in the same forest, with the same unfinished Greek temples for workrooms, and sloughs for roads."[10]

With Baltimore enjoying such fame among literary lions, we can see why neophyte writers were also attracted there. Turning now to this group, we must prepare ourselves with three facts. First, all these authors knew Poe, and most of them competed with him. Those who edited journals bought his writings. Second, nothing they wrote is read today, and only one work, the novel *Ten Nights in a Bar-Room,* is remembered. Third, Poe wrote about their publications in later reviews and in a series analyzing authors' handwriting. Though his words usually made the author squirm, he helps us put this large group in focus.

Two letters help us understand why they squirmed. To a Baltimore journalist, J. Beauchamp Jones, he wrote, "I presume it is the 'Athenaeum' [edited by T. S. Arthur] which has honoured me with its ill-nature. . . . It is always desirable to know *who are* our enemies, and what are the nature of their attacks. I intend to put up with nothing that I can *put down* (excuse the pun) and I am not aware that there is any one in Baltimore whom I have a particular reason to fear in a regular set-to. . . . You speak of 'enemies'—could you give me their names? All the literary people in Baltimore, as far as I know them, have at least *professed* a friendship." [11] To Dr. Joseph Snodgrass he later wrote a more caustic evaluation: "You say some of your monumental writers 'feel *small*'—but is not that, for them, a natural feeling?"[12]

That nasty comment could have meant most men and women in this chapter except Lambert Wilmer. Poe thought well of him and his writing. In *Autography* Poe commented that Wilmer had reaped the usual fruits of a spirit of independence, unpopularity. But better days were in store for him, Poe predicted, and for all who hold the right way "despising the yelping of the small dogs of our literature."[13] Wilmer, on his side, defended Poe in such lines as these:

. . . tho' fortune now
Averts her face, and heedless crowds
To blocks, like senseless Pagans, bow;—
Yet time shall dissipate the clouds,
Dissolve the mist which merit shrouds,
And fix the Laurel on thy *brow.*
There let it grow; and there 'twould be
If justice rul'd and men could see.[14]

Except for Wilmer and one or two others, Poe treated his fellow Baltimore authors as adversaries. Some of them didn't care much for him either. John Hewitt, Poe's rival in the *Saturday Visiter* contests, described Poe's temperament as, "Undoubtedly sanguine, yet morbid.

Remorse brought the 'Raven' to the bust of Pallas, and created the weird forms that continually flitted through his fancy. I always thought Poe a misanthrope, cherishing none of the kindlier feelings of our nature. His criticisms were bitter in the extreme. So freely did he dispense his gall that it was hard to induce publishers of periodicals to publish his essays."[15]

John Hewitt was himself an odd duck. He seems to have been fated to choose the wrong course, whether with Poe or secession or career. His own writing lacked merit. He was a musician, son of a musician, and should have stuck to music, not writing. He wrote the music of one popular Confederate song of the Civil War, "All Quiet Along the Potomac." Though today we sing some songs of his era—Stephen Foster's, for example, and "The Blue-Tail'd Fly"—we don't sing his. He also composed an oratorio called "Jephtha's Daughter." A critic soon destroyed it by observing that Hewitt seemed unawed by knowing that the great Handel had treated the same subject earlier.

Though Hewitt left Baltimore a few years after Poe (and ended up in Washington), he had known local literati well enough to make his memoir worth reading. And he was so wrong in judging Poe in *Shadow on the Wall: Glimpses of the Past* (1877) that we today can see the quality of the prejudice against Poe. For example, Hewitt asserted that Poe had added little to the literary reputation of the country, that the story "Manuscript Found in a Bottle" was only a new version of Coleridge's "Rhyme of the Ancient Mariner," and that reading Poe's verse was like travelling over a pile of brick-bats, so uneven and irregular was the rhythm.

Reading those judgments, we see why Poe disliked him. We also question Hewitt's contention that Poe was overbearing and spiteful. One victim on whom Hewitt said Poe vented his spleen was Dr. John Lofland, who published derivative poems as "The Bard of Milford" (Delaware, his birthplace). According to Hewitt, Lofland "used to demean himself by going into low groggeries and writing off a few stanzas on any subject the barkeeper might suggest for a taste of the liquid fire." Addicted to opium as well as alcohol, he certainly did not need or deserve Poe's contempt. Nevertheless, according to a later biographer, he accepted the challenge Poe laid down to the boys in the back room of the Seven Stars, a tavern on Water Street. That challenge was to write more verses in a given time than Poe could. Lofland accepted for the next afternoon, the wager being liquor for the whole party. Lofland won. Since liquor was said to have started the test, the biographer closed with "the party greeting the dawn of the succeeding day with maudlin recitations and boosy [sic] songs."[16]

Such boozy dawns must have been rare, considering the great quantity of writing done by Poe and the others. Timothy Shay Arthur, for example, turned out six percent of all American fiction for his era, 150 novels and collections of short fiction. He boasted that he had never written a line that he would wish expunged. Time has expunged them all. What is left is the title of his best-selling temperance novel, *Ten Nights in a Bar-Room and What I Saw There* (1854). That book grew out of Arthur's earlier tales about the Washington Temperance Society of Baltimore, *Six Nights with the Washingtonians* (1842), that brought him national notice. It sold over 400,000 copies and was turned into the most popular play in American history: it stayed in production for 100 years. We accept Poe's opinion of Arthur that what little merit he had was negative. Arthur had come to Baltimore as a boy apprentice to a tailor and had taught himself to write. The result you judge from this passage from "Night the Fourth" of the *Ten Nights:*

Mrs. Slade stood near the table, on which burned a lamp. I noticed that her eyes were red, and that there was on her countenance a troubled and sorrowful expression.

"We have just heard," said one of the company, "that little Mary Morgan is dead."

"Yes — it is too true," answered Mrs. Slade, mournfully. "I have just left there. Poor child! She has passed from an evil world."

"Evil it has indeed been to her," was remarked.

"You may well say that. And yet, amid all the evil, she has been an angel of mercy. Her last thought in dying was of her miserable father. For him at any time, she would have laid down her life willingly."

"Her mother must be nearly broken-hearted. Mary is the last of her children."

"And yet the child's death may prove a blessing to her."

"How so?"

"Her father promised Mary, just at the last moment — solemnly promised her — that, henceforth, he would never taste liquor. That was all her trouble. That was the thorn in her dying pillow. But he plucked it out, and she went to sleep, lying against his heart. Oh, gentlemen! it was the most touching sight I ever saw."[17]

Poe liked another of the local literati, John McJilton, better than Arthur as a man, and thought that he had even written one or two very good things. McJilton's poems, Hewitt said, might be placed in competition with the mental efforts of a romantic schoolgirl. He started out life as a cabinetmaker, but veneering and varnish did not suit a mind like his, and he took to the pen in downright earnest. After editing the *Baltimore Monument,* he ran the Floating School of Baltimore, a maritime training program conducted on shipboard in the harbor. He ended up an Episcopal priest in Brooklyn.

Poe also liked the fiction of Frederick W. Thomas, who had grown up in Bel Air, Harford County, and Baltimore. As one of Poe's earliest and best friends, he received the frankest letters. Thomas had begun his literary career at the age of 17 with a poetical lampoon upon certain Baltimore fops. Baltimore was also the setting of some of his fiction. His *Clinton Bradshawe,* Poe said, was "remarkable for a frank, unscrupulous portrait of men and things, in high life and low, and by unusual discrimination and observation in respect to character."[18] Most of the characters were drawn from life.

A number of these writers abandoned Baltimore, as Thomas did. The most prominent emigrant probably was George Henry Calvert, descendant of the original proprietor of Maryland and editor of the Baltimore *American* (1827-1840). He left for Newport, Rhode Island, where he later became mayor. He wrote a lot, including what Poe considered to be feeble and commonplace poetry. Another literary emigré and native Baltimorean, Robert Walsh, edited journals in Philadelphia. There Poe had tried to enlist his aid in publishing his poems. Later Poe praised his *Didactics: Social, Literary, and Political* (1836) as the work of a thinker, scholar, and fine writer. Most of these pieces Walsh composed in Paris, the capital to which he became unofficial American literary ambassador.

Among Poe's group were three stay-at-homes. One of them, Nathan C. Brooks, worked hard at elevating the literary reputation of Maryland. Though born in Elkton, Cecil County, he lived for most of his life in Baltimore. There he knew Poe and later, as editor of the *Baltimore Monument,* printed Poe's favorite short story, "Ligeia." Brooks did write himself, but he was entirely too sensitive for a littérateur, reported Hewitt, and took up the presidency of the first college for women in Maryland, the Female College of Baltimore. Poe commented, "His serious prose is often very good — is always well worked — but in his comic attempts he fails, without appearing to be aware of his failure."[19]

Another stay-at-home of literary bent was the Englishman William Henry Carpenter. Having been a newspaper editor in Baltimore, he left nothing to literature. What he did leave was a charming image of Poe on the occasion of their final meeting: Poe "with a sort of supercilious way he sometimes assumed, stretched out one finger, and Carpenter extended his forefinger and laid it on Poe's, upon which Poe laughed and shook hands."[20]

Brantz Mayer left us no such pictures or solid literary work, though he might have if he hadn't dabbled so much. Born in Baltimore in 1809, he went from law to journalism to soldiering to diplomacy and back to writing. His books were popular for a time. The most lively was called a novel, *Captain Canot, or Twenty Years of the Life of an African Slaver* (1854), though actually it was the memoirs of a French slaveship's captain, Theophilus Conneau, who wrote, "with the flattering expectations that it will bring harvest to my empty treasury." That harvest no doubt was increased by Mayer's taming of the manuscript for genteel readers. Now that the original memoir is in print (1976), however, we discover how Mayer's editing and overblown prose killed Conneau's vigor.[21]

Writing in his room at Susquehanna House in Baltimore, Conneau set down the most complete narrative of trading in slaves — capture, slave factory, Middle Passage, and sale — all. After finishing his book in spring of 1854, Conneau sailed to Liverpool, where he wrote Mayer that he would trade an inch of Baltimore for all of England. Mayer remained in that favored city. There he wrote a memoir of Jared Sparks, erstwhile pastor of the First Unitarian Church on Franklin Street, then president of Harvard, and biographer of Washington. Mayer founded the Maryland Historical Society and, Hewitt reported, "was handsome in person, rather aristocratic, and a great admirer of women, wine, polite literature, the fine arts; saying nothing of his refined taste for music."[22]

Although other male writers probably considered women as Mayer did, as ornaments, several bluestockings contributed to the literary ferment of the place. One was Elizabeth Crawford, the wife of the gifted French architect, Maximilien Godefroy. She published under the nom de plume of Bertha Ironsides. Much better known was another native Maryland woman, Anne Newport Royall, called by President John Quincy Adams a virago errant. She irritated other people too with her attacks on what she considered political corruption. The waspishness of her travel sketches comes out in this comment on Hagerstown, Washington County, in 1827: "The women are short and ill-shaped and have a vacancy of countenance which too evidently shows the want of proper schools."[23] To gather such observations for her ten books she travelled to important settlements.

William Lloyd Garrison was caricatured just before abolition of slavery, the goal for which he wrote and suffered in Baltimore and elsewhere.

R. C. Woodville captured a Baltimore scene about the time Poe used to visit oyster houses there and when newspapers printed literature as well as news.

Top, Wye House, 18th-century plantation house, was built by the politically powerful, rich Lloyd family, Talbot County, Eastern Shore. There Frederick Douglass worked as a slave.

Bottom, Cedar Hill, Anacostia, D.C., was purchased as residence by Frederick Douglass after the Civil War. Note the similarity in appearance between this house and Wye—this one 19th-century and simpler.

Evidence of the Southernness of Maryland is in this rare photograph of buildings at Pratt and Howard Streets, Baltimore, where slaves were lodged before being sold. Near the site today stands a statue of Justice Thurgood Marshall, native Baltimorean and first black to serve on the Supreme Court.

Frances Ellen Watkins Harper, born a free black in Baltimore, went north to write and preach for abolition and other reforms. This photograph was frontispiece for her novel *Iola, or Shadows Uplifted.*

She drove in style — in her own coach with three slaves and a courier — as if to confirm rumors of her descent from King Charles II. At the end of her writing career she was living in a big, bare house in Washington. To the end she was editing a newspaper, the first in the nation edited solely by a woman.

Another of the bluestockings was Mary Barney, who had married a printer. She wrote the biography of her brother Commodore Joshua Barney. Noteworthy was her Baltimore publication, the *National Magazine, or Lady's Emporium* (1830). On its cover she placed a picture of the bust of Sappho surrounded by emblems of the arts. In it she printed a letter to "My dear Mrs. Editor," beginning with a compliment to Mary Barney for being a woman "who has spirit enough to dispute with the lords of creation, (as the fops and dandies who flutter around us proudly style themselves,) the exclusive pretensions to intellect, taste, and genius, and to vindicate the claims of our sex to an equality of rank, at least, in the vast empire of mind."

Female education clearly was a concern of the editor. A "Dialogue on Female Education" rehearsed the arguments, such as the idea that women's "minds were never designed to soar into the higher regions of literature and science." Another point about authorship: she went into writing as "the only alternative to the worse evils of beggary and dependence — a profession, laborious and expensive under the most favorable auspices, and to one of her sex and inexperience doubly vexacious, difficult and hazardous."[24]

Unfortunately, Barney's attempts to publish in Baltimore failed. Like Poe and most of the others in this chapter, she found the task frustrating. Though that city had been stimulating for them all in their formative phases, it could not hold them. For all its urban excitements, it was too much in flux perhaps to sustain literati.

Almost all writers who remained in Baltimore after the 1830s abandoned literature. It would seem that if writers stayed, they gave up writing personal responses to the life going on behind the public façade. Instead, they were drawn into politics or civic enterprises — something public. For example, when John Pendleton Kennedy published his first novel, *Swallow Barn,* anonymously and dedicated it to William Wirt, Wirt's characterization of the author was "a merry young lawyer." Had Kennedy been, like Poe, a serious young *writer,* he wouldn't have settled for a comfortable role as politician and public man.

One reason for the lack of deep literary culture undoubtedly was the relative newness of Baltimore. But more significant probably was the town's being too Southern in spirit. Why that spirit has been many times alien to literature is a question scholars have studied. Commonly aired explanations include these: first, the pre-Civil War South had archaic tastes and wasn't open to new ideas and methods. Second, the staple product cotton made the South a dependency of England and New England factories, an economic fact that undercut independent thought and self-confidence.

Along with cotton came the slave system. That also hindered the critical sense, for Southern writers felt forced to defend slavery. For writers, the time was not stimulating intellectually since the slave system inhibited change. So the Southern mind did not go in for analyzing. Besides, outdoor life and simple rural ways tended to develop types rather than individual people. Then, too, the failure to write down what people were doing and thinking meant a scarcity of raw material for later writers. The Southerner talked and sang, orated and told stories. He did not read much, and so he failed to support magazines, publishing houses, and libraries.

That makes a long list. Some of it will be contradicted in later chapters. But enough of Southernness infused Maryland to prevent its metropolis, Baltimore, from becoming a literary capital like Boston. Writers were "mostly low people," natives thought. You might as well have been bankrupt as an author back in 1820, one of them, John Pendleton Kennedy, reported in his own *Red Book* (1821). He added that poverty would prevail until "some of our fashionables shall make it the mode — which is unlikely to happen in this generation." Kennedy's uncle, Edmund Pendleton, in whose law office he trained, told him, "As to poetical eminence I deem it of no great value in this state of ours."[25]

Happily we can blot out that gloominess with one masterpiece by a Talbot Countian who learned the power of words in Baltimore. It is the best non-fiction book written by a Maryland black, and the chief slave narrative in American literature. That such a classic should have come out of the hectic era of gathering war is a marvel. The book is *The Narrative of the Life and Times of Frederick Douglass, An American Slave, Written by Himself,* published at the Anti-Slavery Office in Boston, 1845.

To see just how outstanding Douglass's book is we must first look at two other Maryland-inspired writings of the same era. These were of good quality, were written by whites, and were, like his, strongly abolitionist in theme. One was a series of poems and essays written by a New England abolitionist who had worked in Baltimore. The other was a novel by a Frenchman, who had visited Baltimore and

Washington.

That Frenchman, Gustav de Beaumont, had accompanied Alexis de Tocqueville on his American tour of 1831–1832 that was basis for his classic study *Democracy in America* (1835). Though the two French travellers had originally planned to write a book together, they ended by producing two. Beaumont's was the novel *Marie or Slavery in the United States* (1835). It figures in local literary history not just because so much of the observed Baltimore scene became part of Beaumont's fiction. Even more significant is his portrayal of the effect of slavery on the townspeople.

It was not much of a novel. Still, it is worth reading for pictures of Maryland life in 1830s as noted by an intelligent foreigner. The following excerpt tells how, at the very moment when the chief character, a Frenchman, is marrying the beautiful Baltimore mulatto Marie in church, a great tumult burst out suddenly at the door:

"The rioters!" cried an apprehensive voice. The cry flew from mouth to mouth; then a dismal silence fell below the sacred vault. The noise of a disorderly multitude could be heard without, sounding like the rumblings of an approaching storm. Driven by an impetuous wind the thundercloud sweeps on, and already the lightning is upon our heads! "Death to the colored people! To the church! To the church!" These terrible shouts re-echoed from all about; terror seized the assembled faithful; the priest grew pale, his knees failed him, the ring that was to unite us fell from his hand! Marie, paralyzed with fear, became insensible and reeled; I gave to the swooning maiden the support of that arm which an instant later would have embraced my beloved wife.[26]

The other writer to set beside Frederick Douglass is William Lloyd Garrison. That New England abolitionist came to Maryland where Quakers and others had long tried to rid the state of slavery. One group of Baltimoreans, including Francis Scott Key, made plans for repatriation for blacks in Liberia. Others, including Garrison, opposed that scheme. Garrison was taking his first step toward becoming the chief American antislavery writer right there in slaveholding Maryland. His initiation was harsh: his incendiary writing with Benjamin Lundy in the Baltimore newspaper *The Genius of Universal Emancipation* landed him in jail, after first being knocked down in the street by a slave dealer.

On the wall of his prison cell Garrison penciled this poem, "The Free Mind — A Prison Sonnet":

High walls and huge the body may confine,

And iron grates obstruct the prisoner's gaze,
And massive bolts may baffle his design,
And watchful keepers mark his devious ways;
Yet scorns th' immortal mind *this base control;*
No chains can bind it, and no cell enclose:
Swifter than light it flies from pole to pole,
And in a flash from earth to heaven it goes!
It leaps from mount to mount, from vale to vale
It wanders, plucking honeyed fruits and flowers;
It visits home, to hear the fire-side tale,
Or in sweet converse pass the joyous hours:
'Tis up before the sun, roaming afar,
And in its watches wearies every star![27]

Of Garrison a local observer said that a halter made of Southern hemp would have frightened him out of his boots: "Had he been disposed of when he ventured as far south as Baltimore, the unfortunate events which have occurred [i.e., the Civil War] might have been avoided."[28] Imagine blaming the War on this one writer! Just add his power with words to that of Harriet Beecher Stowe and Frederick Douglass, and we have sound basis for much blame. Just consider these words by Garrison, for example:

Abolitionism is not a hobby, got up for personal or associated aggrandisement; it is not a political ruse; it is not a spasm of sympathy, which lasts but for a moment, leaving the system weak and worn; it is not a fever of enthusiasm; it is not the fruit of fanaticism; it is not a spirit of faction. It is of heaven, not of men. It lives in the heart as a vital principle. It is an essential part of Christianity, and aside from it there can be no humanity. Its scope is not confined to the slave population of the United States, but embraces mankind. Opposition cannot weary it, force cannot put it down, fire cannot consume it.[29]

Eloquence like that is hard to beat, but within a decade after Garrison had left Maryland after the jailing, he attracted to his side an even better writer, a native Marylander, Frederick Douglass. That he was also a slave made him an ideal spokesman for abolition. That he was articulate, intelligent, and dignified—an impressive public speaker—soon made him a partner with Garrison and other New England writer-abolitionists such as John Greenleaf Whittier and James Russell Lowell.

Six years after he escaped from Baltimore he wrote the first of his three autobiographies. It turned out to be a masterpiece—and not just among slave narratives. In it he told of being reared on a Talbot County plantation, the offspring of a black slave and a white man. As a boy he was sent to Baltimore where he surreptitiously learned to read and thus began his journey to becoming an abolitionist writer.

While still a slave, he changed his name to Douglass, the name of a fugitive chieftain in Sir Walter Scott's *The Lady of the Lake*. The name was apt because he became a fugitive on Monday, September 3, 1838, when he got on the back of a train as it was pulling out of President Street Station, Baltimore. He was dressed as a sailor and carried the identification papers of a friend. At Wilmington, Delaware, he took a steamer to Philadelphia and shortly went on to New York, where he married his Baltimore fiancée, a free black. He himself bought his freedom after he became famous.

His fame arose from his eloquence on lecture platforms and in print. His *Life and Times* became a classic. In college lecture halls today students analyze that book as a masterpiece of rhetoric. An example of his power is this account of how he learned to read as a household slave in Fell's Point, Baltimore:

The frequent hearing of my mistress reading the Bible aloud, for she often read aloud when her husband was absent, awakened my curiosity in respect to this mystery of reading, and roused in me the desire to learn. Up to this time I had known nothing whatever of this wonderful art, and my ignorance and inexperience of what it could do for me, as well as my confidence in my mistress, emboldened me to ask her to teach me to read. With an unconsciousness and inexperience equal to my own, she readily consented, and in an incredibly short time, by her kind assistance, I had mastered the alphabet and could spell words of three or four letters.[30]

Douglass read to unlock the rhetoric of white society. Then he was able to use rhetoric as a weapon against that society's enslaving of blacks. Like Benjamin Franklin, he used autobiography as a means of teaching readers. Behind his persona (his invented self) hides a trickster—the sly underdog with the power to outwit opponents. His book then is truly as revolutionary as anything that Henry David Thoreau wrote, though his approach has much more guile in it.

An example is his account of his return to Talbot County as a famous man and Marshal of the District of Columbia. There he was invited to call on his old owner and father (?) Anthony Auld:

On reaching the house I was met by Mr. Wm. H. Bruff, a son-in-law of Capt. Auld, and Mrs. Louisa Bruff, his daughter, and was conducted by them immediately to the bedroom of Capt. Auld. We addressed each other simultaneously, he calling me "Marshal Douglass," and I, as I had always called him, "Captain Auld." Hearing myself called by him "Marshal Douglass," I instantly broke up the formal nature of the meeting by saying, "Not Marshal, but Frederick to you as formerly." We shook hands cordially, and in the act of doing so, he, having been long stricken with palsy, shed tears as men thus afflicted will do when excited by any deep emotion. The sight of him, the changes which time had wrought in him, his tremulous hands constantly in motion, and all the circumstances of his condition affected me deeply, and for a time choked my voice and made me speechless. We both, however, got the better of our feelings, and conversed freely about the past.

Though broken by age and palsy, the mind of Capt. Auld was remarkably clear and strong. After he had become composed I asked him what he thought of my conduct in running away and going to the North. He hesitated a moment as if to properly formulate his reply, and said: "Frederick, I always knew you were too smart to be a slave, and had I been in your place, I should have done as you did." I said, "Capt. Auld, I am glad to hear you say this. I did not run away from you, but from slavery; it was not that I loved Caesar less, but Rome more."

I told him that I had made a mistake in my narrative, a copy of which I had sent him, in attributing to him ungrateful and cruel treatment of my grandmother — that I had done so on the supposition that in the division of the property of my old master, Mr. Aaron Anthony, my grandmother had fallen to him, and that he had left her in her old age, when she could be no longer of service to him, to pick up her living in solitude with none to help her, or, in other words, had turned her out to die like an old horse. "Ah!" he said, "that was a mistake, I never owned your grandmother; she in the division of slaves was awarded to my brother-in-law, Andrew Anthony, but," he added quickly, "I brought her down here and took care of her long as she lived." The fact is, that, after writing my narrative describing the condition of my grandmother, Capt. Auld's attention being thus called to it, he rescued her from her destitution. I told him that this mistake of mine was corrected as soon as I discovered it, and that I had at no time any wish to do him injustice — that I regarded both of us as victims of a system. "Oh, I never liked slavery," he said, "and I meant to emancipate all of my slaves when they reached the age of twenty-five years."[31]

Douglass's book stands out today as the most alive of local pre-

Civil War writing except for Poe's. It is one of the books, like *Robinson Crusoe,* that readers wish were longer.

Other pieces did come out by Maryland abolitionists. For example, the black poet Frances Ellen Watkins Harper developed her talents for speaking and writing by campaigning in the North for abolition. In 1825 Harper was born free in slave-holding Baltimore, niece of a leader among free black people. She lived there 26 years. Then in 1851 she left to teach in Ohio. But soon she went lecturing for the Anti-Slavery Society, just as her fellow Baltimorean Frederick Douglass did. She also helped run the Underground Railroad, in which another Maryland woman Harriet Tubman was active. Her poem "The Slave Market" presents that era:

The sale began—young girls were there,
Defenceless in their wretchedness,
Whose stifled sobs of deep despair
Revealed their anguish and distress.

And mothers stood with streaming eyes,
And saw their dearest children sold;
Unheeded rose their bitter cries,
While tyrants bartered them for gold.[32]

She undoubtedly knew well the slave market at West Pratt and Howard Streets, near her home on Camden Street.

After the Civil War, she continued agitating for reform, this time for women's suffrage and temperance. By then settled in Philadelphia, she was popular as lecturer and writer. According to literary historians, she may have published the first novel by an American black woman, and the first short story by any black writer.

The colonial sot-weed factor Ebenezer Cook might well have marveled at Frances Ellen Watkins Harper and other poetic descendants of the African slaves he had watched cultivating his tobacco crops. One heir, the poet Paul Laurence Dunbar (1872–1906), once on the staff of the Library of Congress, was descended from slaves on Maryland's Eastern Shore. He himself introduced into his poems old refrains and dialect as well as black folklore.

During the past seventy-five years one of the best known poems by a black was "Incident" (1925), by Countee Cullen:

Once riding in old Baltimore,
Heart-filled, head-filled with glee,
I saw a Baltimorean
Keep looking straight at me.

Now I was eight and very small,
And he was no whit bigger,
And so I smiled, but he poked out
His tongue, and called me, "Nigger."

I saw the whole of Baltimore
From May until December;
Of all the things that happened there
That's all that I remember.[33]

After he became a well-known writer of the 1920s, Cullen again suffered insult when an invitation to address the Baltimore City Club had to be cancelled because no hotel or theatre would admit a black poet. To Carl Van Vechten he wrote that he had not as yet written his second diatribe against Baltimore, but he knew it wouldn't do any good.[34]

Two other sometime residents of Maryland were connected with academic life: Zora Neale Hurston studied at Morgan Academy in Baltimore and supported herself waitressing and by working in the home of a white clergyman and his wife; then she went on to Howard University in the District. Both Baltimore and Washington figure in her memoir *Dust Tracks on a Road* (1942). Some critics rank very high her novel *Their Eyes Were Watching God* (1937).

Another well-known black writer Dudley Randall had been born in Washington in 1914, and in 1954-1956 was associate librarian at Morgan State College. During later years he returned to Detroit, where he had once worked as a foundry worker for Ford Motor Company. There he founded the Broadside Press that has published many black poets. One of his best-known poems is "The Ballad of Birmingham (On the Bombing of a Church in Birmingham, Alabama, 1963)."

An unexpected poet was the famous singer Billie Holiday (called "Lady Day"). She was born in Baltimore on April 7, 1915, as Eleanor Gough McKay, illegitimate daughter of an Irish cleaning woman and a black guitarist with the Fletcher Henderson band. Born into poverty in a tiny rowhouse of the 200 block South Durham Street, she lived in that neighborhood until her singing took her to Harlem. At 15 her career began at the Paradise Club on West Fayette Street. Two of the songs for which she wrote lyrics are famous. One was "Long Gone Blues," with its refrain about a good girl whose love was all wrong. Another was "God Bless the Child That's Got His Own."

Her song's cry of alienation contrasts with the attitude of the so-called Uncle Tom. That epithet for a subservient attitude came from the novel *Uncle Tom's Cabin* (1852), by Harriet Beecher Stowe. And behind the character Uncle Tom stands her model Josiah Henson (1789–1883), a Maryland slave who published a popular pamphlet about his life. That trustworthy slave grew up on a plantation south of Rockville, Montgomery County. His log cabin there was later restored and preserved, an appropriate symbol of pre-Civil War Maryland.[35]

Also appropriate was the choice of Washington as the place to launch the explosive *Uncle Tom's Cabin*. That novel first appeared as a serial in an anti-slavery weekly there from June 8, 1851 to April 1, 1852. Within a year after publication as a book, it sold over 300,000 copies. So influential was the novel that a decade later President Lincoln greeted Stowe with the words, "So this is the little lady who made this big war."

The Civil War's hot, bright noon added great writing in Washington, greater books than *Uncle Tom's Cabin* or *Ten Night's In a Bar-Room* or anything from Baltimore's false dawn. Only Frederick Douglass matched Lincoln and Whitman of the war years.

VI
From Drum Taps to Confederate Diaspora

The forging of Lincoln's prose and Whitman's poems in Civil War Washington; the nurturing of literature by Southern emigrés such as Sidney Lanier in postbellum Baltimore.

"[In 1861 at a Confederate Army camp in Virginia] standing in the tent door under cover of darkness, Miss Jennie Cary [of Baltimore] sang 'Maryland, My Maryland!' The refrain was caught up and tossed back from hundreds of rebel throats. . . . As the last note died away there surged from the gathering throng a wild shout, 'We will break her chains — she shall be free! Three cheers and a tiger for Maryland!'

"There was not a dry eye in the tent — and not a rebel cap with a rim on it in the camp. History does not record another such dramatic inception of a war song on the field of battle!"[1]
— Henry F. Shepherd

"I see the blush upon thy cheek,
    Maryland!
For thou wast ever bravely meek,
    Maryland!
But lo! there surges forth a shriek
From hill to hill, from creek to creek
Potomac calls to Chesapeake —
    Maryland! My Maryland! . . .
I hear the distant thunder hum,
    Maryland!
The Old Line's bugle fife and drum,
    Maryland!
She is not dead, nor deaf, nor dumb —
Huzza! She spurns the Northern scum!
She breathes! she burns! she'll come! she'll come!
    Maryland! My Maryland!"[2]
— James Ryder Randall

The Civil War costume of the guide at Barbara Fritchie's House, Frederick,
recalls the Union heroine of John Greenleaf Whittier's poem. Local literature
also reflected Maryland's having been a battleground as well as a place with
divided sympathies.

Put next to that song what were reported as the dying words of Lincoln's assassin John Wilkes Booth, a villainous actor from Harford County: "Tell mother I died for my country. I did what I thought for the best. Useless, useless."

The Confederate cause was useless in a great sense, but useful in writings that came about between 1860 and 1880. This chapter points up that usefulness to literature during the Civil War and Reconstruction. "Usefulness" is a misnomer: out of wartime Washington came great poems by Walt Whitman and great prose by Abraham Lincoln, and out of postwar Baltimore came harbingers of fine writing such as Sidney Lanier. Clearly war gave a vigorous shake to Maryland's literary kaleidoscope and left fresh designs reflecting the times and place.

Parts of those designs depended on Maryland's location at the tip of the South and the toe of the North. Besides being located just across the Potomac River from Confederate Virginia, Maryland enfolded the national capital. Its problems were compounded because slaveholders there (and some others) sympathized with the South. For them the Civil War was truly fratricidal—brother killed brother. These antagonisms came to a head in Baltimore soon after Lincoln's life had been threatened there as he journeyed through to his inauguration. On April 19, 1861, a crowd of Baltimoreans on Pratt Street attacked troops going to defend Washington. The blood shed there was the first blood shed in the Civil War.

Immediately federal military authorities took over civil authority and occupied the city just as they did New Orleans. They stayed a year longer in Baltimore, perhaps because that city controlled much of the rail system, or maybe because so many residents proved irreconcilably Southern in sympathy. That feeling had inspired the poem "Maryland, My Maryland" when occupation began. Its author, James Ryder Randall (a Baltimorean teaching in Louisiana) called on fellow citizens to spurn the Northern scum: "...avenge the patriotic gore [of Baltimoreans] / That fleck'd the streets of Baltimore" when Yankee troops resisted the crowd's Pratt Street attack. Randall's song was sung only behind closed windows. Singing it gave one little Confederate girl a delicious sense of lurking peril. When quite an old lady, the Baltimore poet Lizette Woodworth Reese recaptured feelings about the Yankees' occupation: (Note: The Confederate colors, red and white, were forbidden to be displayed in combination.)

How softly went we in the sunny hall,
Past the carved wardrobe, where the portraits three

Had hidden been a many a week ago,
Of Beauregard, of Jackson, and of Lee!
Then halted, of a sudden, and stooping low,
Felt in our bosoms small,
For tiny flag with white, with rose-red fair,
Sewn fast by daring fingers overnight;
One pot of red geranium, one of white,
From our front sill proclaimed us rebel there.[3]

Back in the wartime, other Marylanders wrote verses to stir Southern passions. For instance, Abram Joseph Ryan of Hagerstown became the elegist-poet of the Confederacy. Another local poet, John Williamson Palmer, turned out ballads such as "Stonewall Jackson's Way" that circulated in manuscript around the Maryland Club, a secessionist stronghold, even before he printed them under a false name. "The Volunteer Zouave in Baltimore" (1862) came from a "Baltimore Lady" bent on sending that Yankee soldier "hum," though flirtatiously eager to have him back in his own clothes, not a uniform. More solemn was "Coming at Last," by George H. Miles, of Frederick County: it welcomed the rebels as they invaded Maryland. It concluded, "Circling Mac's army, / Three days at work!/Under that smile of theirs / Famine may lurk. / Out with the best you have, / Fill the bowl fast, / For Jeff's ragged Rebels/Are coming at last!"

On the Yankee side, Julia Ward Howe wrote "The Battle Hymn of the Republic" one night after she had heard Union soldiers singing "John Brown's Body" in Washington. It opens with familiar lines, "Mine eyes have seen the glory of the coming of the Lord: / He is trampling out the vintage where the grapes of wrath are stored; / He hath loosed the fateful lightning of His terrible swift sword: / His truth is marching on." A sixth stanza is seldom printed: "He is coming like the glory of the morning on the wave, / He is wisdom to the mighty, He is honor to the brave, / So the world shall be His footstool, and the soul of wrong His slave, / Our God is marching on!"[4]

Later in the war, a Georgetown writer, Mrs. E. D. E. N. Southworth, told the story of a brave Frederick woman, Barbara Fritchie, to a famous New England poet John Greenleaf Whittier. Although we now know that her details weren't accurate, the poet seized on the incident. His patriotic lines aided the Yankees then, and echoed in schoolrooms for generations.[5]

Whittier's poem opened with the first invasion of Maryland by Lee's army: "Up from meadows rich with corn, / Clear in the cool September morn, / The clustered spires of Frederick stand /

Green-walled by the hills of Maryland." At the approach of Stonewall Jackson and his Confederate troops, Frederick townspeople prudently hauled down the Union's Stars and Stripes—all except 70-year-old Mrs. Fritchie. Her heart was defiantly loyal. So when a bullet splintered the staff of her flag and it fell, she "snatched the silken scarf" and leaning "far out on the window sill" shook it forth and said, "'Shoot if you must this old gray head, / But spare your country's flag. . .'" At that, Jackson's nobler nature stirred, and he commanded, "'Who touches a hair of yon gray head / Dies like a dog! March on!. . .'"

Such songs as that give us the passion of the Civil War. Many others give us the sadness, and of these Walt Whitman's endure. He became that war's Homer. Chief among these writings about the war were the prose *Specimen Days and Collect* (1882) and his poems in *Drum Taps* (1865), together with *When Lilacs Last in the Dooryard Bloom'd and Other Pieces,* printed in Washington, 1865–1866.

Whitman went to Washington to find his brother, who was wounded in Virginia, and stayed. In a letter of October 1863 Whitman said that he liked Washington very much. Besides, he wrote, "I like the mission I am on here [i.e. helping to comfort the wounded soldiers in hospitals] & as it is deeply holding me I shall continue." At that time he also wrote, "I . . . rub on free & happy enough. . .walk quite a good deal, & in this weather the rich & splendid environs of Washington are an unfailing fountain."[6]

Though Whitman said the real war would never get into the books, he caught vignettes such as "Cavalry Crossing a Ford." Among his other enduring poems of that period are "Vigil Strange I Kept on the Field One Night," "A Sight in Camp in the Daybreak Gray and Dim," and "Look Down Fair Moon," which goes: "Look down fair moon and bathe this scene, / Pour softly down night's nimbus floods on faces ghastly, swollen, purple, / On the dead on their backs with arms toss'd wide, / Pour down your unstinted nimbus sacred moon."

Besides poems like these, during his 11 years in Washington, 1862–1873, Whitman wrote *Democratic Vistas* (1867), a prose hymn to poets' work in creating future great American women and men. He also published two editions of *Leaves of Grass,* the book of poems that he kept adding to all his life. In the fourth edition (1866) he printed 75 new poems, including war poems of *Drum Taps* and "When Lilacs Last in the Dooryard Bloom'd." The fifth edition of 1871-72 added 13 poems—a major one was "Passage to India." Once again he was his own publisher—no established publishers would issue it.

A telling incident of local and American literary history happened on June 30, 1865 when Whitman was fired from a government clerk-ship because his new boss objected to the frankness of his poetry. Friends found him another job the very next day, and one of them published strong support in *The Good Gray Poet* (1866), one of the first appreciations of his poetry to appear anywhere, as was John Burroughs' *Notes on Walt Whitman as Poet and Person* (1867). (We are happy to find such discerning literary taste in at least a few Washingtonians of that period.)

John Burroughs deserves a special note here partly because so much of the region permeated his early writings and partly because he gave such a good picture of how Whitman looked in Washington: "a large slow-moving figure clad in gray, with broad-brimmed hat and gray beard...He had a hirsute, kindly look, but far removed from the finely-cut traditional poet's face." In turn, Burroughs, as described by Whitman, was a big farm-boy with a face like a field of wheat.

Burroughs tramped the Maryland countryside outside the city, often with Whitman. (He had come to the capital to be near that poet.) While there Burroughs sold milk and garden truck from his small acreage on Capitol Hill, and worked as a guard at the Treasury. More important, he wrote his first nature essays with Whitman's help, and published his first collection *Wake-Robin* (1871). In his prose he captured more than anyone ever had of the wild life of Prince George's and Montgomery Counties. Afterwards Burroughs won a national audience that for 40 years affectionately bought his books and listened to his lectures. Readers liked a man whose characteristic choice was to go to the woods to search for spring flowers instead of attending Lincoln's second inauguration. Burroughs said that he had thought it more desirable to see Spring inaugurated.

Whitman might have approved, though he admired Lincoln. He had seen the President often and had been inspired by his death. Out of the assassination came his popular "O Captain! My Captain!" and his longer elegy "When Lilacs Last in the Dooryard Bloom'd," a classic of American literature. For that elegy he drew two images from walks about the Maryland countryside—lilacs in bloom "with many a pointed blossom rising delicate, with the perfume strong I love," and the planet Venus, "Lustrous and drooping star with the countenance full of woe." A third dominant image, of a hermit thrush, came from John Burroughs.

With these images, Whitman weaves others of battle-corpses and of American places through which Lincoln's funeral train passed.

The whole poem unrolls seamlessly to this ending,
Passing, I leave thee lilac with heart-shaped leaves,
I leave thee there in the dooryard, blooming, returning with spring.
I cease from my song for thee,
From my gaze on thee in the west, fronting the west, communing
* with thee,*
O comrade lustrous with silver face in the night.

Yet each to keep and all, retrievements out of the night,
The song, the wondrous chant of the gray-brown bird,
And the tallying chant, the echo arous'd in my soul,
With the lustrous and drooping star with the countenance full of woe,
With the holders holding my hand hearing the call of the bird,
Comrades mine and I in the midst, and their memory ever to keep,
* for the dead I loved so well,*
For the sweetest, wisest soul of all my days and lands — and this for
* his dear sake,*
Lilac and star and bird twined with the chant of my soul,
There in the fragrant pines and the cedars dusk and dim.

Among Washington writers only Lincoln himself matched
Whitman. Because of experiences in wartime Washington, President
Lincoln himself progressed from being a good stump speaker to great
writer. His Second Inaugural Address, for example, stands as a masterpiece of prose. By the time he gave it in 1865 he had won the war,
freed the slaves, and saved the Union. Yet it is a short speech, one
shorn of flourishes and fireworks. His four years of managing both
the war and the country had made him terse, yet precise and lucid.
In it he distilled large ideas in short sentences, just as he had done
in letters to his generals. A sample of saying what he had to say the
nearest way was his writing to Governor Andrew Curtin of Pennsylvania, April 8, 1861: "I think the necessity of being *ready* increases.—
Look to it." That is all he wrote.

Though devoted to brevity, Lincoln knew how to marry the rhythms
of long sentences to emotion. His Gettysburg Address is one example,
and his conclusion to the Second Inaugural Address is a classic of
rhetoric: "With malice toward none; with charity for all; with firmness
in the right, as God gives us to see the right, let us strive on to finish
the work we are in; to bind up the nation's wounds; to care for him
who shall have borne the battle, and for his widow, and his orphan — to
do all which may achieve and cherish a just and lasting peace among
ourselves, and with all nations."

During the war Lincoln came to Baltimore to address the Sanitary Fair, held at the Maryland Institute, April 18, 1864. Since this example of his writing skill is rarely printed, I quote most of it here:
Ladies and Gentlemen —

Calling to mind that we are in Baltimore, we cannot fail to note that the world moves. Looking upon these many people, assembled here, to serve, as they best may, the soldiers of the Union, it occurs at once that three years ago the same soldiers could not so much as pass through Baltimore. The change from then till now, is both great, and gratifying. Blessings on the brave men who have wrought the change, and the fair women who strive to reward them for it.

But Baltimore suggests more than could happen within Baltimore. The change within Baltimore is part only of a far wider change. When the war began, three years ago, neither party, nor any man, expected it would last till now. Each looked for the end, in some way, long ere to-day. Neither did any anticipate that domestic slavery would be much affected by the war. But here we are; the war has not ended, and slavery has been much affected — how much needs not now to be recounted. So true is it that man proposes, and God disposes.

But we can see the past, though we may not claim to have directed it; and seeing it, in this case, we feel more hopeful and confident for the future.

The world has never had a good definition of the word liberty, and the American people, just now, are much in want of one. We all declare for liberty; but in using the same word we do not all mean the same thing. With some the word liberty may mean for each man to do as he pleases with himself, and the product of his labor; while with others the same word may mean for some men to do as they please with other men, and the product of other men's labor. Here are two, not only different, but incompatible things, called by the same name — liberty. And it follows that each of the things is, by the respective parties, called by two different and incompatible names — liberty and tyranny.

The shepherd drives the wolf from the sheep's throat, for which the sheep thanks the shepherd as a liberator, while the wolf denounces him for the same act as the destroyer of liberty, especially as the sheep was a black one. Plainly the sheep and the wolf are not agreed upon a definition of the word liberty; and precisely the same difference prevails today among us human creatures, even in the North, and all professing to love liberty. Hence we behold the processes by which thousands are daily passing from under the yoke of bondage, hailed

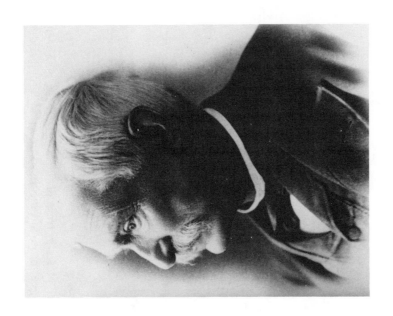

Col. Richard Malcolm Johnston lived out his life in Baltimore as an exile from rural Georgia, a place he captured in local color stories.

Walt Whitman, photographed by Mathew Brady, found that his decade in Washington during the Civil War and after had been "not so much the making as the remaking of the great poet who slept in Whitman's bones." (Mark Van Doren)

In April 1861 the new President, Abraham Lincoln, reviewed Union volunteers in front of the White House, here seen in a contemporary drawing by A. R. Waud. The ensuing war brought forth great prose in Lincoln's letters and formal addresses.

Although Sidney Lanier lived in the center of Baltimore, he celebrated natural beauties of his native Georgia, as is suggested in this monument on the Homewood Campus, Johns Hopkins University.

At the time Sidney Lanier was writing some of his finest poems, he was teaching boys at Pen Lucy School, housed for a time in one or two of these 1400 Block Eutaw Place mansions and run by Col. Richard Malcolm Johnston.

by some as the advance of liberty, and bewailed by others as the destruction of all liberty. Recently, as it seems, the people of Maryland have been doing something to define liberty; and thanks to them that, in what they have done, the wolf's dictionary, has been repudiated.

With this Lincolnian prose echoing down the decades, we close a section about wartime writing and turn to that of the troubled Reconstruction era. The gulf of 100 years since then may be no greater than the one made by the Civil War in one generation. The 19th-century historian George Ticknor said that postwar America didn't seem to be the same country he had been born in.

After federal occupation of their city ended, Baltimoreans faced in their own way the cataclysmic changes the war had wrought. They had not profited from a war boom as Cincinnati had, and they didn't suffer destruction as Richmond did. Baltimore's ambiguous position between North and South enforced its insularity, its solidarity, and its self-absorption. Above all, the town—and state—suffered from memories of divided loyalties. On Baltimore's Mount Royal Avenue stood one monument to the Confederate dead and another to the Union dead. The advent of refugees from Southern states only complicated matters.

But that diaspora of ex-Confederates brought benefits to literature. Although they arrived with no baggage save good manners and empty stomachs, as Mencken later noted, they greatly enriched Baltimore culturally and materially. He also credited them with keeping his city less corrupt than most other large American cities.

In another modern view, Baltimore was the lying-in hospital for the New South. It was just the right place for talented Southerners to make a new life. One reason was that it made them comfortable. Its social air was Southern, and old amenities hadn't yet disappeared, partly because the city had not shifted from commerce to industry, as more Northern cities had done.

For all that Southernness, Baltimore gave perspective and with it a chance to criticize the Old South. In doing so, writers such as Sidney Lanier nurtured the New South there. When he arrived in town after the war to seek work, he wrote to his wife in Georgia how happy they would be to "dwell in the beautiful city, among the great libraries, and midst the music, the religion, and the art we love." Once there, he found something better, what he called "enough attrition of mind on mind," to bring out "many sparks from a man."[7] More than that a writer cannot ask of any place.

With Sidney Lanier we see one more major kaleidoscopic design in 19th-century literary history. This one came from literary ex-Confederates who brought richness in talent and theme to Maryland. Lanier made one of that diaspora of ex-Confederates. Three other representatives will give us the quality of literary riches they brought to Maryland: Susan Dabney Smedes (from Mississippi), Colonel Richard Malcolm Johnston (Georgia born), and John Bannister Tabb (Virginia born).

The word *diaspora* is too grand for this small group; *coterie* is better. They resembled American writers after World War I who fled to Paris. Baltimore, like Paris, stimulated writers partly because exiles mingled with their own kind. They liked native Marylanders, but they loved their fellow expatriates. And they could applaud a Baltimore editor's sentiment: "Great God! It makes my blood boil in my veins when I think of the South flinging away just the priceless jewels of which no force can deprive her: her individuality, her Southern character, her Southern honor."[8]

These jewels appeared in the setting of *Memorials of a Southern Planter* (1887), written by Susan Dabney Smedes and published in Baltimore. That Southern planter, Mrs. Smedes's father Thomas Dabney, lived from Washington's administration to Cleveland's — 87 years. Details in his letters build up a self-portrait of an honorable man. He had developed character while creating a cotton plantation of 4,000 acres out of the Mississippi wilderness, and then losing it after the Civil War. An aspect of his character that fascinated readers in the 1880s was how well he had treated his 500 slaves on that plantation. Readers today find the theme of the benevolent despot less palatable. Even so, this memoir made a fine epitaph for the romantic plantation myth. Isn't it appropriate that the city of the creators of that myth, John Pendleton Kennedy and William Wirt, should be the place where its epitaph was composed?

This excerpt shows why Susan Smedes's book ranks with other fine personal narratives such as *Mary Chesnut's Civil War.* (Note: the women of Thomas Dabney's family stayed on his plantation while the battle for the Mississippi River engulfed them.)

In the midst of all this Mrs. Allen's baby died. One of the plantation carpenters made a coffin, and the Burleigh family buried the little child. No clergyman was to be had. Many of them were gone as chaplains in the army. Our pastor led his company into the first battle of Manassas.

The baby was buried in the park under a small oak-tree. The deer, seeing the procession of the family and the coffin borne by the Negro men come in, with the curiosity of their species drew near. The gentler ones mingled with the group around the open grave, one special pet licking the hands of her human friends and stretching out her beautiful neck to reach the flowers that the young children had brought to strew on the little coffin.

The rude coffin and the absence of the minister, and of any white man save one silvery-haired one, spoke of war. But it was a beautiful and peaceful scene. The setting sun threw its slanting rays on the deer as they stood in the background near the forest trees, and on the little group gathered close to the grave. A woman's voice was repeating the solemn ritual of the Episcopal Church for the burial of the dead.[9]

Moving though Smedes's narrative is, she never pretended to be the artist that Sidney Lanier was: he now ranks as the best of these Southern writers-in-exile. He came up from Georgia, where he had been born in 1842, the son of a cultivated Macon lawyer. There he loved music and poetry early, matriculated at Oglethorpe University, and planned to study in Germany.

Instead, he enlisted in the Confederate Army at 19 and served actively until captured in 1864. His imprisonment under cruel conditions at Point Lookout, St. Mary's County, led to his lifelong fight against tuberculosis. Another lifelong fight, against poverty, also began then. In these battles he resembled Poe. Like Poe, too, he made the heroic decision to become a writer, and he threw up a career in law. Just how bad off he was comes out in a letter to the Northern writer Bayard Taylor: "Perhaps you know that with us of the younger generation in the South since the war, pretty much the whole of life has been merely not dying."[10]

In his first published book, a novel *Tiger Lilies* (1867), he drew on wartime experiences as scout and blockade runner. It did not fare well with readers. Then, to support a wife and children, he came to Baltimore as flutist with the Peabody Conservatory Orchestra. Once there, he also earned money editing what he called "boy's books — pot boilers all," including the popular *The Boy's King Arthur* (1880). He also taught at the Pen Lucy School and gave public lectures. After he became a reputable poet with publication of "Corn" and "The Symphony" (1875) and *Poems* (1877), he persuaded President Daniel Coit Gilman of the new Johns Hopkins University to appoint him lecturer in English. Lanier had even lowered himself to write a poem celebrating that university. (It was poor.)

Unfortunately, Baltimore at the time gave little real notice of Lanier because the town then was not a literary center. Some people say that it has never known quite what to do with a non-conformist, especially an intellectual. Still, Lanier found advantages in his exile. One was his social circle of people with literary tastes. Some were Southerners such as Father John Bannister Tabb. Other ex-Confederates joined the Wednesday Club with him (Innes Randolph, for one) to meet with prominent artists and musicians. Another refuge in town was the Turnbull family of Beethoven Terrace. In their huge townhouse he made music and friends.

Another advantage of coming to Baltimore was stimulation from Hopkins faculty. Like some of them, he read widely in science and became interested in mending the broken economy of the South. He used the phrase "New South" early in the growth of that concept. Some critics believe that Lanier should have escaped the Old South earlier so that he could have missed falling in love with his idea of Chivalry and with the inflated language of romanticism so dear to readers of Sir Walter Scott. Much of Lanier's verse seems to us today insipid, flowery, and long-winded.

One poem that is read today is "From the Flats" (1877). It could have come from his stay in Southern Maryland as prisoner-of-war. In it Lanier subdues sentimentalism, gives a feeling for Southern nature and shows his mastery of rhythm:

What heartache — ne'er a hill!
Inexorable, vapid, vague and chill
The drear sand-levels drain my spirit low.
With one poor word they tell me all they know;
Whereat their stupid tongues, to tease my pain,
Do drawl it o'er again and o'er again.
They hurt my heart with griefs I cannot name:
Always the same, the same.

Nature hath no surprise,
No ambuscade of beauty 'gainst mine eyes
From brake or lurking dell or deep defile;
No humors, frolic forms — this mile, that mile;
No rich reserves or happy-valley hopes
Beyond the bend of roads, the distant slopes.
Her fancy falls, her wild is all run tame:
Ever the same, the same.

Oh might I through these tears

But glimpse some hill my Georgia high uprears,
Where white the quartz and pink the pebble shine,
The hickory heavenward strives, the muscadine
Swings o'er the slope, the oak's far-falling shade
Darkens the dogwood in the bottom glade,
And down the hollow from a ferny nook
  Bright leaps a living brook!

Lyric richness like this gave promise of future greatness. So did his poems in Negro dialect, forerunners of works of regional realism by other Americans. Again, in a book on prosody, *The Science of English Verse* (1880), he opened a door. His thesis was that poetry and music have identical rules and that verse is "in all respects a phenomenon of sound." Serious interest in prosody had been long of interest to Southern writers like Poe. Such an interest meant that poetry writing had to be a serious pursuit, not a casual accomplishment such as painting china at home. Unfortunately, death at 39 stopped Lanier's pioneering.

Mourners in Lanier's Southern circle helped him raise the level of literary Baltimore and Maryland. One of them was Basil Gildersleeve, a philologist, from Charleston, South Carolina, and Princeton College, who had served in the Confederate cavalry. After he became professor of Greek on the first faculty of Johns Hopkins, he wrote essays defending *The Creed of the Old South.* That region, he argued, had given color to the life of the country. With that view in mind, he encouraged another Confederate exile Colonel Richard Malcolm Johnston to write stories about middle-class Georgians. These stories Johnston's friend Sidney Lanier sent off to Northern magazines where they were printed. They appeared as *Dukesborough Tales.*

Johnston was 57 when he got his first story published nationally in *Scribner's Monthly*, June 1879. His earlier pieces in the Baltimore *Southern Magazine* had brought in no money and not much notice; luckily, the Yankees paid. Though money was a spur to write, so was homesickness for rural Georgia. Coming to Baltimore in 1867, he brought with him the nucleus of the school that he had run down there. The Pen Lucy School prospered, partly because Georgians sent their sons to him to be educated. After 1875 the school's fortunes declined, and Johnston gave it up the year Harper & Brothers brought out an enlarged edition of *Dukesborough Tales* (1883). Afterwards his daughters supported him in Baltimore: their father "never knew the value of a dollar." They also asserted that "father's personality was greater than his writings."

When Alexander Stephens, ex-Vice President of the Confederacy, also came to Baltimore, Johnston renewed their friendship. Later Johnston and William Hand Browne published a biography of Stephens. And Stephens joined the group that criticized and presumably improved Johnston's tales. So did an editor of *The Century* in New York, the daughter of Alfred Bledsoe, a friendly Southern writer-editor in Baltimore.

Johnston recorded why he came to write his fiction:

I said that I began writing after my removal to Baltimore, partly for the sake of subduing as far as possible the sense of homesickness. I might add, of alleviating the burden of misapprehension which soon befell me, that perhaps after all I had made a mistake in coming so far away from the other people who knew me, and setting out to maintain my large family among strangers, by practice of my profession, my entire competency for which was not known outside of my native State. In the fall of 1867 the price of cotton began to decline rapidly, and foreseeing that planters and others who had sustained me heretofore must lessen in numbers, I became intensely apprehensive of the consequences upon my fortunes. I knew well that if I were to return to Georgia I could reinstate myself without difficulty or delay. But my wife, who was always my most earnest, trusted, and efficient counselor, decided to remain, a decision which after all I feel confident was the better.

I mention this fact in connection with the preceding to show the frame of mind in which I wrote some of my stories, in which only the humorous appears. This was the case, I remember well, particularly with that called "The Early Majority of Mr. Thomas Watts," which perhaps was the most popular of all my platform readings, although I wrote it when most heavily weighed down by a load of apprehension. The work did its part in rescuing me from entire despondency. I suppose that many writers of humorous tales have had like experiences.[11]

Johnston's stories of Dukesborough helped bring the South into American literature. He performed this feat just at the time — between late 1860s and 1900 — when local color stories dominated magazines and book lists. Such dominance occurred abroad as well. What Johnston and several other Southern writers added were tales about plain folks to put next to older ones about plantations. Without Johnston, later Southerners could not have so readily focused on people other than gentry and blacks. Imagine no Flannery O'Connor or Eudora Welty!

Johnston also provides a revealing footnote to this book. He was once the cause of the greatest gesture of friendship in Maryland literary history since the time John Pendleton Kennedy helped Poe find a job. The gesture was Mark Twain's: he filled in for Thomas Nelson Page, in a duet of public readings. Though Twain had sworn off such shows, he came to the Academy of Music on Howard Street and read from manuscript part of his *Connecticut Yankee at King Arthur's Court*. The *Sun* review praised the way Twain read "on a recall" a dueling experience when he was a reporter on the Virginia City *Enterprise*: "His delightful drawl, persuasive comedy powers and purposely committed speech impediments made the evening a great go." Johnston won approval too: his "inimitable reproduction of dialect" and "his intellectual veiling of the funny in commonplace event" made his reading of his story "The Early Majority of Mr. Thomas Watts" memorable.

Gossip had it that Twain gave all receipts from a full house to Johnston, who was in need. (He always was in need.) Money wasn't the sole boon: another treat was the Johnston family having Twain spend the evening before the reading with them at their rowhouse on St. Paul Street.

No such warmth attached to the last notable Southern literary emigré, Father John Bannister Tabb, who probably was the oddest. He wore and wore his cassock — until it was green with age, it is said, and threadbare. In appearance he was ugly: he was tall, ascetic, and thin like a rail. He must have been sensitive about his homeliness because once he stopped a stranger walking with him on the street in Baltimore and said laughingly, "How do you do, friend? Until I saw you, I thought I was the ugliest man alive."[12]

Tabb, a Virginian, enriched Maryland literary history with his verse and with his support of other writers. He wrote defending Poe's reputation, and he attended the ceremony at the reinterment of Poe's body in Westminster Burying Ground. (Other invited poets failed to show up — except Walt Whitman.)

Best of all, Tabb befriended Lanier. When both were under 20, love of music brought them together in the prison camp at Point Lookout. Tabb had left his rural Virginia home, "The Forest" in Amelia County, to join the Confederate Navy. At night he ran the blockade of 20 or 30 Union vessels protecting Wilmington, North Carolina. He brought in supplies from Bermuda and Nassau 18 or 20 times, a risky business, he later recalled, especially when the load was ammunition. His runs ended June 1864 when he was captured and put in the bull pen of the prison camp at Point Lookout, St. Mary's County, on Chesapeake Bay.

There he became seriously ill. And there he also met Lanier, supposedly because he followed the sound of Lanier's flute. (Both young men had planned to study music in Germany but the war interfered. Later, Tabb wrote seven poems to Lanier, and in Baltimore they renewed acquaintance.) In the fall of 1864 Tabb escaped prison by hiding under a garbage tub as it floated out. Back on shore outside the camp he found Southern sympathizers to help complete his escape.

After the war Tabb came to Baltimore to study music. What he got besides music was a chance to imbibe High Church instruction. Then after being received in the Roman Catholic Church in 1872, he came as a student to St. Charles College outside Baltimore, entered the priesthood, and subsequently became a professor.

At St. Charles College he taught among many students George Sterling, later a prominent poet in San Francisco. And there he wrote witty epigrams about fellow teachers; his published verse is also epigrammatic. As an example, one about himself went, "It is a cruel stab / With Edgar Poe to measure Tabb:/As well with Tennyson to rate / The present Poet-Laureate." On "Lanier's Flute" (1897) he wrote: "When palsied at the pool of thought / The Poet's words were found, / Thy voice the healing Angel brought / To touch them into sound."

By a curious twist of the literary kaleidoscope, no poem by Tabb or Lanier had the currency of a song by an erstwhile Confederate captain of engineers on Jeb Stuart's staff, Innes Randolph, who later joined literati in Baltimore. His song became popular with Western cowboys, some of them ex-Confederate soldiers who doubtless carried it with them to the range. Called "The Good Old Rebel," this song had only four stanzas at first. As happens with songs passed around, singers added to them, but retained the bitterness of the South after defeat. "The Good Old Rebel," as he wrote it, began: "O I'm a good old rebel, / Now that's just what I am; / For the 'fair land of freedom,' / I do not care a damn; / I'm glad I fit against it, / I only wish we'd won, / And I don't want no pardon / For anything I done."[13]

Randolph's words expressed the feeling of many Marylanders. They and other Confederates had done what they thought best for their country and were bitter. Sadly, the bloodletting on both sides left a people deprived of who knows what talents—literary and other.

VII
No Peace and Claret

Washington literature's odd coming of literary age with *The Education of Henry Adams* and *Little Lord Fauntleroy;* Baltimore's deflection from literature to become a social and scientific Athens.

"They [the powers-that-be in late 19th-century Washington] knew not how to amuse themselves; they could not conceive how other people were amused. Work, whiskey, and cards were life."[1]
— Henry Adams

From A Photograph
             "All shadows once were free
             But wingless now are we,
             And doomed henceforth to be
             In Light's Captivity."[2]
                         — John Banister Tabb

W&S Lᵀᴴ   PERMANENT

Frances Hodgson Burnett, a popular novelist and sometime resident of Washington, was photographed in London dressed for presentation at court in an era when such things mattered.

Readers of 1900 might well have echoed Sidney Lanier's yearning for the mountains in his poem "From the Flats." Sadly for literature, Lincoln, Whitman, and Lanier were receding like distant mountain peaks. In front of those peaks stretched a flat valley. New heights of local achievement were not literary, but scientific. And chief peaks of the youngest, most exciting science, medicine, were Johns Hopkins University Medical School and Hospital. Right from their founding in late 19th-century Baltimore, these institutions attracted worshipful pilgrims.

The expatriate writer Logan Pearsall Smith, for example, came from London for a prostatectomy, performed by a world-famous Hopkins surgeon. In a letter from his hospital bed, Smith complained to his friend George Santayana, author and philosopher, about how sophomoric and ineffectual American culture and "mind" were. The place was empty of books. In reply, Santayana pointed out that the Baltimore surgeon, a great expert, really knew how to do things. In the service of the material life, he added, all the arts and sciences were prosperous in America. But Smith had been a friend of Whitman and Henry James, and he knew that a gilded age had replaced the golden literary age. He lamented the decline. Though science saved his life, it failed to give the heroic feeling that he found in books such as *Leaves of Grass*.[3]

Smith wasn't alone in lamenting this loss. Mark Twain had even created the phrase "The Gilded Age" as title for his novel describing post-Civil War America. Under this title he satirized political corruption in Washington and wild financial speculation everywhere. He knew both evils well because he had lived many places, including Washington. There in the capital he wrote the first book to make him famous, *Innocents Abroad* (1869).

Twain's pessimism was expressed by other authors in this literary history, most eloquently in *The Education of Henry Adams* (1906). For Henry Adams as well as Logan Pearsall Smith, 19th-century American culture had lost sparkle. One reason was that London then set the style in literature. London also offered freedom from censorship of the sort that prevented Whitman's printing *Leaves of Grass* in Boston. No wonder gifted writers such as Henry James, Stephen Crane, and Bret Harte expatriated themselves in England. Other writers retreated in different ways. Henry Adams, for instance, turned to art of long ago or far away. (His Washington circle worshipped its Tintorettos.)

Complaints about lack of sparkle found Maryland spokesmen, too.

For example, a literary critic of the 1870s reported that Baltimore sparkled only as "the Social Athens of America." That city's social graces and accomplishments outshone literary culture. And all for want of encouragement, that critic scornfully asserted. He lamented the lack of literary periodicals, and found hardly a single publishing house worthy of the name. The upshot was that local writers went north to New York and Philadelphia. The critic added, "We could name one or two Baltimore writers who are better known in Boston than in their native city."[4]

Such complaints about thin literary culture left out of account the town's relative youth. In 1800 Baltimore, after all, had only a fraction of the population of Philadelphia. And, seen in perspective, the literary circle of Poe's day was ending its span just when Mencken was born. Those 70 years, interrupted by the cataclysmic Civil War, were not enough for a literary culture—audience, critics, writers—to grow and season.

That fact did not comfort an anonymous Baltimore writer who decried the lot of late 19th-century authors in this couplet: "While your polished pen scarce can earn a garret/Double-entry points to peace and claret." Double-entry bookkeeping meant profits in business: claret was the drink of the well-settled.

Ironically, this poet's cry arose just when a Baltimore invention made possible the making of big money by writers. For them, Ottmar Mergenthaler, a German immigrant, working in his shop on Wilkes Lane, invented the linotype. That invention revolutionized printing, and made possible a profitable flood of books around the world. What's more, it coincided with two more forces for change besides Johns Hopkins: 1) the emergence of Washington as an urban center, and so a place with the potential of generating literature, and 2) the birth of Henry Louis Mencken, on September 13, 1880.

Before examining these forces, we benefit by listening to three witnesses of both life and literature in those days. One observer, a literary historian of 1894, contrasted the doleful state of literature then with happier times before the Civil War.[5] Back in the 1830s, he recalled, Baltimoreans had held no prejudice against literati. Writers had been welcomed to the drawing-rooms of the best society, their faults excused on account of their talents. In the eyes of the public their calling was not a mean one. We remember how well Poe had been received by John Pendleton Kennedy and William Wirt, authors in the Establishment. But by 1880 all that hospitality had vanished.

Another witness, an early Hopkins medical student, Dr. Bertram

M. Bernheim, remembered that Baltimore made a fetish of tradition, family, and good breeding, to say nothing of good eating and good living. That all stemmed from the South. He felt that the new and old blended unusually well and in quite a different way from that in any other American city. He concluded that Baltimoreans never compromised in the slightest with ideas of their own importance. Beyond a doubt, natives *knew* who they were.[6]

A third witness, Henry James, the expatriate novelist, discovered that the city had the real Southern glow without the usual Southern looseness. (He had been travelling in the South.) The glow of rowhouses, white marble steps, and tree-lined streets and squares made him think of quiet old ladies at old-fashioned tea-parties, seated with toes tucked-up on uniform footstools. For good reason, though, he did not mention having met any writers there.[7]

Nor did he mention devotion to science at Johns Hopkins University, only two blocks west of his haunts on ladylike Mount Vernon Place. There, however, a graduate student of the Professor of Chemistry, Ira Remsen, was about to discover saccharine. And there an advocate of the New South, Woodrow Wilson, wrote a Ph.D. thesis about the role of Congress. Both men were fulfilling Hopkins' President Gilman's determination, in his words, to "open things up."

Many Marylanders, of course, didn't want things opened up. Certain of the Baltimore elite, for example, criticized the Peabody Institute Library for not being a popular circulating library. In reply, Provost Nathaniel Holmes Morison, a New Englander, told them that his library was aimed at the highest and best — for instance, a young man of genius but poor: "To strangers unacquainted with our local prejudices [i.e. against learning and letters], the present feeling of some of our respectable people is utterly incomprehensible."[8]

Still, signs of improvement came with the founding of the Peabody Library. It formed a part of a gift from a Massachusetts man, George Peabody, who had made his first fortune in Baltimore. This gift filled several gaps, for that Southern city was the only major American one without a scholars' library, conservatory of music with orchestra, and art gallery. Luckily, he chose the most literate and literary native, John Pendleton Kennedy, to oversee the creation of his institute. And Kennedy had the wisdom to choose Morison from Massachusetts to build a collection of 100,000 volumes, now much expanded and still a city treasure.

In 1876, it was a particular treasure for Johns Hopkins University, just then opening three blocks west of it: it provided books for the outstanding early faculty as well as a haven for writing their own. Some of the seminal works thus produced came from the logician Charles Sanders Peirce and the historians Herbert Baxter Adams and Frederick Jackson Turner.

Late in the century great talents also worked at Johns Hopkins Hospital to revolutionize modern medicine and medical education. Advances ranged from discovery of the first six vitamins to the inauguration of surgical gloves, subcutaneous surgery, radical mastectomy, and the essential tenets of behaviorism. More to our purposes, the physician-in-chief Dr. William Osler bridged science and humanism in lectures and essays. In that he resembled his great contemporary William James of Harvard. He was greater, though, by becoming the most beloved Marylander of the day. So popular was he that his waiting room, Mencken noted, should have been Druid Hill Park.

A literary footnote: several other scientists with literary talent have studied at Hopkins over the years and should have been persuaded to stay and teach there. Among them were Leo Stein (Gertrude Stein's brother), Dr. Lewis Thomas, and Rachel Carson. In *The Youngest Science,* his recent memoir, Thomas evaluated places he had lived — New York, Minneapolis, New Orleans, New Haven — and ranked Baltimore best. A major reason was the literary and intellectual conversation of Hopkins men not on the medical faculty.

For all this new scholarship, some Baltimoreans were quick to criticize Hopkins as offering the youth of Maryland the glittering stone of elegant culture, instead of the substantial bread of well-rounded education. Soon Hopkins' faculty outdistanced all others in the state and District of Columbia. Since the university's opening, Hopkins has stressed research and science, not strong connections with Baltimore intellectual life. Nor did the university lead in literary matters: Hopkins failed to become a Harvard nurturing writers.

True, the first president, Daniel Coit Gilman, did hire the poet Sidney Lanier to lecture — a solitary littérateur. And, be it ever to his glory, Gilman gave his faculty enormous freedom both in research and in their public lectures. Not all the results were what he hoped for. For instance, think of local literary culture after the Professor of Mathematics James Sylvester gave a public reading from his own poetry. The story goes that he prefaced reading his 400-line poem "Rosalind" by reading aloud footnotes. Each note required, he thought, additional remarks, so an hour and a half went to footnotes alone. We don't know what happened when he at some point invited anyone to leave — if they wanted to. We do know that the reading went on into the night. And we do know that the poem had but one rhyme: every line ended in "ind." This repetition, Sylvester thought, had the effect of the dash and splash of waves on the seashore.

With such goings-on at the opening of Hopkins, why should we be surprised by the dearth of first-rate poetry there? Not until the era of world wars did a Hopkins writer find a national audience for anything but academic writing. (Hopkins professors' medical texts have no doubt sold more copies than any other Maryland books.) As for belles lettres, Hopkins names of note today are Russell Baker, author of *Growing Up* (1983), Karl Shapiro, poet and critic, and John Barth, novelist, who teaches the Writing Seminar that long was conducted by Elliott Coleman. Would literature at Hopkins have been different and more abundant if H. L. Mencken had accepted his father's offer to send him there? To another bright Baltimorean without a B.A., Huntington Cairns, Mencken confided that college only addled your brains.

Then, in 1889, Hopkins gave a boost to local literary culture with the Percy Turnbull Memorial Lectureship on Poetry. It was given by a local publisher Lawrence Turnbull and his wife Frances Hubbard Litchfield Turnbull of New York. This lecture series attracted scholars and writers from all over the Atlantic world. Most of them discussed great writers of the past, as T. S. Eliot did in his three lectures in February 1933 on "The 'Metaphysical' Poets." Nearly every year brought others then formulating critical literary opinion, such as H. J. C. Grierson (University of Edinburgh) and R. W. Chambers (University of London).

The very first lecturer, Edmund Clarence Stedman, admitted that (in his words) the very best of the learned, poetic, and epigrammatic would be none too good for a Johns Hopkins and Baltimore audience. The fourth lecturer, Charles Eliot Norton of Harvard, always made a mission of being useful, the way Massachusetts people do. His goal was to bring the religion of aesthetics to benighted towns like Baltimore and Washington. Surely his six Turnbull lectures on Dante elevated local taste. At least the lectures and the Turnbulls' evening reception for him must have been well attended because he had great reputation as Dante scholar and as literary executor of John Ruskin, Thomas Carlyle, and James Russell Lowell. In Norton the Turnbulls had captured a literary lion of the first rank.

Other lions later joined Norton among lecturers in bringing world literature to Maryland. Popular poets came: Robert Frost, Marianne

Moore, A. E., and W. H. Auden, to name examples from the 20th century. Topics of lectures ranged through the ages from Chaucer and Dante to French poetics and the New Criticism to the writing of Sylvia Plath. The Baltimore poet Lizette Woodworth Reese noted that the Turnbull Lectureship of Poetry was "one of the most beautiful, far-seeing things ever done in Baltimore. For poetry, more than any other art, except music, has a compelling hold upon the spiritual side of life."[9]

In 1923 this literary series was joined by another, sponsored by the Tudor and Stuart Club. That club was founded by Sir William and Lady Osler in memory of their son and of happy years they had in Baltimore. They gave this club books and money to promote good fellowship and love of literature. To carry out their wishes, club members brought lecturers of the calibre of Turnbull lecturers, men such as E. M. W. Tillyard (Cambridge), Hardin Craig (Stanford), and Sir Walter Raleigh (Oxford). That club still meets to hear visiting literary scholars. Some visitors remark afterwards on the rigor of post-lecture questioning by T. & S. members.

Just at the time Johns Hopkins became a force in Maryland, another force entered regional literary history: Washington's growth had finally made it the second big city to emerge on Maryland soil. It grew from just the national village with strong Maryland traits into a fairly cosmopolitan city after the Civil War. As national capital, it attracted many writers, and still does.

From two journalists there we get useful pictures of what Washington was like in its 1880s adolescence as a literary center. One newspaperman found more men of distinction in science in Washington than in any other American city. And the Smithsonian, he noted, was the nucleus of both scientific and literary operations.

The other journalist, Frank G. Carpenter ("Carp") of the *Cleveland Leader,* explored the literary side fully. He called this capital a living curiosity, made up of the strangest and most incongruous elements. It had a fairy-tale sense of instability about it. One strangeness was the proliferation of as many literary societies and socials as Society functions. But some topics for discussion in the club called The Literary Society seem not to have been very literary: one topic was "The Metamorphosis of Negative Matter." During its first 100 years, 1874-1974, it enrolled bookish politicians (President James A. Garfield) and popular authors (Mary Roberts Rinehart). Still, an authority on intellectual life in Washington recorded that the social side made up three quarters of existence.

The sky-lighted stacks of the Peabody Library are to the left of the Peabody Institute's main entrance on Mount Vernon Place. In the late 19th century that library was a mainstay of the new Johns Hopkins University nearby. More recently it has served as haven for writers as prominent as John Dos Passos. In the right half of the building, Sidney Lanier played flute at the Peabody Conservatory of Music.

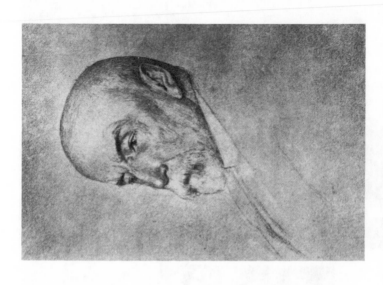

Here is an intellectual adopted Washingtonian with Maryland roots, Henry Adams. The drawing by John Briggs Potter shows him old, when he wrote *The Education of Henry Adams* and had it privately printed in Baltimore.

Ottmar Mergenthaler, sculpted by Hans Schuler, entered literary history through his invention of the linotype, a machine that led to mass production of books. He invented it in his shop on Wilkes Lane, Baltimore.

The corner house, Eutaw Place at West Lanvale Street, Baltimore, was residence of Daniel Coit Gilman, first President of Johns Hopkins University. Here he and his wife entertained the stellar faculty that stimulated intellectual life in Baltimore. He created the first university press in the country.

In this bird's-eye view of Washington (ca. 1871) the capital looks like a real city at last. As the town grew, it attracted writers from elsewhere, such as Joachim Miller and Henry Adams. In contrast to Baltimore, it nurtured few indigenous authors.

In a mansion on Beethoven Terrace, Park Avenue, Baltimore, the Lawrence Turnbull family befriended musicians and writers, including Sidney Lanier. Here they entertained the Turnbull Lecturers on Poetry, stimulants to local literary life, and here Mrs. Turnbull met with the Woman's Literary Society of Baltimore.

That authority was Henry Adams, recollecting his salad days in the capital, where he had expected political power. As an Adams he had grown up expecting to become President like his grandfather and great-grandfather. Yet he never held political office. Ironically, his power turned out to be literary and posthumous, expressed in *The Education of Henry Adams* (1906), a classic autobiography and analysis of scientific revolution in his time.

In this book he also caught significant sides of Maryland character. One side he portrayed through his favorite grandparent, Louisa (called Madame), the wife of President John Quincy Adams. Her father was a native Marylander, and she was niece of Maryland Governor Thomas Johnson. (He also coordinated the establishment of the new capital Washington.) To her grandson she seemed a charming Romney portrait of a woman juxtaposed with harsh-lined engravings of Adamses. There in Washington he knew her at 70, a vision of silver gray. He described her as exotic, like her Sevres china, presiding over her old President and her Queen Anne mahogany: "The boy knew nothing of her interior life, which had been, as the venerable Abigail [Adams], long since at peace, foresaw, one of severe stress and little pure satisfaction. He never dreamed that from her might come some of those doubts and self-questionings, those hesitations, those rebellions against law and discipline, which marked more than one of her descendants."[10]

That rebellion must have seemed part of what he ironically called the taint of Maryland blood in himself. Part of his dislike of New England restraint came out in hymns on Maryland seasons. Even austere Bostonians, he said, became almost genial in the softness of spring in Montgomery County: "The Potomac and its tributaries squandered beauty. Rock Creek was as wild as the Rocky Mountains. Here and there a negro log cabin alone disturbed the dogwood and the judas-tree, the azalea and the laurel. The tulip and the chestnut gave no sense of struggle against a stingy nature. The soft, full outlines of the landscape carried no hidden horror of glaciers in its bosom."[11]

Such lyrical outbursts showed his literary powers. They and much else in *The Education* reveal how he helped make Washington such a strange, incongruous center for literature. For one thing, he wrote that book and parts of his other best books there. Although those products of his first-rate mind perhaps cannot be called indigenous, they could have come only from someone of long residence — from someone experiencing, understanding, and loving the place. Adams remains a superb example of the Washingtonian writer. Coming back each fall to his red brick mansion on Lafayette Square was, he wrote, like a horse going back to its stable.

Adams lived in Washington first in 1850–1854 when his father was Congressman. At that time the capital looked as though white Greek temples rose in abandoned gravel pits of a deserted Syrian city. Only an earth-road with wheel-tracks meandered from the Treasury to the Patent Office. So it seemed to Adams. The capital had grown by the time he settled there (1868) and, until his death in 1918, lived there as the stablemate to statesmen, as he put it. So positioned, he tried to use writing as a means to get power. The Adams legacy of talent for thinking and writing helped him. His *Democracy: An American Novel* (1880), published anonymously, exposed scandals and corruption of the Grant era. It failed to bring reform in a place where, he said, the blackmailer alone prospered. He felt that Adamses were foredoomed: neither Adams President had been successful in office.

Still, he found writing amusing — but not amusing enough to pursue seriously as career. Not until he was past 50 did he write his two classics. In preparation for the first, *Mont-Saint-Michel and Chartres* (1904), he tutored for years with the artist John LaFarge to educate his senses. In his scholarly study of those two French medieval buildings, Adams pursued his thesis about the force of the patron Virgin, the ideal of human perfection. He contrasted the resulting unity of the 13th century with the multiplicity of the 20th.

That multiplicity became his theme in *The Education of Henry Adams* (1906). His treatment of that theme, combined with his mood of cynicism and skepticism, struck responsive chords. It remains a classic and a curious recollection, but classic in a way quite different from the memoirs of Jean Jacques Rousseau or John Stuart Mill. To give one difference: Adams views not only his own life but also America's decline from optimism in 1800 to decadence in 1870.

Another reason for this classic's popularity was Adams's ironic style. For this his models were Montaigne and Voltaire: like their prose, his sentences echoed the colloquial verve of familiar letters and brought in learning and philosophy wittily. His style holds up well. Moreover, out of this style Adams created a persona, a Henry Adams at once self-deprecating and endearing, tragic yet comic. By contrast, people other than intimates saw him as a man desolated by the suicide of his wife, then as a wanderer over the earth in search of Nirvana, and finally as a recluse. To the world he was short, bearded, and saturnine. Maybe Saint Gaudens, the sculptor, caught his image best in a mock heraldic device of a porcupine with angel's wings.

Characteristically, Adams said he didn't want fame, and so had his two masterpieces printed privately. For printer he chose J. H. Furst & Co. of Baltimore. Although he hesitated to pay $1,000 for 100 copies of *Mont-Saint-Michel and Chartres,* he must have been pleased with Furst's work because he also got them to print the 40 copies of his *Education.* He later increased the order to 60, so that he could send copies to men and women he talked about in the book.

A local footnote to the publication of these masterpieces is worth adding here: After working six hours a day revising his *Mont-Saint-Michel* he finally completed the work begun in 1899. The date was April 20, 1903, and to celebrate, Adams rode out into Maryland's countryside to look at his beloved dogwood and redbud. No one, he said, loved those flowering trees more than he did. Very soon afterwards he conceived *The Education.* That fall he was still adding to the first book while going ahead with the second. Then in January he sent the manuscript of the first to Baltimore, just in time to have part of it burned up in the Big Fire of February 1904. Resupplying the text delayed publication until mid-December. Once out, it circulated among the few people whose praise he counted worth having. He said that there weren't more than a score of them in the whole country. Despite his small hopes, both books found audiences everywhere and still do.

For us, Adams provides a granite outcropping in the flat valley of literary Washington. We will explore that flatness briefly in order to see what strange literati came there in the late 19th century. None was much affected by the place. Here is a prime illustration as recorded by "Carp":

In the 1880s Joaquin Miller built a log cabin on Meridian Hill at the opposite end of 16th Street from the White House and across the District boundary. As the very model of a California poet – he was called "the poet of the Sierras"– he did some writing there. Mostly, however, he was so much bothered by curious visitors that he had to lock his front gate. No wonder they came: he made a picturesque Westerner with his flowing hair under a slouch hat (or sometimes a tasseled sombrero), high-heeled boots, and a solitaire diamond, said to be of purest water, and larger than any owned by the belles of Washington.[12]

Fellow writer and Washingtonian-from-the-West Ambrose Bierce called Miller the greatest living liar. Ambrose Bierce himself lived and wrote in Washington for more than a decade at the beginning of this century. At the Olympia Apartments he gave Sunday breakfasts to cronies in journalism and to others. (Mencken knew him then.)

In Washington Bierce prepared 12 volumes of his *Collected Works* for a local publisher. No reader of this literary history will need to wade through these 12 volumes. If the author had printed only literature, not the journalism, his reputation would now be higher. As it is, *The Devil's Dictionary* (1906) and stories in *In the Midst of Life* (1891) are worth reading for their mordant view, conveyed in crisp style. Take, for example, his definition of lawsuit: "A machine which you go into as a pig and come out as a sausage." We might deduce from the examples of Bierce and Adams that living in Washington generally aggravated a writer's misanthropy. Maybe politics does that. But Bierce was already far gone in despair when he moved there at 60.

Worse than despair would visit a reader today picking up a sentimental novel by Mrs. E. D. E. N. Southworth, of Georgetown. Any of her 65 books will serve to represent the female novelists that abounded in Washington in the 1880s. To the journalist "Carp" she boasted that when she outlined her plot, she just let her pen flow on and on, page after page, until she had enough manuscript for her purpose. He noted that she scarcely ever erased, and that she was not, like some writers, subject to fits of genius.[13]

On the other hand, another popular female novelist of this era in Washington, Frances Hodgson Burnett, was subject to lucrative fits of genius. She made enough money from *Little Lord Fauntleroy* (1886) (dramatized two years later) to build a mansion at 1770 Massachusetts Avenue. Her other romantic stories—many, such as *The Secret Garden* (1911), for children—proved popular, also. She often set these stories in England because she had been born and lived there until she was 16.

While living at 1219 I Street, Washington, she wrote in an attic room with a tiger skin on the floor and warm red curtains at the windows. Downstairs she gave afternoon receptions, including one attended by Oscar Wilde in 1882. He dressed the part of a poet in flowered dark waistcoat, knee breeches, silk stockings, and patent leather pumps with broad buckles. Doubtless that wit met his match in Mrs. Burnett, a vivacious and strong-willed talker. To illustrate: at 15 she had sent a story to a magazine, only to have the editors say they would print it but couldn't pay her. She demanded the return of her manuscript because, she realized, if the story was good enough to publish, it was worth paying for.

Money was to be made then by Burnett, and plenty more by the Maryland novelist Martha Finley. She had been skimping along teaching school and writing religious stories for children, when in 1867 she published the first of 28 books about a Southern orphan, Elsie Dinsmore, on a plantation. This Elsie series reached 25 million readers. With profits from sales, she bought a big house in Elkton, Cecil County, where the Finleys had always lived. Apart from making money, Finley had the satisfaction of instilling feminist ideas as well as her pro-Unionist stand. As art, though, her novels resembled Southworth's "wishy-washy sentimental tales," as "Carp" called them.

Yet we do wrong to make fun of writers such as Southworth and Finley, for they commanded vast provinces of readers. Their books satisfied. One reason was that many women had idle time to fill after manufactured articles cut down on the hours of housework. Another reason was the spread of female education. Though the newly literate first sought books of practical and social instruction, they also wanted sentiment. To please them, publishers took advantage of advances in printing like Baltimorean Ottmar Mergenthaler's linotype to lower prices on novels. Novelists responded by pouring out a river of what Twain called tears and flapdoodle.

Some locally produced novels, however, were meant to teach good values. An example was Mrs. May Agnes Early Fleming's *Worth and Its Reward, a Story of a Life* (1856). Another, *Doings in Maryland* (1871), came from a school teacher Emily Jours McAlpin, who wrote to expose evils in public education in Baltimore, a fresh subject then. A novel of 1886, *Revoked Vengeance!*, by "J. E. Heard, M.D. of Baltimore, Md." assured the reader that "Did every man confine himself to truth, friendship would be saved many pangs, virtue many wounds, and his memory many reproaches." Unfortunately, it is even duller to read than McAlpin's novel. Nor did it titillate the vulgar as did the anonymous book that bore on its title page this synopsis: "Baltimore scandal and awful social tragedy, being the history of the Hinds and James affair in Baltimore, Maryland, which is now exciting social circles. The betrayal of the lovely Lizzie James, her sad confession to her mother, her heartrending death... the shooting of her brother. Also the tragic death of her father while avenging his daughter's ruin."[14]

Quite another direction — into history — attracted other writers. Such a tack should not surprise anyone aware of Marylanders' rootedness. Among the most popular were George Alfred Townsend's novels *The Entailed Hat* (1884) and *Katy of Catoctin* (1886). In them Townsend exploited his firsthand acquaintance with both the Eastern Shore and Western Maryland. He had lived in both places and retired to Gap-land, an estate with mountain views of Pleasant Valley above Frederick. He used local history, embroidered with imagination. In *The Entailed Hat,* for example, he portrayed the historical and infamous Patty Cannon, a murderer and a kidnapper of slaves, whom she resold. The tavern that was her headquarters stood at Reliance, on the line between Maryland and Delaware.

Here is a sample of Townsend's tone from the opening of *Katy of Catoctin* in a Western Maryland setting:

"Maryland is only a rim of shore, a shell of mountain, but all gold!"

So said Lloyd Quantrell, the gunner, looking down from the South Mountain upon Middletown or Catoctin Valley, an October Saturday in the year 1859.

The mellow light of afternoon touched or bathed the hundred farms, the bridges, barns, hamlets, stacks, corn-rows, brown woods, streams and stone walls, and with a fruity smell, as of cider-presses, seemed to come up the tone of bells ringing the Marylanders home from the labors of the week.

He saw the red and white spires of Middletown in the lap of the valley like its babe, and thought he saw, beyond its Catoctin Mountain knees, the father Frederick, the good old burgher, holding his devout fingers up, like index boards at the junction of his many pike roads.

Then fancy spread other terraces of Maryland, farther and farther on, like descending steps of gold and marble, beyond the hills of Sugarloaf and Linganore, to where Potomac and Patapsco blended their cascades and ocean-tides at the shrines of Washington and Baltimore.

Lloyd Quantrell's dog put his nose in the air silently, looking also downward, as if he scented, with the pheasants of the mountain, the sea-fowl of the Chesapeake.[15]

With this Civil War novel, Townsend was following a vogue because historical fiction about the American past caught on following the Centennial of 1876. All of it was sentimental, wooden, and false. A master of nostalgia, Thomas Nelson Page re-created life *In Ole Virginia* (1887), writing from his library in the colonial-style mansion he built at 1759 R Street, Georgetown. There he lived out most of his 30-year exile from Virginia.

Another popular example, Winston Churchill's *Richard Carvel* (1899), put Maryland on the nostalgia map. The author had fallen in love with Annapolis while a midshipman at the United States Naval Academy (1890–1894). He then got to know Annapolitans, their narrow streets and mouldering mansions, and their ancestral legends.

He returned three years later to soak up atmosphere for *Richard Carvel*. Happily for lovers of old Maryland, his first great literary success portrayed a Maryland upper-class family, who wintered in Annapolis and summered at Carvel Hall, Queen Anne's County. There on the Eastern Shore they lived the ideal 18th-century planter's life — hunting foxes and reading Swift and Addison. Churchill painted the scene well. From their mansion's 100-foot-long front the Carvel Hall family welcomed friendly neighbors like Mr. Lloyd and Mr. Bordley, who arrived by private barge rowed by ten velvet-capped slaves. At tea these planters talked of the coming American Revolution. So nostalgic was this author for colonial times that in 1904 he put his large royalties into a reproduction of that imaginary Carvel Hall. He had the well-known architect Charles Plant build it in the White Mountains at Cornish, New Hampshire. What a site for a Tidewater Maryland plantation house![16]

Richard Carvel lacked the high literary quality that the Turnbull lecturers were preaching. It also didn't endure, as *The Education of Henry Adams* has. Certainly all the sentimental fiction of the time has faded, though *The Entailed Hat* still meets antiquarian tastes and remains popular at the Enoch Pratt Free Library.

Even though so much of late 19th-century writing lies gathering dust, we value that era for impact on the future. Many new resources developed for writers then: the Smithsonian Institution and the Library of Congress expanded, and Johns Hopkins University and Hospital set high standards for learning and research. Furthermore, just the great growth of Baltimore and Washington meant increased chances for literary life. With a little study we can regard much of what happened in those decades as preparation for the next major writer, H. L. Mencken.

As we shall see, he became *the* writer of the Upper Chesapeake. If history is place as well as time, then his house at 1524 Hollins Street has become historic. (Today it is a house museum.) In the 1880s its predecessors as literary historic houses were Henry Adams's on Lafayette Square, Washington, and, in Baltimore, the Turnbulls' at 1530 Park Avenue, a rowhouse in Beethoven Terrace, Bolton Hill.

A survey of what this hospitable Baltimore house meant to Maryland culture will make a happy conclusion to an era that offered writers too little peace and claret. Beethoven Terrace of 11 mansions served as a cultured island. The corner building at McMechen Street housed the first college for women in Maryland. Running south along Park Avenue were ten residences in which cultivated Victorians abounded.

For example, at the north end lived Frank Frick, who led in founding the Lyric Opera House and was a collector of paintings. Best of all, near the south end of the Terrace gathered the Woman's Literary Club of Baltimore. Members were entertained there by the founder, Mrs. Laurence Turnbull. All of those women read and discussed their own writing. And a number of writings were published, including those of Lizette Woodworth Reese.

Of all the arts, music and literature flourished best on the Terrace when the poet Sidney Lanier visited the Turnbulls, as he did often. Today Beethoven Terrace, together with the Peabody, is all that remains of places associated with Lanier. Although Baltimore treated him fairly well (and the Turnbulls, very well) Lanier was poor and sick throughout his stay. Just before he died, he wrote a touching note from North Carolina to the Turnbulls: he sent them "the whole valley full of green-leaf wishes and summer longings."[17] He wanted them to be with him, camping on "this great mountain that lifts us into the air, 2,000 feet higher than the corner of McMechen Street and Park Avenue." But they could not join him on his mountain top, and later that year Lanier, only 39, died of tuberculosis. He was buried in the Turnbull lot at Green Mount Cemetery with an epitaph from one of his poems: "How dark, how dark so ever the race that must need be run, / I am lit with the sun."

Culture in the Upper Chesapeake and Potomac region needed more sun. And just then a bringer of light — a new writer — was born on West Lexington Street, Baltimore. The baby was Henry Louis Mencken.

VIII
The Perfect Lady and a Sort of Devil

Baltimorean Henry L. Mencken as *genius loci,* a national gadfly, and memoirist supreme of his town's orderly domesticity.

"What I contend is that in Baltimore, under a slow-moving and cautious social organization, such contacts are more enduring than elsewhere, and that life in consequence is more charming. Of the external embellishments of life we have a plenty — as great a supply, indeed, to any rational taste, as New York itself. But we have something much better: we have a tradition of sound and comfortable living."[1]

— H. L. Mencken

"The old town will not give you the time of your life; it is not a brazen hussy among cities, blinding you with its xanthous curls, kicking up its legs, inviting you to exquisite deviltries. Not at all. It is, if the truth must come out, a Perfect Lady. . . .it has, at bottom, . . . the impalpable, indefinable, irresistible quality of charm."[2]

— H. L. Mencken

"To this day, in Baltimore, the Babbitts regard me as a sort of devil."[3]

— H. L. Mencken

A photograph of H. L. Mencken, by A. Aubrey Bodine, that has never been printed — that, in fact, was pulled from Bodine's wastebasket by Edward L. Bafford. Mencken himself evidently didn't have the chance to destroy it, although what seems revealed in his eyes might have made him want to.

Twenty years after H. L. Mencken died, the Baltimore City Council voted to name a plaza in Charles Center after him. But one of the Powers-That-Be vetoed the plan. Such a slap Mencken would have expected. The world, he said, has very little liking for the habitual truth-teller and truth-seeker, and in 1925 he noted, "to this day, in Baltimore, the Babbitts regard me as a sort of devil."

This whole literary history could well begin with this truth-teller in his study at 1524 Hollins Street, facing Union Square in West Baltimore. A useful opening scene would be an August day in 1940 when the writer is typing a letter. He can't ignore the humid heat, for suspenders bind b.v.d.'s to his sweaty hide. From three large windows he catches breezes off park trees. He thinks of his trees and garden out back screening furnace-hot brick houses.

In the letter he says that this enclosure of green helped formulate his view of life: "I have never had any sense of being hemmed in, and I have never been confronted with down-right hideousness."[4] We can interpret his sentence as analysis of why he wrote as he did. Maybe the tight rows of houses baking in the sun represent the society that was so stifling. And maybe the natural scene was like his own spirit, open and delightful. Those park trees were separate yet integrated into complexes of streets and parks. By analogy, Mencken was separate from his town, and yet he too was a part of its great design.

He and Baltimore go together like good local hard crabs and beer. Writing as a native, he called his city a perfect lady. He refused to leave her, even though editorial duties took him to Manhattan several times a month. Because of his well-known attachment to Baltimore, he enhanced its reputation. Already by 1910 the name of Baltimore shone because the scholars and doctors of Johns Hopkins had proved and advertised the humane uses of intellect. We now see that their influence on the city and nation served as prelude to Mencken's explorations of politics, religion, and morals.

To illustrate: as editor of *The Smart Set* and later *The American Mercury,* he fought censorship, promoted new writers (Theodore Dreiser and Joseph Conrad for two), and generally led Americans out of what he saw as an Age of Superstition. For his weekly column about local issues in the Baltimore *Evening Sun* he was often reviled, because he was ever the truth-seeker. Yet he was lover as well as scourge. What's more, he had become *genius loci* — the embodiment of his place and a master at capturing the spirit of his city on paper. In doing so he found himself as a writer. There in his hometown, too, he impressed his earliest readers with his talent: soon his writings from there put him on the American literary map.

Small wonder then that Mencken loved Baltimore, and that this love affair lasted 75 years. That is a long time for any affair, especially if the man is a native-born writer. Rarely does such a gifted author stay home. James Joyce, for example, left Dublin to live in exile and to describe his city's decay. By contrast, Mencken was born in Baltimore, grew up there, went to school there, worked on newspapers there for 50 years, married there, and died and was buried there. He was pure Baltimore.

Frequently he noted advantages of living there. What he liked he called his city's slow-moving, cautious, and enduring social organization. And home-life (Maryland style) was "spacious, charming, full of creature comforts, and highly conducive to the facile and orderly propagation of the species."[5] Notice his praise of orderliness, an ideal he attained in Baltimore.

Once we recognize how much orderliness meant to Mencken, we aren't surprised that he chose to live where people valued regular habits. Looking back from 1935 to 1905, he recalled that he had indeed been favored by fortune. He had then had a good job, and had known everyone he considered worth knowing, such as bordello madams. He spent evenings in "theatres, breweries and other cultural establishments of the town,"[6] and lived comfortably in his mother's home. Mencken loved that house at 1524 Hollins Street. Standing near the middle of a row of 12, it symbolized his way of looking at the world. Both rowhouse and Menckenian view are paradoxical. The contradiction is that a rowhouse is for leaning out of — for being part of the community. Yet it remains private because it presents only a discreet facade to the world. The rest is hidden behind that wall.

So it was with the private Mencken. Orderliness of neat rows echoed the orderliness in routine within those walls. He ordered his day thus: rising, cold bath, breakfast; work; stop work at 10 p.m.; have a beer with the boys. Though frequent commuting to New York editorial offices interrupted routine, he always returned with relief. Escaping to so ancient and solid a town as Baltimore, he wrote, was like "coming out of a football crowd into the quiet communion with a fair one who is also amiable, and has the gift of consolation for hard-beset and despairing men."[7]

Most observers then wouldn't have called him hard-beset and certainly not despairing. Lucky man! He happened along at the right time: he arrived before the advent of mass communication. Back then a place stamped a writer with a local seal. That lets us center on a time when Maryland, and indeed the entire Northeast, had more influence on the country than it does now. (Just 100 years earlier, in 1820, the center of America's population was Ellicott City, Howard County, Maryland.) As late as 1920 a powerful national editor such as Mencken was could work in Baltimore, not New York. His city wasn't as provincial then as it had been 50 years before. Just when Mencken arrived in 1880, cultural life took a belated spurt forward, thanks to benefactions of local multimillionaires. Mencken benefited from George Peabody's creating the Peabody Institute with its music conservatory, concert hall, and scholars' library. Peabody's example inspired Johns Hopkins to leave a fortune to endow both a university and a hospital. Men attached to these institutions, particularly the School of Medicine, influenced Mencken.

Then Enoch Pratt founded the first public library, one with branches and one from which books could be borrowed. Mencken recalled that as a youngster he was the best customer. At the branch library three blocks from home, Mencken idolized Thomas Henry Huxley, an English popularizer of science and a writer who put clarity above everything: "He even made metaphysics intelligible, and, what is more, charming. Nietzsche did the same thing in German, but I can recall no one else in English."

Mencken emulated him, and by the age of 30 felt that he too had developed a clear and lively style. Few readers knew that Mencken had taken Huxley as guide: "The imbeciles who have printed acres of comment on my books have seldom noticed the chief character of my style. It is that I write with almost scientific precision — that my meaning is never obscure. The ignorant have often complained that my vocabulary is beyond them, but that is simply because my ideas cover a wider range than theirs do. Once they have consulted the dictionary they always know exactly what I intend to say. I am as far as any writer can get from the muffled sonorities of, say, John Dewey."[8]

For all his love of books — and order — literary culture wasn't uppermost in Mencken's mind as a young man. Looking back to 1900 in 1926, Mencken told readers of *The Evening Sun,*

I am glad I was born long enough ago to remember, now, the days when the town had genuine color, and life here was worth living. I remember Guy's Hotel. I remember the Concordia Opera House. I remember the old Courthouse. Better still, I remember Mike Sheehan's old saloon in Light Street — then a medieval and lovely alley; now a horror borrowed from the boom towns of the Middle West.

Was there ever a better saloon in this world? Don't argue: I refuse to listen. The decay of Baltimore, I believe, may be very accurately measured by the distance separating Mike's incomparable bar from the soda-fountains which now pollute the neighborhood—above all, by the distance separating its noble customers (with their gold watch-chains and their elegant boiled shirts!) from the poor fish who now lap up Coca-Cola.[9]

Mencken was 46 years old when he wrote that. Already behind him stretched an orderly progress in journalism as well as in literature. That advance came, of course, from talent and competence, a virtue Mencken valued as much as orderliness. All his qualities he put to use when at 18 he reported for the Baltimore *Morning Herald* (1899–1902). His prose first appeared in print in 1899 when he reported a theft. Although the writer was only 18, his talent showed: "A horse, a buggy and several sets of harness, valued in all at about $250, were stolen last night from the stable of Howard Quinlan, near Kingsville. The county police are at work on the case, but so far no trace of either thieves or booty has been found."

After serving as city editor (1903–1905) he became managing editor of the Baltimore *Evening Herald* (1905–1906) and then in 1906 joined the *Sun.* In his spare time he wrote a book on Bernard Shaw's plays and one on Nietzsche's philosophy. He also became literary critic of *The Smart Set*, a popular New York magazine. When the Baltimore *Evening Sun* was born in 1910, he joined its staff as columnist. Thirty-eight years later he wrote his final column (just before his crippling stroke in 1948). He interrupted this column only during wars with Germany, when his views diverged from those of the paper. Not one to break his routine of writing, he employed those years creating his classic *The American Language* (1918) and his memoirs.

During 20 of his *Sun* years Mencken also competently edited two national magazines, first *The Smart Set* (1914–1923) and then *The American Mercury* (1924–1933). From 1914 until 1925 his co-editor was the most famous drama critic in New York, George Jean Nathan. Then Mencken had the help of Charles Angoff, a young Harvard graduate from Boston. Even with such aid, he astonishes with both quantity and quality of work.

Just during the decade of editing *The American Mercury*, for instance, every month he wrote several book reviews and essays (he was contributing editor of *The Nation* then too), he read hundreds of manuscripts and a score of novels and other books, he collected notes for supplements to his *The American Language*, he collected and edited his essays in six volumes of *Prejudices,* and he published *Notes on Democracy* (1926), *Treatise on the Gods* (1930), and *Treatise on Right and Wrong* (1934). He was efficient and tireless.

Once when asked why he, one of America's literary lights, stayed in provincial Baltimore, Mencken replied, "To work." From his work place on Hollins Street, he sent forth 100,000 letters, numerous short pieces, and more than 30 books. His first book was *Ventures Into Verse* (1903), a work he later ignored. The reason we can see from two examples. Both display a young writer's competency and imitativeness. The first, "Madrigal," harks back to 17th-century English Cavalier poets:

Ah! what were all the running brooks
From ocean-side to ocean-side,
And what were all the chattering wrens
That wake the wood with song,
And what were all the roses red
In all the flowery meadows wide,
And what were all the fairy clouds
That 'cross the heavens throng —
And what were all the joys that bide
In meadow, wood and down,
To me, if I were at your side
Within the joyless town?

A second poem echoes Rudyard Kipling, although the title "Im Hinterland" could have pointed to rural Maryland. (This poem was printed in "Knocks and Jollies," a column in the Baltimore *Herald,* January 20, 1901.)

Im hinterland, im hinterland,
Where roosters crow and porkers grunt,
And cows engage the toothsome cud,
And carrots bloom and turnips bud,
And ways are rough and speech is blunt,
Im hinterland, im hinterland.
But let a man with fairish front
Set out to do a three-card stunt,
Im hinterland, im hinterland,
And plenteous coin will flow his way,
For every coruscated jay —
Im hinterland, im hinterland —
Will buck the game and gladly pay
For opportunity to play

His luck ag'in a certaintay —
Im hinterland, im hinterland;
And that's the way they are today,
And that's the way they'll be for aye —
You cannot civilize a jay
Or from his belfry pluck the hay,
Alas, alack, alackaday —
Im hinterland, im hinterland.

After Mencken gave up writing poetry, he created a prose that led to national influence. With that style he also shaped the persona that set the Genteel Tradition on its delicate ear. Certainly, he stirred up the strife in which literature thrives, just as Poe had done three generations before him. Both critics, Mencken and Poe, picked up a raucous, iconoclastic spirit in this port city. Evidence of Mencken's spirit comes from an editor, Theodore Dreiser: he met Mencken in 1908 when he recalled

. . .there appeared in my office a taut, ruddy, blue-eyed, snub-nosed youth of twenty-eight or nine whose brisk gait and ingratiating smile proved to me at once enormously intriguing and amusing. I had, for some reason not connected with his basic mentality you may be sure, the sense of a small town roisterer or a college sophomore of the crudest and yet most disturbing charm and impishness, who, for some reason, had strayed into the field of letters. More than anything else he reminded me of a spoiled and petted and possibly over-financed brewer's or wholesale grocer's son who was out for a lark.

With the sang-froid of a Caesar or a Napoleon he made himself comfortable in a large and impressive chair which was designed primarily to reduce the over-confidence of the average beginner. And from that particular and unintended vantage point he beamed on me with the confidence of a smirking fox about to devour a chicken. So I was the editor of the Butterick Publications. He had been told about me. However, in spite of Sister Carrie, *I doubt if he had ever heard of me before this. After studying him in that almost arch-episcopal setting which the chair provided, I began to laugh. "Well, well," I said, "if it isn't Anheuser's own brightest boy out to see the town." And with that unfailing readiness for any nonsensical flight that has always characterized him, he proceeded to insist that this was true. "Certainly he* was *Baltimore's richest brewer's son and the yellow shoes and bright tie he was wearing were characteristic of the jack-dandies and rowdy-dows of his native town. Why not. What else did I expect? His father brewed the best beer in the world."*

All thought of the original purpose of the conference was at once dismissed and instead we proceeded to palaver and yoo-hoo anent the more general phases and ridiculosities of life, with the result that an understanding based on a mutual liking was established, and from then on I counted him among those whom I most prized — temperamentally as well as intellectually.[10]

Certainly what that brash youth experienced — and then wrote about — affected the nation, not just Baltimore. Writings of his heyday, 1917–1930, reached the best audience in the nation. Through them Mencken changed the whole country. More to the point of this book, his literary criticism and editing changed literature. Here is what he did for literature as taste-maker and liberator:

— In place of a genteel tradition in books, he substituted realistic portrayals such as Dreiser's and Sinclair Lewis's.
— He freed Southern writers from control by churches, and encouraged the Southern Renaissance by prodding them to dare.
— He woke writers to use what he called the prodigal and gorgeous life of America.
— He got after sentimentality, hypocrisy, Puritanism, and stuffy academia.
— He introduced major European writers such as George Bernard Shaw and Frederick Nietzsche to America, and promoted such authors as Joseph Conrad, Dashiell Hammett, and James M. Cain. In fact, he launched both Hammett and Cain in his magazines.
— He made American writing respected and respectable abroad.
— He forced writers to discuss tough ideas openly.
— He helped black writers by printing their work and by telling them to portray life honestly, from the inside, and artistically.

Parallel with his national publications were Mencken's 50 years of newspaper work in Baltimore. In weekly columns he gave a cosmopolitan perspective on local issues. He used his intelligence to raise consciousness. After five years of writing the column "The Free Lance," he wrote: "General aim: to combat, chiefly by ridicule, American piety, stupidity, tin-pot morality, cheap chauvinism in all their forms. Attacked moralists, progressives, boomers, patriots, reformers, and finally Methodists, etc., by name. . . Defended alcohol, regulated prostitution, Sunday sports, vivisection, war, etc. Often tackled osteopathy, Christian Science, direct primary, single tax, socialism."[11]

Though wary of "Do-Gooders," he himself helped make Baltimore better. In doing this he fits the picture painted by a recent critic of

Mencken as the quintessential American: "vulgar, outspoken, salty, well meaning, and compassionate."[12] One way such a man managed to make Baltimore better was by educating young bright readers. A case in point: Victor Weybright, a New York publisher, told him that he had been responsible for the precociousness of some 25 Carroll County boys even before they went to high school: "I have never in all my life forgotten the iconoclastic highlight of the period which reached us daily through the early skeptical writing of H. L. Mencken in the Baltimore *Sunpapers*, then the daily gospel of upland Maryland."[13]

Mencken was aware of many advantages he had by not living in Carroll County or any other rural Maryland spot. A letter of 1935 gave his attitude toward country yokels in Western Maryland: some residents of that mountainous region, he wrote — tongue in cheek — practised cannibalism, and others (violent Baptists) often drowned a neophyte during baptism by immersion. Worse practices characterized dwellers on the Eastern Shore, he often assured readers.

To show Mencken as a cockney whose hide was saturated with common life, here is a sample from one of his early columns that is pure urban Baltimore. It is testimony to local waiters' independence:

The waiters at the Back River parks are not like the groveling sycophants of the hotels. Like the waiters of the Spring Gardens and Curtis Bay resorts, they are free American citizens, and they seem to be eager that everyone recognize the fact and applaud it. When one of them is halted in his mad career and pauses to take an order, he does not pause long, nor does he offer respectful suggestions. The most he can be induced to say is, "Well, sport, what do you want?" If you don't tell him at once he passes on and a good deal of bawling and arm-waving is necessary to get him back. He has no time to waste upon the soft flatteries of the ordinary waiter. If you offer him a tip he takes it, but usually in a shamefaced sort of way. He wants it distinctly understood that he is the equal of any man in the house, bar none. At Hollywood last Sunday night a waiter in the casino demanded the loan of a spectator's cigar to light a cigarette.[14]

This excerpt proves that the air Mencken breathed at the Baltimore *Herald* practically forced a writer to dissent from the prevailing genteel tradition in literature. In his dissent, Mencken joined other American writers trained by newspaper work — Ambrose Bierce, Stephen Crane, Frank Norris, and Theodore Dreiser. Newsrooms were their Harvards and Yales.

Those newsmen wrote for male readers, who expected to read

colorful accounts of sin in their town. They also found much to muck-rake, and plenty of encouragement to do so. Such literate newsmen used the 19th-century French novelists Gustave Flaubert and Emile Zola as models. Those men writing for the *Herald* went in for imaginative setting down of human interest stories, complete with personal impressions.

As Mencken joined journalists covering a large port, his life, he said, was "the maddest, gladdest, damnedest existence ever enjoyed by mortal youth." Reporters collected a daily budget of fires, assaults, and drownings. The Central police district offered the busiest police courts, a downtown hospital, the jail, and the morgue. At first he was shocked at City Hospital—people with arms torn off, throats cut, eyes gouged out—but then, he said, no more.

James M. Cain and Russell Baker later endured the same initiation as *Sun* reporters. They and Mencken got more than initiation to mayhem and blood: Mencken was taught by his editors. One of them was charming, subdued, and highly respectable Lynn Meekins. He not only commanded a first-rate style, but also gave sound advice. As an example of Meekins's understanding, when proofs of Mencken's first book arrived, Meekins gave him the day off. He said it was one of the most important days of any life, and work shouldn't interfere with enjoyment of it.

Since Meekins had read widely, he introduced Mencken to many books. Another editor, Robert I. Carter, a Harvard graduate, encouraged Mencken, then drama critic, to praise the first Baltimore production of Ibsen's *Ghosts,* a play other critics then found immoral. Next, the local man behind that production, Will A. Page, stirred Mencken's interest in George Bernard Shaw as well. As a result, Shaw influenced Mencken's essays, and was the subject of his first prose book, *George Bernard Shaw, His Plays* (1905). Most important, Shaw was catalyst for finding a vocation. That vocation was analyzing ideas.

Mencken developed ideas such as that of the "Superman" in his second prose work, *The Philosophy of Friedrich Nietzsche* (1908). Ideas swarmed in Mencken's head then. Soon he began writing them down to enlighten and frighten readers. By chance, just at that time Baltimoreans were exerting themselves to bring their town into modern times. That same goal perhaps was Mencken's in his local column.

The five years on either side of his inaugurating a column serve as vantage place for viewing Mencken in Baltimore as he approached his prime. He himself recorded much of those good times in *Newspaper Days* and *Heathen Days.* Two events of national news later made lively chapters. The first event was the Big Fire of February 1904. That conflagration roared and sputtered for ten days and burned out a square mile of downtown. Every day Mencken as city editor had to marshal his staff — scattered in three cities (Baltimore, Washington, and Philadelphia) — to publish a paper. In his chapter, "Fire Alarm," he recalled that he had been a boy when the fire alarm called him to his office that cold Sunday, and that he emerged a sleepless week later "a settled and indeed almost a middle-aged man."[15]

His city had changed, too. By 1910 the rebuilt downtown looked like Cleveland or Seattle. City population had risen to well over half a million, and a new sewer system put Baltimore ahead of all other cities. Mencken lamented the boosterism surging around town.

In another chapter in his *Days* books, Mencken made a good story out of what such boosterism did to him and to his city in July 1912. Local boosters, especially the mayor, then carried Baltimore to what they said was a high plateau of civilization: they persuaded the Democrats to hold their nominating convention in the Fifth Regiment Armory. Their coming gave Mencken "A Dip Into Statecraft" and a delightful tale. This story turned on his almost being nominated for Vice President of the United States, with Woodrow Wilson as President. Anyone who knows Mencken realizes how incongruous such an arrangement would have been. As Mencken tells the story, he was groomed by his editor secretly as a dark horse. As such he was to prevent the editor's enemy Mayor J. Harry Preston's being presented to the convention as Maryland's official nominee.

Mencken concludes his account of how he missed his purple moment — and maybe even immortality — by calling on the publicists of liberal journals such as the *New Masses* to speculate upon the effects "upon history — nay, upon the very security and salvation of humanity"[16] if the editor's scheme had worked.

As it was, the mayor lost, though he became the state's nominee. And Baltimore boosters also lost because delegates spread word of a dreadful tropical climate that they had endured without benefit of air conditioning. Their complaints kept away generations of tourists. Native Marylanders continued as before, careless of reputation. Like Mencken, they felt comfortable within their redbrick fortress of rowhouses. In summer they relaxed in Druid Hill and other parks or else took a Bay steamboat to Betterton or other water resorts to cool off. What's more, to Mencken and other observers such as Gerald W. Johnson, the town then "shone as glamorous, full of wickedness but shining, full of wine and women, but also full of song."[17]

In the third-floor apartment of this brownstone at 704 Cathedral Street, Mencken spent his five years of married life with Sara Haardt. He also stopped editing *The American Mercury* then.

Mencken's beloved house at 1524 Hollins Street, Union Square, still has the lyre displayed on his steps and the pseudo-colonial fanlight over the front door that he had placed there. Through that door passed most of the prominent authors of his day, either in person or in manuscripts.

Here in the second-floor front room of 1524 Hollins Street, on the park, Mencken wrote.

Photographed November 25, 1930, Mencken stands in the dining room on Cathedral Street with Clarence Darrow, defense attorney at the Scopes trial in Tennessee, at which Mencken had been chief reporter. Mrs. Mencken delighted in exuberant Victoriana (note the Pabst advertisement) and Mr. Mencken, in the beer.

A good friend of Mencken's and a native Baltimorean, Huntington Cairns promoted such advanced writers as Ezra Pound, and inaugurated the intellectual radio program "Invitation to Learning." In the picture he is just taking up a new job in Washington, October 1934.

Gerald W. Johnson was snapped in 1978 opposite his Bolton Street house, where his friend and colleague Mencken always paid a Christmas call.

Following Mencken's custom, Gerald W. Johnson had set in the wall of his property an emblem of love. This plaque was given to him by Mayor T. R. McKeldin, who rescued it from who knows which demolition in town.

Obviously contented with his liveable city, Mencken posed in 1936 next to the fireplace of the downstairs sitting room at 1524 Hollins Street.

Reading Mencken's memoirs, we find that accounts of such profound and alarming experiences as the Big Fire of 1904 and the 1912 Convention give us the man in his place. We sense also that in those good times he was expanding his powers. Back then he was fully exercising his brisk, witty style. In the pages of the brand-new Baltimore *Evening Sun*, appeared in all its richness Mencken's characteristic public attitude — often noted as cynical without being bitter, iconoclastic without being anarchistic. That tone drew thousands of readers.

In his column "The Free Lance" Mencken gave those readers much pleasure. Three classic columns he wrote *in memoriam*. These columns are often reprinted as prose models. One was "In Memoriam: W.J.B.," about the death in 1925 of a perennial presidential candidate William Jennings Bryan, and about what a fool he made of himself in the Scopes "monkey trial." Mencken summed up Bryan's career of 40 years in one sentence: "Wherever the flambeaux of Chautauqua smoked and guttered, and the bilge of idealism ran in the veins, and Baptist pastors dammed the brooks with the sanctified, and men gathered who were weary and heavy laden, and their wives who were full of Peruna and as fecund as the shad *(Alosa Sapidissima),* there the indefatigable Jennings set up his traps and spread his bait."[18]

Another classic column marked the death of a film idol, Rudolph Valentino (1926). The two men had met and talked a week before the death, and Mencken decided that the actor had been killed by "the whole grotesque futility of his life": "Valentino's agony was the agony of a man of relatively civilized feelings thrown into a situation of intolerable vulgarity, destructive alike to his peace and to his dignity — nay, into a whole series of such situations."[19]

In a third postmortem marking the passing of Calvin Coolidge (1933), Mencken lighted on that President's gift for sleeping a lot: "Nero fiddled, but Coolidge only snored.... There were no thrills while he reigned, but neither were there any headaches." Mencken concluded, "He had no ideas, and he was not a nuisance."[20]

Such columns naturally brought charges of insensitivity. To that, his defenders answered by noting Mencken's unfreezing courage. They also pointed out how well he suited language to audience and occasion. Certainly most Baltimoreans knew how to take him. They delighted in his love of manipulating words, in metaphor, and in imaginative analogies. And they enjoyed his witty two-liners, such as, "Women always excel men in that sort of wisdom which comes from experience. To be a woman is itself a terrible experience."[21]

After 1930 and the coming of the Depression, Baltimoreans found Mencken harder to defend. His style remained alive; his views he maintained as before. He hadn't changed, but his readers had. Those eager readers of the 1920s he lost to worries about breadlines and the growth of fascism. So Mencken gave up editing *The American Mercury* in December 1933.

Fortunately for readers, Mencken in 1930 had married a Southern writer, Sara Haardt. Perhaps because she was writing stories out of her Alabama past, she encouraged him to reminisce. For years he regaled guests with accounts of his Baltimore youth. Then after his wife's death in 1935, he was left bereft and sad. He moved back to live with his brother August in the Mencken family house on Hollins Street. There he began looking in cupboards and odd corners, all filled, he discovered, with memorabilia of mother and father and, of course, of his own formative days.

Mencken then began mining that residue of years in pieces for *The New Yorker.* His series of recollections ran to 60 chapters. They came out in one small book, *A Christmas Story* (1946) and three big books — *Happy Days* (1940), *Newspaper Days* (1942), and *Heathen Days* (1943). This autobiography approaches the heights of Mark Twain's *Life on the Mississippi* in humor, vividness, and style. Like Twain, what he told was mainly true, but with occasional stretchers.

The *Days* chapters touch a full register of Baltimore life. In them appear dwellers in alleys, both immigrant whites and native blacks. Also there are Proper Baltimoreans, in and out of their Sunday best. These people come across to us, as one critic noted, like the lively individuals in a Brueghel painting, distinct and often comic. To illustrate, I choose a passage from the first volume, an account of young Baltimore males' reading habits and one reminiscent of Mencken's favorite novel, Mark Twain's *Huckleberry Finn:*

We Hollins street boys spent many a pleasant afternoon roving and exploring this territory, which had the name of Steuart's Hill. We liked to watch the operation of the lime-kilns, all of them burning oyster shells, and the work of the carpet-beaters and sod-cutters. But best of all we liked to visit the slaughter-houses at the far western end. There was a whole row of them, and their revolting slops drained down into a deep gully that we called the Canyon. This Canyon was the Wild West of West Baltimore, and the center of all its romance. Whenever a boy came to the age when it became incumbent on him to defy God, the laws of the land and his father by smoking his first cigarette, he went out there for the operation. It was commonly a considerable ceremony, with a ring of older boys observing and advising. If the neophyte got sick he was laid out on one of the lower shelves of the Canyon until he recovered. If he began crying for his mother he was pelted with nigger-lice and clods of lime.

The Canyon was also a favorite resort of boys who read dime novels. This practice was regarded with horror by the best moral opinion of the time, and a boy who indulged it openly was given up as lost beyond hope. The best thing expected of him was that he would run away from home and go west to fight the Indians; the worst was that he would end on the gallows. In the more elderly years of my infancy I tried a few dime novels, trembling like a virgin boarding an airship for Hollywood, but I found them so dull that I could scarcely get through them. There were other boys, however, who appeared to be able to bear them, and even to like them, and these addicts often took them out to the Canyon to read in peace. No cops ever showed themselves in that vicinity, which was probably, in fact, outside the city limits of Baltimore. It was an Alsatia without laws, and tolerated every sort of hellment. I have seen a dozen boys stretched on the grass within a circumference of fifty feet, all of them smoking cigarettes and reading dime novels. It was a scene of inspiring debauchery, even to the most craven spectator.[22]

While writing these recollections for publication, Mencken was also adding lengthy notes embroidering on them. These notes he carefully locked away. By his last will and testament, he kept them secret until 1981. Here are two excerpts from notes to page 4 of *Newspaper Days* about the time when he worked in his father's cigar factory on Greene Street:

In 1897 my father tried to launch me as a city salesman, but I hated the job and made a failure at it. I was by this time fully determined to leave the cigar business for newspaper work, but I knew that it would be difficult to break away, and I can recall a despairing moment when I contemplated suicide. Soon afterward I revealed my desire to my mother, and was heartened by her approval, though she was well aware that my father's plans for the future were all grounded on the assumption that I would remain with him. Her support emboldened me to open the subject to my father himself. This must have been toward the end of the Summer of 1898. He was naturally pretty well dashed, but he did not protest with any rancor, and it was understood between us that we were to resume the discussion in a year or so. His unexpected death early in 1899 saved me from what must have been a painful unpleasantness, for even if he had consented to my leaving it would have been at the cost of his long-cherished plans. Looking back, indeed, I am convinced that his death was the luckiest thing that ever happened to me, though we were on good terms and I missed him sorely after he was gone.

This passage continues with frank statements about his own outlook:

There was never a time in my youth when I succumbed to the Socialist sentimentalities that so often fetch the young of the bourgeoisie. My attitude toward the world and its people is and always has been that of the self-sustaining and solvent class. It requires a conscious effort for me to pump up any genuine sympathy for the downtrodden, and in the end I usually conclude that they have their own follies and incapacities to thank for their troubles. I don't think it would be fair to call me heartless, but my feelings for others are certainly concentrated upon my own class, and I am a good deal less moved by the woes of other classes. In brief, my attitude in the latter case is substantially analogous to that of a Christian toward the sufferings of Jews, or that of an Englishman toward those of Germans, or that of a German toward those of Russians. This is the common human way, but there is a hypocritical tendency to deny it. When I am aware of such prejudices I never deny them. In the present case my attitude has colored and conditioned my whole life. In so far as I have been free to choose my everyday associates I have chosen only men who knew how to do what seemed to me to be some useful thing in a workmanlike manner, and who got a respectable living out of it. Among newspaper men I have always dismissed the poor fish as mere ciphers, and among writers I have never had anything to do with the failures.[23]

Passages like these are now stirring up curiosity about other recently opened manuscripts. Many of these treat of Mencken's *Sunpapers* years, and are frank about the cadre there. Maybe even franker is his diary. Commencing in the year of his marriage and ending with his incapacitating stroke, it fills 2,100 typed pages, double-spaced. Mencken recorded pungent observations about Baltimoreans, with an attitude only distantly related to the one caught in the *Days* books that he was writing during much of that time. The tone is matter of fact, not humorous. And certain places show some of that attitude towards the Proper Baltimorean that will be noticed in the next chapter about three streetwise writers who left Baltimore after their early years, Upton Sinclair, Dashiell Hammett, and James M. Cain. Like them, Mencken knew a negative side of Maryland life.

The positive side, however, attracted literati from all over to be entertained by Mencken. Some of them he invited to drink beer and hear music at the Saturday Night Club. All of them savored the famous crabs from the Chesapeake. One anecdote suggests that Maryland rye whiskey inspired Sinclair Lewis to deliver Babbitt's "Booster Speech" to Mencken and others gathered in the men's room of the Rennert Hotel on Saratoga Street. The tall gaunt Lewis delivered the speech while standing in a washbowl. Lewis and other guests, of course, gobbled up something better even than Chesapeake crabs: visitors also enjoyed the feast of conversation.

Two friends who feasted told me what being with Mencken was like. One of these men, Gerald W. Johnson, first read Mencken in 1913 at age 23 and thus discovered a new planet. Down in North Carolina, he realized that Baltimore, that old capital of the Upper South, had produced a prodigy. Mencken, the prodigious writer-critic, stirred up Southerners, just as he had planned, and won Johnson's admiration. After 1926 when Mencken persuaded him to write for the *Sun*, Johnson moved to Baltimore and fell in love with it. There he wrote his series of histories, commentaries on current events, and biographies. Johnson lived almost a quarter century after Mencken and died full of honors of the kind Mencken had refused, especially honorary university degrees. Indeed the two men contrasted in everything except in their enthusiasm for the American parade and for American realism.

In his later years, Mencken always visited the Johnsons in their big Victorian rowhouse on Bolton Street on Christmas day. That was after he had made his annual pilgrimage to the Mencken lot in Loudon Park Cemetery on Wilkens Avenue, West Baltimore. The Johnson party was the only frivolity on a day Mencken hated. His going to it shows how well he and Johnson got along. One tie was their love of music. Johnson played flute and Mencken, piano, and both wrote about music.

A greater tie was respect for each other's professional writing. This regard endured even though they were opposed in politics. Their friendship survived even the months of January to May, 1938, when Mencken filled in as editor of *The Evening Sun*. Johnson said of those days that Mencken was consistently genial and helpful to the smaller fry there, although he was sometimes sardonic. Once he told Johnson in a deliberately bland tone, "He [Duffy] is a great cartoonist but in politics, of course, Duffy is an idiot." Johnson commented that since Duffy's politics and his were identical "I got it, all right." For all that, Johnson's epitaph stands out: Mencken, he wrote, "touched the dull fabric of our days and gave it a silken sheen."[24]

Another old friend, Huntington Cairns, recalled how quick and lively Mencken's physical movements were. Mencken's body was packed with the vitality of 20 ordinary men: Johnson remembered that "He was surcharged, and the fact was evident in whatever he did, even in the way he put his foot down in walking, or the flip of a hand when he returned a greeting...to observers it seemed that he could extract more, and more profound, pleasure out of one seidel of beer than most men could from a gallon; certainly he could extract energy and encouragement from apparent defeat; and certainly he could detect and savor lusty humors in situations which to most men meant only tragedy and despair." This savoring of lusty humors also made Cairns laugh at such Menckenian advice as, "There is always a well-known solution to every problem — neat, plausible and wrong."

Recalling how he used to take summer trips with Mencken to visit Joseph Hergesheimer in West Chester, Pennsylvania, Cairns said, "He was a wonderful companion, one of the best to take a trip you ever heard of — kept us hilarious." He also said, "Mencken was a lovely man. He was always quick and witty, but I never saw him lash out at anyone with his tongue as he so often did with his pen." This conclusion fits Gerald W. Johnson's idea that there were two distinct Menckens: one was the public force, the other was the polite, hospitable Baltimorean.

Cairns's last visit with Mencken was sad. About a week before Mencken died, Cairns came to lunch on Hollins Street: "I remember coming to the door that day, and Henry was coming down the stairs. I arrived at the same time the mailman arrived. Henry always gives you a boisterous greeting. He attempted it then in his ill condition. But his mind was really on that mail. He grabbed the mail and couldn't read it. But August told him there were only three or four letters. Henry used to get a hundred letters, and he still wanted that mail."

After the meal, Mencken excused himself to go upstairs. Cairns recalled, "As he was walking out of the room I called out, 'I'll be seeing you, Henry.' He turned and said, 'Maybe,' and went on upstairs. That was the last word I had from him. He died ten days later."

When I asked Cairns what he thought Mencken's place was in literary history, he said, "I know what *he* thought: it was *permanent*." Cairns's own view is that Mencken's strength was his comic genius. "He was an awfully funny fellow...as funny as Twain, though he may not have been the artist that Twain was." Mencken also will be remembered as writer of the best prose of the first half of the 20th century. The possible exception, said Cairns, would be the prose of Hemingway's early fiction.

Cairns concluded by saying that Mencken had made himself the most provocative writer of his day in America: his social and political criticism had educated a generation; he raised burlesque to an art, and he forced attention on the American language as separate from the English; he sorted out ideas like Nietzsche's and other European intellectuals for general consumption.[25]

In all of these achievements we see results of orderliness provided by the Perfect Lady, Baltimore, for that sort of devil, Mencken. The stability and tolerance of his city supported him. A resulting shelf of books reflected true freedom and sophistication. Writers he helped added a lengthening shelf of realistic novels and plays. To illustrate Mencken's far-reaching effect on American writing, here is an anecdote about the black novelist Richard Wright. By chance Wright read an article attacking H. L. Mencken in ugly words that the young black man had thought white people used only on blacks. He was eager to find out why, but in Memphis at that time blacks couldn't take out library books. In desperation, he borrowed a library card from a white co-worker and forged a note from him asking for some books by H. L. Mencken. That night of reading in *Prejudices* launched his writing career.[26]

Such wide and public results of Mencken's orderly creation of literature as that are well known. Less known but more important to his Baltimore-Maryland circle was the private Henry Mencken. One of that circle, Gerald W. Johnson, saw both the public and private man. In remembering the private man, Johnson said that Mencken's talk was better than his writing — "lightly, ironically, extravagantly, but with a flashing perception that illuminated whatever it touched, and it touched everything. A display of intellectual pyrotechnics it was, certainly, but like any fine fireworks display it created in an ordinary place on an ordinary night a glittering illusion; momentarily, at least, life sparkled and blazed, and the knowledge that it can ever sparkle and blaze is worth having. In fact, it is one of the best things a man can have."[27]

Not all of Mencken's writing reached such heights. But all of it bore his hallmark. Usually he wrote as he did in *Newspaper Days* — extravagantly and humorously. In that book he captured the gaudy life of a young reporter at large in a wicked seaport "getting earfuls and eyefuls of instruction in a hundred giddy arcana, none of them taught in schools."[28]

By contrast, Mencken wrote quite a different style in recently opened records of *Sunpapers* events and people, and in certain other pieces. That unadorned style he used in the following essay from the Bradford F. Swan Collection at Yale. (So far as I know, it has not been published before.) It brings out again Mencken's concern for competence and orderliness. It also brings us back to where we began this chapter, to the house that was as much a part of him as his two hands.

The fireplace in the downstairs sitting-room at 1524 Hollins street has been in service since 1917, and my brother August and I still sit in front of it, talking, smoking and taking a modest dram, every night when we are both at home. The chimney which serves it goes back to the building of the house in 1883. For ten years or more afterward that chimney provided the draft for a Latrobe stove burning anthracite coal. I still remember the cheerful glow of its mica windows on a Winter night, and I also recall the battered coal-scuttle that stood beside it, and the hired girl's morning struggle with the ashes. When my father equipped the house with steam heat the old stove was taken out and the gap under the black slate mantel was closed with a large sheet of similar slate, rounded over the top. We appreciated the superior efficiency of steam heat, but we missed the red pleasantness of the old fire, and when I undertook a general overhauling of the house in 1915 or thereabout, one of my first projects was the substitution of an open wood-fire.

It took me more than a year to find just the mantel I wanted. It had to be small, for the chimney-breast was not wide, and it had to be harmonious in design with the Eighteenth Century chairs and tables I had in mind. One day I found it in a Eutaw street store window. It turned out to be a precise fit, to an inch, and it was very simple and charming. A little while later I found a mirror to go above it, also of exactly the right size. Where I got that mirror I forget, but I think it was from Henry Herche, the Baltimore cabinet-maker whose shop produced most of the Heppelwhite imitations (and very good ones they are) that are still in the house. In the center of the old mantel there had stood a curious little cigar- and match-holder of glazed earthware, apparently from Dresden, that was one of my mother's wedding presents in 1879. It was transferred to the same place on the new mantel, and remains there to this day. It has outlived all her other wedding presents, and also several subsequent generations of decorative ceramics.

The little fire-place has not only warmed and cheered us for nearly thirty years; it has also served admirably as a household incinerator. About the time it went into place we substituted gas for coal in the steam boiler down cellar, and so the first wood that went into it came from the old wood-bin, followed soon afterward by the bin itself, along with the adjacent coal-bin. I well remember the heavy labor of sawing up the sturdy joists and tough unplaned planks of which these bins were made. There followed during the next twenty years all the debris of my operations in the back-yard, and of the constant rebuildings and refittings that went on inside the house. These enterprises furnished enough good fire wood first and last, to load a couple of large gondola cars—for example, the floor, posts, rails and roof of the old Summer house in the yard; the original floor of my third-floor back bedroom, and the joists under it that had begun to sag; the whole of the old backyard fence—at least 150 feet of it; the grape-arbor; the wooden Summer kitchen that, after years of service, gave way to brick; the backyard servants' privy, which my mother always called the Post Office, the original wainscoting of the dining-room; a built-in china closet; a dozen or more doors that were replaced by better ones; the wooden steps that used to be laid over the marble front steps in Winter; the wooden wall that once separated a bed room from a hall room on the third floor; the frames of the doors aforesaid; the old cellar steps, replaced when they wore out; an assortment of shutters; the old ash-house at the lower end of the yard; a wooden bathroom floor replaced by tiles; several condemned bookcases, and so on and so on.

I had an agreement with my mother that every time I bought a new chair or table or other article of furniture for the house I should be free to dispose of what ever it displaced. Most of the things then displaced were monstrosities of the late 70's and early 80's, so I usually broke them up, and they went into the fire. Along with them went all of my discarded concrete forms in the days when I was building a fence and a pergola in the yard. Also, all the wood cut from the three trees in the yard or as brought down by storms. Also, the debris of my brother's workshop in the days when he was making ship-models and experimenting with parquetry. Also, the frequent logs (usually half rotten) that I brought in from the river road along the Patapsco. . . .

When I think of the enormous pleasure that little fireplace has given us, and then figure out how little it has cost, I am impressed all over again with the fact that the most durable delights of life are *cheap. It is my recollection that the mantel, the fire-dogs, the cast-iron box, the red tiles, the screen and the fire-tools, and the cost of labor all ran to no more than $100. All the fittings of the fireplace, at the start, were of iron, but when I moved back from Cathedral street in 1936 I brought along the brass dogs, tools, folding screen and front rail that had been in use there. (I gave them to Sara before we were married, and she had used them in her apartment in Read street). We paid out nothing for wood until about 1940, and since then its cost has not been more than $30. All the rest of our fuel has consisted of the debris aforesaid and we not only got it for nothing but saved the expense of having it hauled away. Thus at a total cost of not more than $150 we have had a cheery fire burning for nearly 28 years. It burns, on an average, about 100 nights a year, which works out to 5½ cents a night...* [29]

The significance of such a domestic essay stressing order won't be lost on readers of this chapter. At home in his city he found order always. Paradoxically, as we have seen, Mencken both transcended his city and embodied it. Yet for him there was no place like his native hearth. Every sentence of his essay announces him a Baltimorean of 1524 Hollins Street, Union Square, West Baltimore, Baltimore City, Maryland, U.S.A.

IX
"Shallow, Kittenish Fellows" And Other Traditionalists

The carrying on of old forms of writing, usually with pleasure in the past, by — among others — Christopher Morley, Lizette Woodworth Reese, William Force Stead, and the Poetry Society of Maryland.

"Down in Maryland, I get on very well with the native gentry, but the bogus intellectuals pain me severely. The virtue of the gentry lies in the simple fact that a back-ground is behind them.... In such matters I am extremely reactionary. I believe that a man's great-grandfather influences him enormously more than the people he ordinarily meets with in his life."[1]
— H. L. Mencken

"The dignified writers of that time [the end of the 19th century] were such shallow, kittenish fellows as [William Dean] Howells, F. Hopkinson Smith and Frank R. Stockton, with Richard Gilder as their high priest.... The Gilders of his time left only trash."[2]
— H. L. Mencken

William Force Stead is shown here in the 1950s lunching at the French villa of his Baltimore hostess, Mrs. Nancy Howard DeFord Venable (left). He wrote most of his poetry abroad. After Stead returned to Maryland from consorting with T. S. Eliot and the like he stated that he knew he was not a great poet, but that he *was* a poet.

When I knew them on Bolton Hill, they were old. They lived together but never married, presumably because his wife lived on in an English religious order. She — Nancy Deford Venable — had been put in a play by her friend Tennessee Williams. He — William Force Stead — had baptized his friend and fellow poet T. S. Eliot. Together they brought to town the excitement of international literary lions. Once he said to her, "Let's invite T. S. Eliot and Tennessee Williams to dinner — and watch the fun!"

In appearance both of them were tall, gawky, unsmiling; they looked at one as if from a distance, or as people separated by the glass walls of an aquarium. They had not aged as most people do: she kept her hair blonde, in page-boy style; he looked much as he did in an I.D. photograph of 20 years before.

Walking slowly along the edge of new housing sites, they resembled almost extinct sea creatures washed up on shore and allowed to walk for a time on land, a marvel. At other times I saw them setting off in their tall, tan, old-fashioned coupe, sometimes driven by the black man-servant. Or I would come upon them contemplating their garden plot, blooming with spring bulbs. From May to October they retired to better gardens abroad.

Small wonder that they fascinated: they were so out of place. Her fate was to see her traditional Society all but vanish, to spend time chiefly with eccentric men, some of them downright irascible, and to spat with "upstart neighbors." His fate was to teach girls in a small Catholic college in Washington, to witness the end of the donnish life, to see his kind of poetry discredited.

Seeing your life's work discredited does, of course, hurt — even if changing taste is to blame. A shift in readers' taste simply makes more difficult the evaluating of poetry like Stead's. Yet evaluation is needed if readers are to find good books especially among neglected authors.

To place Stead in perspective, imagine a classroom full of 20th-century Maryland authors. At the head of the class H. L. Mencken and F. Scott Fitzgerald would receive A's. Many others would earn a C or less. (F. Hopkinson Smith would get F.) The class would be remarkable, though, for the number of B's and B+'s. Shining there would be innovators such as Dashiell Hammett, James M. Cain, and Ogden Nash.

Next to those pioneers would sit a more traditional group, some also earning B's. Three of good quality would occupy front row seats in this chapter: Christopher Morley, Lizette Woodworth Reese, and William Force Stead. Those authors would head a group writing in conventional form and styles. That group usually stuck to familiar themes and to local settings and people, although certain members of the Poetry Society of Maryland ventured way beyond those bounds. So did a stellar faculty of women, including Edith Hamilton, Julia Randall, Ola Winslow, and Mencken's wife, Sara Haardt.

A majority of that group showed a predilection for history. Pleasure in the past also showed in earlier Maryland books such as John Pendleton Kennedy's novels. That habit of looking back led one modern observer to say that citizens of the Old Line State are inclined to think yesterday more important and more divine than tomorrow.[3]

Looking back didn't excite everybody. Even a loyal Old Line Stater like Mencken found certain Maryland writers disappointing: they lacked good sense — or perhaps James M. Cain's guts and gusto. But Mencken didn't condemn all writing outside his favored category of realism. He supported local memorialists such as Meredith Janvier and Lizette Woodworth Reese, for example.

In doing so, Mencken helps make an important distinction in literary histories: writers tend to fall into either national or local categories. Many competently written books of purely local note balance those others, also well written, of most interest to readers beyond the region. This chapter includes a long look at the local writers. Some have held up well despite the years — Hulbert Footner and Laura Lee Davidson, for instance. Those holding up less well for reading today are represented by Belle Caples Morris and Eugene Lemoine Didier.

Mid-20th century examples by competent local writers came from the Baltimore press of Mary Owings. She published not only a prose memoir by Elizabeth Sewall Glenn, *The Curtains of Yesterday* (1957), but also slim volumes by local poets such as early poems of Josephine Jacobsen. Doubtless Owings assured quality by having as advisor the English poet W. H. Auden.

Mencken apparently did not object to Owings's series of poets. But certain other traditional authors did earn his scorn; these he called shallow, kittenish fellows. One example was Francis Hopkinson Smith, a well-born Baltimorean of Franklin Square. His fiction was pap. In *Kennedy Square* (1911), he tried, and failed, to re-create Poe's Baltimore friendship with John Pendleton Kennedy. Maybe a reason for failure lay in Smith's having taken up writing at 50 as a sideline to engineering projects such as his constructing the Statue of Liberty's foundation and pedestal (1886). His fictions were less solidly built. They collapsed from weakness of plot, characterization, and style, though they had a vogue when published. Reading them was for

Mencken an experience that was almost terrible.

Another D student and target of Mencken's attack was Eugene Lemoine Didier. Mencken called him one of Baltimore's two or three low comedy literati. In 1909 Didier set up a new target when he published at his own expense *The Poe Cult and Other Poe Papers.* That book justified Mencken's scorn of him as a locally celebrated Baltimore bug — an angry, foolish defender of Poe. Mencken scoffed because Didier praised Poe for the wrong things. Also, Didier, like some other Baltimoreans, was too much caught up in details of Poe's death and posthumous ill-fame to recognize with Mencken his true genius as literary critic.

A third "shallow, kittenish fellow,"—but one earning a higher grade—was Christopher Morley. Like other traditionalists, he looked to England for models; he liked Rupert Brooke, Hilaire Belloc, and Robert Louis Stevenson. Unlike the others, he found many readers. Although Morley and Mencken grew up only a mile apart, they came from different worlds. Mencken's was a world of streets and German-American cigar businesses. Morley's was a world of Quakers, Haverford College, and Oxford (his parents were English). With their differences, we aren't surprised to hear Mencken telling a colleague in 1930, "This is not a decent country. Christopher Morley flourishes, but poor Ring Lardner rots away."[4]

Time proved Mencken's evaluation right. Morley's whimsy lies on the shelf; Lardner's ironies keep echoing in our ears. Such novels as Morley's *Where the Blue Begins* (1922) came under Mencken's epithet "artful emptiness." This stricture applies also to *Parnassus on Wheels* (1917), with a Marylander hero who was a kind of 20th-century Parson Weems still selling books from a cart traversing America.

Novels like that only partly filled Morley's shelf of more than 50 books. All of them reflected a whimsical, bookish, pipe-smoking uncle. In his books of essays such as *Mandarin in Manhattan* (1933), he combined gossip, strong enthusiasm, and crotchets. His poetry was sentimental, though occasionally winning in style. His style in prose too used to charm readers with its ease.

That style ideally suited him as shaper of literary taste. He pointed beginning readers the way to writers such as Sir Arthur Conan Doyle and Joseph Conrad. As guide, he helped found the *Saturday Review of Literature.* He also served as judge for the Book-of-the-Month Club. Always his theme in essays and novels was the importance of relating literature to ordinary life.

Morley departed from that theme in his popular *Kitty Foyle* (1939).

For us it documents the entrance of young women into the business world of men. The author imagined what it was like to be one of those white collar girls. Yet even his imagination and his aphoristic style couldn't make the book a classic.

Morley's wit, however, kept the novel lively with such lines as, "You see a lot in the papers about the Man's point of view and the Woman's, etc., as if they were never the same. That's just a gag to keep women from being a nuisance, or getting too many of the good jobs." (The year, remember, was 1939.)[5]

Kitty Foyle was made into an Oscar-winning movie starring Ginger Rogers, who also won an Oscar for her portrayal of the witty young woman from Frankfort, a working-class section of Philadelphia. Her affair with the scion of a rich Quaker family from the Main Line reached a climax when she decided to have an abortion rather than, as she saw it, ruin the man's life. The ending was teary.

Clearly Morley's portrayal of Kitty Foyle required more imagination and maybe more knowledge of the poor than he apparently had. As it was, his boyhood and youth in Baltimore provided no such information — only a warm, academic cocoon. Since his father held the chair of mathematics at Johns Hopkins University, he belonged in the upper-middle-class neighborhood of Park Avenue. There the writing Morley brothers — Christopher, Felix, and Frank — lived the life described affectionately in Christopher's novel *Thorofare* (1943).

Why the writer chose to use the form of a novel for this memoir is a mystery. The book is so leisurely, so anecdotal, so nostalgic, so uneventful, that one would hang oneself if in need of a plot. Did novels sell better than reminiscences did during World War II? The kind of book *Thorofare* is comes out in how Morley integrated the Big Fire of 1904 when his characters watched from four miles away:

No citizen has ever forgotten the great fog of smoke and burning that lasted so long. "It smells worse than Friends' Meeting," said Ingram...The flames were so alive, so terrifying, it was hard not to think them conscious with malevolence. "The big fiends," Ingram muttered, standing in his long overcoat against the railing of the bridge.

Aunt Bee agreed. "It really looks like hell-fire," she said. "I dessay it's a judgment." In the panorama of rioting flame stood momentary outlines of shattered masonry, jagged and black against fury beyond...It looked indeed like the end of their world, and long later Jeff remembered how his boyhood closed with a curtain of red light.[6]

These urban sights contrasted with bucolic scenes at Blue Ridge

Summit, Western Maryland, where Morley's family summered. The amused tone of those scenes permeates an account of one hot afternoon when a fictional little sister busied herself floating chips of bark down rushing Hunting Creek. She called them what her older brothers did, "A letter for the government!" That phrase came from the creek's flowing into the Monocacy River and then into the Potomac, where it finally entered the sea of politics at Washington. Morley noted, "The boys would have been amused to hear her utter this innocent ejaculation; in confidential moments they had adapted the phrase for private reinforcements of the stream [urinating]."[7]

Living so near the Mason and Dixon Line and to Gettysburg, these children felt that they were living Civil War history. Their ex-Confederate friend the Major even refused to cross the line into the North; to him the nearby town of Blue Ridge Summit, straddling the Pennsylvania border, was foreign country. More forgiving were local veterans marching in Fourth of July parades side by side, blue and gray.

Just as amiably, Morleyan bookishness combined with nostalgia throughout *Thorofare*. Bookishness began early for all three Morley brothers. When as Baltimore boys they made their mile-long pilgrimage to the Enoch Pratt Free Library, they read as they walked. Not only did they read, but they also raced to see who could read the most pages in a block.

Although we don't know how often Christopher won, he led in another literary venture. At age 12 he dragooned his brothers and friends into publishing a neighborhood newspaper. They had to write all copies by hand. From that paper come these samples of early Morley prose, rare items reprinted from the original Home Notes of 1905:

In the twenty seventh of December a club entitled the "Park Avenue Literary Club" was established. The members, at present, are: C. D. Morley (President), F. M. Morley, F. A. Davis. The purpose of this Club is "the promulgation of literary instinct in the youthful mind."

On Saturday morning a meeting of "The Sign of the Four" was held at 1812 Eutaw Place.

Mr. C. D. Morley went skating with Mr. Benjamin Tappan on Friday afternoon in Druid Hill Park (at the Boat Lake). The ice was moderately good, but an immense crowd made the pond rather unattractive.

Toto [the baby] wants to know if he is deceitful. Lizzie [his black nurse] says, "No, bless his heart, he isn't."[8]

Toto (Frank) became a well-known publisher and writer and lived mostly in England. His books included *My One Contribution to Chess* (1945), a mystery novel *Death in Dwelly Lane* (1952), and *The Great North Road: A Journey in History* (1961). *Literary Britain: A Reader's Guide to Its Writers and Landmarks* (1980) he dedicated to an old Baltimore sweetheart, Cynthia J. Stevens, a nice touch to a labor of love. As publisher, he founded Faber & Faber with others, including his friend T. S. Eliot. He helped put together Eliot's influential *Selected Essays* (1932). Eliot, in turn, dedicated *Old Possum's Book of Practical Cats* (1939) to Morley's daughter Susana. The popular musical *Cats* was based on that book of poems.

Frank's brother Felix also followed a career in letters. He wrote for the Baltimore *Sun,* edited *The Washington Post,* and served as president of Haverford College. Then, retired to Gibson Island, Anne Arundel County, he published a novel, *Gumption Island* (1956), and his memoirs, *For the Record* (1979). In these recollections he covered childhood years already captured in his brother's *Thorofare,* as well as a newspaper career close to Mencken's. But probably no straight autobiography could compete for charm with *Thorofare* and *Newspaper Days.* For both Christopher Morley and H. L. Mencken used imagination to create a town that never was, and a place to envy.

Similarly, many other writers tried to charm readers with descriptions of marshes and mountains beyond Baltimore, but with less success. Collections such as George C. Perine's *Poets and Verse Writers of Maryland* (1898) showed the writers' sincerity. But sincerity — even free of sentimentality — wasn't enough. Long ago a Baltimore critic judged a number of sincere poetic celebrations of Maryland's outdoors as having "the quaint but rather awful charm of a badly stuffed owl."[9]

Part of that awful charm came from writers' imitating 19th-century nature poets such as William Wordsworth. One Western Maryland poet even revived the favorite 18th-century form, the couplet, in "From Braddock Heights." Among the droning lines that poet, T. C. Harbaugh, composed two startling, Freudian lines: "Where Shenandoah's crystal tides Potomac's ripples wed / And Maryland Heights in grandeur rise above the nuptial bed."[10]

Few versifiers have addressed the beauties of the Eastern Shore with less than Tennysonian ardor. Most were nostalgic. Consider, for instance, just the titles in *Songs of the Sassafras* (1940), by Belle Caples Morris: "Song For Maryland Day," "Springtime in Kent," "When the Raven Of Your Hair Has Turned To Snow," "When Mary Baked the Bread," and "Take Me Back To Baltimore." The poem called "Old Times, Old Loves, Old Friends" closes, "Come! All aboard for

Sassafras, the boat swings in the stream / And Captain Cundiff's at the wheel, bound for the land of dream; / Brice, Griffith, Boyer, Morris, Foard, I see them go aboard— / The mist has gathered in my eyes and slowly fall the tears. . ."[11]

Richard Hart's approving advice to readers in 1942 is still sound: "There is no vice less harmful than the writing of bad verse." Hart asserted, "In a democracy no one is compelled to read it, and the honest pleasure, excitement, and gratified vanity which result from unskilled wrestling with English prosody are probably good for the glands."[12]

Nostalgic newspaper readers also took pleasure in that wrestling, skilled or unskilled. Baltimoreans enjoyed the verse of Amy Greif, for one, and read numerous nostalgic rhymes by the "Bentztown Bard," Folger McKinsey. Here is the opening of "Going for the Boat" (1909), a piece from days when steamboats out of Baltimore threaded the Chesapeake and its rivers:

Oh, they hurried with a song, with a light still sweet
Of the dreams in their hearts, as they hurried through the street;
Going for the boat, while their eyes burned bright,
For the old bay boat that was blowing down at Light:
  Oh, they hurried with a song, they were going for the boat,
  And my heart felt the song as it echoed in my throat:
    Song of the shine and sweet of the bay,
    The low green shores where the dreams dance gay,
    The isles of the bloom and the fruit and the gleam
    Where the Kentland lies in the deep, sweet dream—
    Pumpkins in the cornfield, honey out of reach,
    And the ruddy rainbow cheek of the early Crawford peach!

Luckily for readers now, not all nostalgic writing has faded. In fiction, for instance, some people still savor romantic vignettes of early times at Johns Hopkins Hospital in Augusta Tucker's *Miss Susie Slagle's* (1939) and *The Man Miss Susie Loved* (1942).

A number of nostalgic poems survive also. Examples of considerable quality came from Waters Turpin, Sally Bruce Kinsolving, Gilbert Byron, and Elinor Glenn Wallis, to name only a few out of many.

An illustration is "Farm In Autumn," a Marylander's imagining colonial life. The farm could well have been her ancestors' in Baltimore County near Stemmer's Run, where she spent summers. Here is the first stanza of three by Elinor Glenn Wallis:

The smell of batter cakes
  and bacon frying,

Crackle of hickory wood,
  a martingale,
And pair of gloves upon the fender, drying,
A cough, a knock
  a lazy thumping tail.
And Tom, apologetic,
  black of feature:
"Marse Eddie, whah de skim milk
fo' de preacher?"[13]

Two other Baltimore poets, both still writing, have puzzled over Maryland's past impinging on the present. Josephine Jacobsen's "Arrival of My Cousin" contrasts a serene relic of Victorian Baltimore, Green Mount Cemetery, with street life outside its walls. The day is typical of summertime Maryland—humid and very hot. The poet reports that the dead sleep under cool grass and thousands of white stones, crosses, and angels of granite, but, "Traffic sweats and stalls on Oliver Street, / and Hargrove, Dolphin, Bethel Streets; the dirty bars / sweat, and the usual accidents in the accident-rooms / are glazed by July, as are the gutters and the junk-man's / horse, jerked up the tar-soft mountain of July. / My cousin, however, is in / the green city of the dead."[14]

Another poem, this one by Julia Randall, called "Maryland" itemizes inescapable inheritances from the past: "It is ours now, the silver / the heart-trouble, the entrée / to the Mount Vernon Club. We took it for granted, / knowing from whom, by whom descended / manners, the cellarette, red hair."[15] During the rest of the poem Julia Randall brings out further significance of a grandmother and other ancestors. In that harking back she supported a report that Old Guard Baltimoreans were second only to Boston in valuing ancestors. Even Baltimore's internationally known authors had a strong interest in forebears—witness Poe, Mencken, Fitzgerald, and Gertrude Stein.

Of these four, Fitzgerald alone made fun of Marylanders' obsession with ancestors. But that was before he moved to Baltimore. His spoof, a short story called "The Curious Case of Benjamin Button," tells of a problem faced by a young couple on Mount Vernon Place, a proper pair, he noted, connected with that enormous peerage that largely populated the Confederacy. Their problem was Mrs. Button's giving birth to a gentlemanly old man, not a wailing baby. Their offspring Benjamin grew younger every year and so threw their careful order out of kilter. Really, Old Baltimoreans said, we can't tolerate such disorder.

Stead's home place in Howard County, The Gables, Lawyers Hill, evidently provided little food for his imagination. But from other Maryland villas like this one came a spate of works of polite literature on local themes.

Ogden Nash, right, and Christopher Morley, second from the right, showed their newest books to Princess Paul Supieka, December 21, 1943.

The boyhood home of the Writing Morleys still stands at 2026 Park Avenue. Its neighborhood was the chief setting in Christopher Morley's autobiographical novel *Thorofare*.

A literary center of 1920s Baltimore was Old St. Paul's Church Rectory, center, with stone wall, where the Poetry Society of Maryland often met and heard visiting poets. The house with the flag at the right was earlier the home of Johns Hopkins, the wealthy bachelor who endowed both university and hospital.

Lizette Woodworth Reese lived her last years in this house on Harford Road with her sisters. It still faces Herring Run Park, whose natural beauty couldn't match that of her Waverly girlhood home (demolished), also in the northeast quadrant of Baltimore.

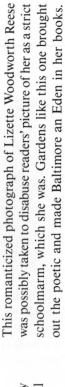

This romanticized photograph of Lizette Woodworth Reese was possibly taken to disabuse readers' picture of her as a strict schoolmarm, which she was. Gardens like this one brought out the poetic and made Baltimore an Eden in her books.

Sally Bruce Kinsolving, poet, founder of the Poetry Society of Maryland, and wife of the rector of Old St. Paul's Episcopal Church in whose rectory poets gathered.

As one way to keep out disorder in the real world, Marylanders have long supported conservative private schools and colleges. Many institutions had religious foundations, and most were segregated by sex and race. Also, they were snobbish once. These schools assume importance for this history because their teachers promoted polite letters, and many graduates became steady readers. Their early faculties included Sidney Lanier and Colonel Richard Malcolm Johnston in the 19th century. Later, a teacher at Boys' Latin School, Edward Lucas White, wrote popular historical novels such as *El Supremo* (1916). (White was the great-grandson of a well-known Baltimore publisher, Fielding Lucas, Jr.) Happily, he doubled his value to literary culture by instilling love of literature in his students and appreciation of the past in his readers.

Literary culture depended mostly, however, on women teacher-writers. One example, Ola Winslow, headed the English Department at Goucher College, and wrote during summers. Her biography of Jonathan Edwards won the Pulitzer Prize in 1941. When that award came, she told a reporter that she earned her living teaching the young, but there was nothing she would rather do than write. That reporter doubtless told an editor, and the paper then editorialized that hard-working intellectuals like her probably outnumbered "the elderly gentlemen with a glass of Madeira in one hand and a copy of the Racing Form in the other, who are supposed to typify Baltimore."[16]

Another teacher, Laura Lee Davidson, justified that boast. Her books count among Maryland's undiscovered treasures. Although now forgotten, her *Winter of Content* (1922) and *Isles of Eden* (1924) deserved prizes, the first one especially. In it she told about her winter of living on an island in Ontario all alone. In her very first lines she sets her tone and invites the reader: "A small, rocky island in a lake, a canoe paddling away across the blue water, a woman standing on a narrow strip of beach, looking after it. I was the women left on the shore, the canoe held my companions of the past summer, the island was to be my home until another summer should bring them back again."[17] The ensuing pages belong with classics of solitary adventuring in nature, such as Joshua Slocum's *Sailing Alone Around the World* (1900). There an educated woman from Bolton Street, Baltimore, brought her Canadian winter to life. Her companion deer mice, rabbit, and red squirrel stir on the page.

Another of these female writer-teachers, Edith Hamilton, was as well known as Davidson was obscure. Although she began to write only after retiring from teaching, by age 90 she was a celebrated author. Yale cited her for having taken the nation to school: "Your scholarly love of Greek culture is no repining for a dead past, but a new dimension of depth and beauty in our civilization." In her major work *The Greek Way* (1930), she showed how the ancient Greeks arrived at the clarity of their thought and the affirmation of their art. About the permanence of Greek drama she had this to say: "It is ever to be borne in mind that though the outside of human life changes much, the inside changes little, and the lesson-book we cannot graduate from is human experience."[18] She added other insights in *The Roman Way* (1932), translations of Greek plays (1937), and *Mythology* (1942). Later her translation of Plato's writings came about because in Washington she had the custom of dining Sunday nights with another ex-Baltimorean, Huntington Cairns, and his wife. One night he proposed that they together might do for Plato what had been done for the Bible: that is, put all the works in one volume. Much later Cairns reported that Hamilton "jumped at the idea of it, and we did it."[19] Their *Plato: The Collected Dialogues, Including the Letters* came out in 1961. Cairns's summing up of Hamilton was, "She was a highly intelligent woman." Her success rested on mastery of her own tongue; her prose flowed simply, lucidly, classically.

These books contributed perhaps no more to the literary culture of Maryland than what she had already done in her Baltimore school by creating readers with rigorous critical standards; her graduates could think. They had done so since 1884 when a Baltimore lady, M. Carey Thomas, and friends had founded the Baltimore Bryn Mawr School as feeder for Bryn Mawr College, where she was dean. Soon Edith Hamilton came to run that school, the only strictly college preparatory school for girls in the whole country.

As one graduate recalled, Baltimore was a most unlikely place to conduct such an experiment. The natives then showed little enthusiasm for literature and learning. And besides, noted this graduate, most people in that Southern place thought girls should not learn anything in particular. When one parent asked Carey Thomas why young women should learn Greek, she told them it was so that they could read Homer.[20]

During Edith Hamilton's reign at Bryn Mawr School, another well-known female writer, Lizette Woodworth Reese, was teaching English ten blocks to the west at Western High School for Girls. She had won Mencken's praise for the same reason Sidney Lanier had: she sang sweetly and softly and also had a muffled kettle drum. Throughout much of her career she counted on Mencken's supporting puffs to sell her books.

With or without boosting critics, she pleased readers with delicate ruminations on the green fields and simple rural folk in Waverly on York Road. In thus pleasing, she reminded some readers of her younger contemporaries Edna St. Vincent Millay and Elinor Wylie. That came out especially in excited lyrics such as "The White Fury of the Spring":

Oh now, the white fury of the spring
Whirls at each door, and on each flowering plot —
The pear, the cherry, the grave apricot!
The lane's held in a storm, and is a thing
To take into a grave, a lantern light
To fasten there, by which to stumble out,
And race in the new grass, and hear about
The crash of bough with bough, of white with white.
Were I to run, I could not run so fast,
But that the spring would overtake me still;
Halfway I go to meet it on the stair.
For certainly it will rush in at last,
And in my own house seize me at its will,
And drag me out to the white fury there.[21]

To one fellow poet then Reese seemed strangely out of place: she resembled a good tart winter apple in a dish of wax fruit.[22] Another poet (not a local one), Louise Bogan, singled Reese out for sounding an authentic and good feminine song. Reese's first poetry, *A Branch of May* (1887), dropped the usual faded ornaments and romantic locutions of her era. She substituted, Bogan said, an almost weightless diction: "expression is molded by feeling as the liquid in a glass is shaped by the glass itself."[23] Here is an example from *A Quiet Road* (1896), "In Time of Grief":

Dark, thinned, beside the wall of stone,
The box dripped in the air;
Its odor through my house was blown
Into the chamber there.

Remote and yet distinct the scent,
The sole thing of the kind,
As though one spoke a word half meant
That left a sting behind.

I knew not Grief would go from me,

And naught of it be plain,
Except how keen the box can be
After a fall of rain.

What poetry Reese expressed she gathered with the daffodils along York Road, northeast of Baltimore. Her fiefdom there is now city but in her youth was Baltimore County and rural. One of her two prose memoirs she aptly called *A Victorian Village* (1929). The other memoir, *York Road* (1933), centered on that main artery for farm wagons lumbering down to the port. The road passed just west of her rose-draped low cottage.

There she was born in 1856, and there she grew up close to nature. The family orchard behind the house was at once, she said, a sanctuary, a playground, a closet, and a stage. She loved to look at it: "At dusk, any time of the year, stretched out against a west of honeysuckle-yellow, it has the effect of medieval carving. There is a grave loveliness about it then that makes you think of a strain of music coming out of a half-closed door. It is as full of secrets as an old house."[24]

Her house there in Waverly gave her the same satisfactions that Mencken's rowhouse on Union Square did him; the two Baltimore writers wrote about home the same way. Of the pleasures there, she wrote, "When your gate clanged behind you, and your foot touched ancestral gravel, your democratic warmth began to cool a little. The aristocracy of possessions demanded upon you. It was good to remember a bedstead."[25]

From that house she set out to teach at the nearby St. John's School even before she published her first poem at 19. Teaching and writing were thereafter her twin lives. Most days during the 45 years she taught public school, she was too tired to sit and compose. So she developed a method of composing a whole page in her mind before committing it to paper. Still, composition was just as hard after she had retired from teaching and wrote her prose memoirs.

Her very first poem, "The Deserted House," took her weeks to write. Then one Saturday morning she set off with another female teacher to present it to the editor of the *Southern Magazine* on East Baltimore Street. That editor was William Hand Browne, a defender of Poe's reputation and later English professor at Johns Hopkins University. He published her poem in the June 1874 issue. For it she received no remuneration because, she said, it was as much as Browne could do to pay the bills.

Her true reward came from seeing her name staring at her from the bottom of the broad magazine page. That satisfaction recurred often after that. She soon found readers for her poems, particularly her sonnets. After the success of her first collection — "a pinched little dove-colored volume," sold at 75 cents — she published poems in popular magazines. Her poem "Tears" stirred the widest audience, though some readers today find other pieces less sentimental.[26]

If she is read at all now, it is for vignettes of Maryland nature and Maryland working people. Old, stooped black Eli, for instance, lived in a one-room hut on a half acre of herbs and flowers — "Scarlet, or hot king's purple, orange, blue." Once a slave, he later earned a living mending village roofs. But by night he came to his true calling, reading palms: Although he was a plain carpenter by day, by night he loomed a master of all fate.[27]

Despite her success, Reese told the Poetry Society of Maryland that only the few really care for poetry. There are no more now, she said, than there have always been. She served as honorary president of that society for a time, and at one evening meeting was the subject of a talk by Mencken. How many sessions she attended we don't know. We do know that Society meetings attracted widely read poets — William Butler Yeats, T. S. Eliot, Robert Frost, Edna St. Vincent Millay, and Amy Lowell.

This Society met first in January 1923 in the 18th-century St. Paul's Church Rectory at the northeast corner of Cathedral and Saratoga Streets, Baltimore. The rector's wife, Sally Bruce Kinsolving, was one of the two women in charge; the other was Mary C. Goodwillie. They brought together people interested in hearing and discussing poetry. For $2 dues a year members mingled with travelling writers, including Padraic Colum, Walter de la Mare, Stephen Vincent Benét and his brother William Rose Benét, Vachel Lindsay, Edgar Lee Masters, Harriet Monroe, and Carl Sandburg.

The Society faltered after 11 years. One reason, according to Sally Bruce Kinsolving, was that a special moment in literary history — a real renaissance of poetry — had passed by 1933.[28] That flourishing was like the brief blooming of the Jacquotte rose in Gilman Paul's garden on Blythewood Road, always the time and scene of the Society's spring executive meeting.

Luckily the Society had a second blooming beginning in 1938, according to Richard Hart, then head of the Literature Department of the Enoch Pratt Free Library. Hart noted that in a sizeable city like Baltimore, people of a common occupation and purpose are bound to have a certain amount of association. A case in point: this Poetry Society and the library's literature department gave poets an excuse and place for meeting. (Among poets who met were Karl Shapiro and William Force Stead.)

Local writers had lacked both before World War I. Hart's explanation for that state of affairs ranged from the town's deeply rooted provincialism to its Toryism, both cultural and political. A major deterrent to nurturing poets, he said, was "the domination of a clique of polite society which was on the whole rich in pride as only an elite of middle class origins can be."[29]

In the 1920s, Hart recalls, "some fresh air circulated when a window was opened by Mencken, the *Sunpapers,* the partial liberalization of the Johns Hopkins, the rebirth of the Pratt Library in 1926, and, in the thirties, the movement to Baltimore of a number of distinguished European men of letters."

One of this international group, William Force Stead, both begins and epitomizes this chapter on traditional writing, though not solely for any of Hart's reasons. Stead contributed literary friendships of international significance, he discovered and edited for publication a lost masterpiece of English literature, he wrote fine poems, and he left behind him in letters and essays a record of one writer's life in Maryland and abroad.

In poetry he left few Maryland vignettes. An example is "Southern Idyll" that begins:

Down on the Eastern Shore of Maryland
The oyster-fishers in the Chesapeake Bay
Bring home such boat-loads, that the pearly shells
Are thrown upon the road and trampled into
A surface white and hard. By such a road
I found an old frame Quaker Meeting House.
Its date was sixteen-eighty. All within
Was timber of a brown and reverend hue,
Darkness and peace. And everywhere without
Was light and peace.[30]

Stead had roots in Washington, though his family house, The Gables on Lawyer's Hill, Howard County, was his home. His ancestor Peter Force came to the young nation's capital in 1815 and established a printing business. At the end of his life (1857) Force was paid $100,000 to add to the Library of Congress his great collection of Americana — 1,000 bound volumes of early pamphlets, 1,000 volumes of 18th- and 19th-century newspapers, and more than 22,000 books. Force also served as mayor of Washington, a post not usually held by a bibliophile.

Peter Force's literary descendant William Force Stead reported that an early enthusiasm for poetry lured him away to the English countryside and the Parisian cafe. After college he lived abroad, first as Anglican priest in Florence, Italy, and then as Chaplain of Worcester College, Oxford.

At the onset of World War II he was trapped on this side of the Atlantic. Then he remembered his father's telling him he would never feel at home again once he lived so many years abroad. That may be why in 1939 Baltimore seemed a dull place. From time to time the dullness was alleviated somewhat by visiting literati from England such as W. H. Auden and Charles Morgan.

Stead himself enlivened the town when he joined forces with another former expatriate, Nancy Howard DeFord Venable, his Bolton Hill hostess. When she entertained in her tiny, bay-windowed dining room at what we called Villa Caprice, 232 West Lanvale Street, she let her guests know that Tennessee Williams had written a part for her in *Camino Reale,* and that he had begged her to play the part on stage. A recording of her reading the role was as far as that proposal went. Some people wondered if Williams had named his villainess in *Suddenly Last Summer* Mrs. Venable after her.

When Williams visited the Venable-Stead villa, he was entertained as were Stead's literary English friends. From that house Stead kept in touch with his Oxford circle. That group included William Butler Yeats, William Golding, Robert Graves, John Masefield, Edmund Blunden, and T. S. Eliot. Three of them subsequently won Nobel Prizes in Literature — Yeats, Eliot, and Golding.[31]

Stead's own prize arrived when two of his poems were chosen by Yeats for his edition of the *Oxford Book of Modern Verse (1892-1935).* One poem was "How Infinite Are Thy Ways" and the other "I Closed My Eyes To-Day and Saw," quoted here:

I closed my eyes to-day and saw
A dark land fringed with flame,
A sky of grey with ochre swirls
Down to the dark land came.

No wind, no sound, no man, no bird,
No grass, no hill, no wood:
Tall as a pine amid the plain
One giant sunflower stood.

Its disk was large with ripened seed:

A red line on the grey,
The flames, as yet afar, I knew
Would gnaw the world away.

In vain the seed were ripe; the stem,
With singed leaves hung around,
Relaxed; and all the big flower stooped
And stared upon the ground.[32]

Even before this poem appeared in the Oxford anthology, Stead had published a number of small volumes, including *Moonflowers: A Book of Fancies* (1909) and *Verd Antique* (1920), all of them in England. His religious themes attracted readers, including T. S. Eliot. The two poets, Stead and Eliot, became friends. Then in 1927 Eliot asked Stead's help in becoming an Anglican, a major step for his poetry and, therefore, an event in world literary history.

Stead made no claim for Eliot's conversion, but he did set up one milestone by baptizing him. He wrote that because "it seemed odd to have such a large though infant Christian at the baptismal font, to avoid embarrassment, we locked the front door of the little parish church and posted the verger on guard in the vestry."

That night after dinner, Stead recalled, "we went for a twilight walk through Wychwood, an ancient haunted forest, 'savage and enchanted.' I can see Eliot pacing under mighty oaks and pushing his way through hazel thicket attired in a smart suit, a bowler hat, and a gray spats."[33]

Stead's second claim to notice in world literary history came about when he was invited into an English country house to examine "inherited treasures." Among them was a manuscript poem, whose merit he recognized and whose author he spotted as the famous 18th-century mad poet Christopher Smart. This poem he edited and published in 1939 as *Rejoice in the Lamb*. He thus added a major work to Christopher Smart's *A Song of David* (1763).

Introducing his edition, Stead said that he especially liked Smart's "child-like innocence, a bright celestial vision, a heart which was always affectionate, and a faith which survived years of misery and humiliation."[34] Such qualities, combined with genius, placed Smart up with his contemporary mystical poet William Blake. Stead's sure instincts as critic singled out for praise Smart's now famous tribute to his cat Jeoffry, a companion of solitary hours:

"For I will consider my Cat Jeoffry. / For he is the servant of the Living God, duly and daily serving him. / For at the first glance of

the glory of God in the East he worships in his way. / For is this done by wreathing his body seven times round with elegant quickness. / ...For he purrs in thankfulness when God tells him he's a good Cat. / For he is an instrument for the children to learn benevolence upon. / For every house is incomplete without him, and a blessing is lacking in the spirit. / For the Lord commanded Moses concerning the cats at the departure of the Children of Israel from Egypt. / For every family had one cat in the bag."[35]

After *Rejoice in the Lamb* was published, a well-known English composer, Benjamin Britten, set it to music. By that time Stead had returned to live and write in his native Maryland. There in an 1850s villa on Bolton Hill he and his Baltimore hostess, Nancy Venable, lived on into the 1960s. As exotic relics of the Jazz Age they added to the legend of their neighborhood's specialness. In Bolton Hill he was always the "Oxford Poet" — after all, he knew Eliot and Golding and the rest. And she conveyed the elegance of the chatelaine of Manoir De La Hulotais, her old house on the coast of Brittany, where she summered.

Stead wrote a number of poems to Nancy, lyrical compliments like this one called "Her Powder Box":

This powder-box might seem to be
A sign of Nancy's vanity:
Not so, say I, who understand
How exquisitely she is planned,
At once to be
Yet not to see
Herself the beauty of perfection,
And still to show
Yet not to know
Such beauty cannot need correction:
Nothing but Innocence would dress
In dust her native loveliness.[36]

During Stead's last quarter century, living in Baltimore, he wrote many poems but published little. He also wrote recollections, some of them about his youth in Howard County. If these pages are ever published, they will add to a long shelf of Maryland memoirs. Some are indeed the work of Mencken's *bêtes noires,* those "shallow, kittenish fellows" of the genteel past. Others deserve a B+, and Mencken's own *Days* books, an A.

Few American states have been so blessed with books giving their true flavor. A capturing of Maryland by memorialists makes a fit ending for a chapter on traditional writers. Most prolific of the group, Hulbert Footner published *Maryland Main and Eastern Shore* (1935) and *Rivers of the Eastern Shore* (1944). In them sounds the same personal voice—chatty and humorous—that makes his *Charles' Gift* (1939) such a pleasure to read today. Here is a sample from that Calvert County memoir:

It was delightful house to visit. They were poor, but they had a civilized outlook. Miss Euphemia was a great lady in the best tradition; broad-minded, discerning and generous-hearted. From the waist up she was of the usual matronly dimensions, but when she sat down she covered all of two plain chairs. Being of a hospitable disposition, she gave many parties in a pavilion that she had built on her brother's place.

It was at this time that the dancing craze was gathering its first momentum, and many a night that summer Miss Mollie's daughter and I paddled up the quiet river to dance at Miss Euphemia's. Our great-hearted hostess caught the craze just like any smaller woman, and somewhere she learned to dance. She refused, however, to dance with me or with any of the men guests, because, she said, she had not invited us for the purpose of imposing such a penance. Instead, she tipped the young hired men on her brother's farm, and one of them appeared each night, freshly bathed and slicked up, to steer the monumental Miss Euphemia through the turkey trot and the waltz.[37]

In contrast with Footner's rural vignette, here is one about Lexington Market by another memorialist, a native-born poet Letitia Stockett in her *Baltimore: A Not Too Serious History* (1929):

The market people, too, are worth knowing. There was the old horseradish and cocoanut man who had a stand on Paca Street. I loved to hear the rub-a-dub-dub of his flying wooden wheel. He threw out with a rapid circular motion a fine spray of rich cocoanut drippings not despised by the ragged darkey children who flit across the background of every Baltimore picture. This old man had a fine ruddy face like an English squire's; I have not seen him for several months now. Perhaps he has passed on; if so, God rest his soul![38]

The horseradish and cocoanut man died and joined a literary parade with old black Eli, with Folger McKinsey's Bay steamboat travellers, and with other creations of backward-looking Marylanders. Certain of their creators might have deserved the grade of F that Mencken gave to shallow, kittenish fellows. But Christopher Morley, Lizette Woodworth Reese, William Force Stead, and several other tradition-alists may receive a better grade from new readers.

X
Square Houses, Circle Lives

Low life, class, and protest in stories by native-born novelists Upton Sinclair, James M. Cain, and Dashiell Hammett.

"Baltimore is multifarious, has the attractive dirt of a fishing town, the nightmare horizons of a great industrial town; it is very old, sordid, traditional, and proud. It despises no sort of traffic that can be conceived of; it is not fanatical; it has a self-sufficiency as towns of old Europe, even in the hideous yellow waste bays full of abandoned shacks, the mazy sameness of its mean, white-stepped streets, its traffic in pleasures both respectable and disreputable."[1]
— Christina Stead

"His nursery had been haunted by such musty phantoms [of the old aristocracy]...but...in earliest childhood the fates had given... [him] the gift of seeing beneath the shams of things, and to him this dead Aristocracy cried out loudly for burial.... These people came and went, an endless procession of them...through the boy's life, and unconsciously he judged them, and hated them and feared them."[2]
— Upton Sinclair

When a reporter asked Dashiell Hammett which of his books was his favorite, the author picked *The Glass Key,* "because the clues were nicely placed, although nobody seemed to see them."[3]

This photograph of 1903 shows Light Street Wharves, Baltimore, with other evidence of an industrial port that made a city of blue collar grittiness and rowdiness.

It's as though Dashiell Hammett sent *The Glass Key* as a valentine to fellow Baltimoreans, but they didn't realize it was meant for them. Local readers still don't clasp that novel to their hearts as they surely would if they knew its secret: it is that this classic of crime and bossism was based on the city election of 1919. One reason readers don't know the secret is Hammett's neglecting to name the city of the key murder and its resulting violence, though street names give clues.

Also, his biographers failed to note the novel's reliance on Baltimore political warfare. This chapter reveals that link, thanks to the recent sleuthing of one of my students.

Another reason Baltimoreans didn't early seize *The Glass Key* as their own was its seaminess. When published in 1931 it offended genteel taste. Squeamish readers were put off by its opening with gamblers rolling green dice on a green table. After that, low-life characters stirred up every sort of disreputable traffic—words chosen by the novelist Christina Stead to suggest Baltimore's intriguing multifariousness.

Genteel readers of the 1930s rejected not only *The Glass Key*, but also all such books as the offal of literature. They ignored a whole shelf of novels mirroring sordid America and originating in Baltimore. More perceptive readers such as H. L. Mencken praised those books for realism. And some titles still sell in the thousands and appear on college reading lists. *The Glass Key* is one and so is Hammett's *The Maltese Falcon* (1930), Upton Sinclair's *The Jungle* (1906), and James M. Cain's *The Postman Always Rings Twice* (1934).

Today it is hard to understand earlier critics' dismissal of those authors as dirty little boys with a piece of chalk and a board fence and nobody looking. A kinder critic in 1930 called Cain a Proust in greasy overalls. But French novelists Andre Gide, Albert Camus, and Jean Paul Sartre accepted Cain, grease and all, and imitated him.

Those Frenchmen could understand the origin of what was then called "tough guy" fiction. Its beginnings went back before World War I to a clash between polite Baltimore and rowdy, bawdy street life. That conflict lay behind Dashiell Hammett's saying that Baltimore held only square houses and circle lives.

He said that when he left home and moved West. For him San Francisco proved geometrically more compatible because he began to write shortly after moving there. But he took his inheritance with him, whether he wanted to or not. Those restricting Maryland squares and circles continued to stimulate. For him and the other two writers, Baltimore's hard geometry provided something to kick against.

Because of that kicking, their novels pioneered realistic fiction. The three Marylanders dared explore low life in print, just as they had done in Baltimore streets. Their stories told about prostitutes and con men, marital infidelity and the best way to track down a killer. Their subjects explain Hammett's and Cain's finding an early welcome in Mencken's magazines. Mencken discovered them both: he sized up their talents at once, and he encouraged them to ditch the genteel tradition in literature. And they did.

Their abandoning an established path may surprise readers who know them as native-born Marylanders. Other readers may be astonished at discovering them in Maryland. But Sinclair was indeed born in Baltimore, Cain in Annapolis, and Hammett in St. Mary's County on a tobacco farm. More important, all three spent formative years mostly in Baltimore. Though Sinclair moved away younger, Hammett called Baltimore home until age 25. Cain stayed until he was 32 and returned at 56 to spend his last 30 years in Hyattsville, Prince George's County.

Strangely enough, biographers devote little space to Maryland beginnings and the place's usefulness to their books. An extreme case in point appears in the Hammett listing of the *Oxford Companion to American Literature* (1984): his birthplace is given as Connecticut. No mention at all is made of Maryland. What a gap that makes in his annals because Baltimore's marks are on many stories. In *The Glass Key*, for instance, Hammett proved he knew that town all too well. So did Cain and Sinclair.

Their knowledge of the patrician side of town came in part from newspapers' rotogravures and Society columns. In them a young writer could learn about Old Families, fashionable balls, and dandies adorning a leisure class. For example, one white-haired dandy, Walter DeCurzon Poultney, appeared everywhere faultlessly attired and with gold-headed cane and waxed mustache. Often a columnist noted his costume — something dazzling like an Alice-blue [bright] shirt with pink bow tie.

Such a frivolous costume disguised his class's rigid code. Based on Maryland pride, that rigidity had earlier shocked a pioneering sociologist, Thorstein Veblen. Out of his experiences with the Baltimore upper class came *The Theory of the Leisure Class* (1899). He boarded with a "proper" but impoverished family when he did graduate work in the 1880s at Johns Hopkins University.

Keeping a boarding house for money didn't ruin that family socially. Many Old Baltimoreans then took boarders, including the socially well-connected mother of the future Duchess of Windsor. Veblen's hosts sacrificed to keep up the elaborate style of antebellum days. Doubtless their servants came cheap, but wine and show did not. That host family spent far more on style at table than they ever collected in board money. From that family Veblen supposedly formed his idea of what he called "conspicuous consumption."

Consumption wasn't usually conspicuous among Maryland gentry. To them a display of wealth showed bad taste. What mattered was lineage, not money. Still, they did have to keep up appearances. A novelist who knew about that attitude, Edith Wharton, once topped her social pyramid with an Old Marylander. In the New York of *The Age of Innocence* (1921) she put the crown on a dowager, Louisa Dagonet, from Trevenna, her ancient Maryland estate, where she and her husband spent part of each year. Even though that good lady was rather dim, she was socially superior even to Virginians. Furthermore, she had the gift of her class for covering up unpleasant facts ever so skillfully and politely. No one did that better than an Old Marylander.

Aware though Sinclair, Cain, and Hammett were of that polite tradition, their education came from a second major Maryland tradition. That was the one that Mencken found in sinister alleys and in an infinite oddity and extravagance of Baltimore's streets. There Hammett and the others became streetwise.

Their education drew on that city's reputation as Mobtown. For decades, riots and threats of riots had occupied police. When rival fire companies fought each other instead of the fire, police clubbed firemen into insensibility. Outside Baltimore, violence accompanied the beginning of the great 1877 strike against the Baltimore and Ohio Railroad. In town both police and National Guard were buffaloed often by strikers and sympathizers. Once a mob attacked the Sixth Regiment of the Guard as they left their armory on Fayette and Front Streets. In the fight 12 men died.

Later, in the 20th century, teenage gangs fought with sling shots in Patterson Park, and the highest clay hill there was even called Bunker Hill. An old account asserts that these young gangsters advanced to safe-blowing throughout rural Maryland. Unlike that gang, legions of illegal bookmakers, political bosses' henchmen, and prostitutes flourished forever and a day. Baltimore thus earned a name for sin and for tolerance of sin — and for offering a good time.

Local novelists promoted that reputation: gambling figures in Sidney Offit's *The Other Side of the Street* (1962) and in William

Manchester's *City of Anger* (1953); sex on The Block makes a humorous center in Bernard Livingstone's *Papa's Burlesque House* (1971); sex and sordidness also suffuse Patrick O'Mara's *Taxi Heaven* (1932) and the film *Diner* (1982), written and produced by a Baltimorean, Barry Levinson. That film was shot in Baltimore.

Such an old, sordid inheritance mixed with an old, polite one to create the world of the first of the three streetwise writers, Upton Sinclair. (Note that Marylanders accented the first syllable of his last name.) He wrote to rid society of what was worst in both traditions: he admired neither exploiter nor exploited. And he wanted to make over a sordid, unjust world. That goal shone through 80-odd books and 250,000 letters, which documented his career from age 13 to 89.

Characterizing him as a Baltimore non-conformist, Gerald W. Johnson noted that such people are the yeast in our intellectual bread, "and yeast, with a villainous taste taken straight, is yet indispensable to fine cooking."[4] Yeasty Sinclair wrote fiction to bring political and social reform. His novel *The Jungle* (1906) did in fact do just that. It helped prevent sale of rotten meat, and it pushed along enactment of the Pure Food and Drug Act. In other books he also sought to make the world change its values. That romantic theme of breaking down barriers found a big audience abroad and on college campuses. In America he was chief muckraker before World War I. Even such a vocal reformer as President Theodore Roosevelt remonstrated with him, "Really, Mr. Sinclair, you must keep your head!"

Years before that moment in the White House, Baltimore gentlemen of Sinclair's class — some of them — wanted reform but their group had lost political control to lower-class bosses. Also, the city itself had lost some ground by 1910; it no longer ranked in the top three in size. But, strangely enough, just then Baltimore gained in symbolic importance. For it was something to be from Baltimore. One case in point: the artist James Abbott McNeill Whistler even lied that he had been born there rather than give his true birthplace, Fall River, Massachusetts.[5]

Such snobbishness was reflected in newspapers when Sinclair was growing up. Society columnists then could reject socially ambitious matrons or they could welcome amusing people such as Harry Lehr, son of a Baltimore snuff merchant, impecunious though he was. Lehr moved on from local Paint and Powder productions to Newport extravaganzas, such as the one to which he brought as guest of honor a monkey in full dress.

With Society's amusement at such goings on, it isn't surprising that a Society columnist triggered Sinclair's rebellion. That happened one day in his grandfather's large townhouse on Maryland Avenue, Baltimore. Young Sinclair eavesdropped as his relatives gossiped with a male Society columnist from a local paper: "I sat in a corner and heard the talk — whose grandfather was a grocer and whose cousin eloped with a fiddler. I breathed that atmosphere of pride and scorn, of values based upon material possessions preserved for two generations or more, and the longer the better. I do not know why I came to hate it, but I know that I did hate it from my earliest days. And everything in my later life confirmed my resolve never to 'sell out' to that class."

Sinclair's revolt against polite society thus began in Baltimore, where he was born in 1878 (two years before Mencken). Born of upper-class Southern stock, he was quite aware that seven relatives had served in the Confederate Navy. He was brought up, of course, to hate the sadness of Reconstruction. Even more embittering was the contrast between his parents' scrimping, complicated by his father's alcoholism, and his maternal kin's plutocratic routine. His mother's father was John S. Harden, secretary-treasurer of the Western Maryland Railroad. And her sister married a wealthy banker, John Randolph Bland, a founder of the United States Fidelity and Guaranty Company. Sinclair later recalled, "No Cophetuna or Aladdin in fairy lore ever stepped back and forth between the hovel and the palace as frequently as I."[6]

Sinclair himself certainly thought that stepping back and forth a formative experience. But of course writers can't always themselves tell what influenced their work. Sinclair's fiction probably did come in part from his individual psyche. It also relied on his imagination. And another source was reading. Like Poe, Mencken, and Hammett, Sinclair took up reading — voracious reading — in Baltimore. At age 11 he discovered Shakespeare in his Uncle John Randolph Bland's library on Maryland Avenue. There he read all the plays in two weeks. Later in life he said that he had lost his soul in that Shakespearean wonderland.

Even more affecting than Shakespeare was discovering Percy Bysshe Shelley's works. From that English Romantic poet, Sinclair drew zeal and plans for political and social reform. Shelley even appeared to him in a vision. That happened when the future reformer, Upton, was walking one winter night in Baltimore's Druid Hill Park. He recorded that his mind "was on fire with high poetry," and he walked through crunching snow and with occasional crackling of the black and naked tree branches. He stood enjoying a moment of silence when "suddenly this thing came to me, startling and wonderful beyond any power to tell; the opening of gates in the soul, the pouring in of music, of light, of joy which was unlike anything else, and therefore not to be conveyed in metaphors. I stood riveted to one spot, and a trembling seized me, a dizziness, a happiness so intense that the distinction between pleasure and pain was lost."

In his ecstasy he saw Shelley and heard him converse with Hamlet and Don Quixote, favorite characters from reading. Those three conversed, "each in his own character, yet glorified, more so than in the books."[7] Sinclair then knew what literature was — real literature, far above the potboilers he had been writing. He then felt his genius rising.

By then the neophyte author was living with his parents in New York, though he spent a lot of time visiting wealthy relatives in Baltimore. He was then considered handsome by some people, with blue-gray eyes and an aristocratic nose. (Years later Charlie Chaplin, the entertainer, knew him and used to amuse friends by imitating Sinclair speaking through a smile.) As a teenager he was precocious. He graduated from college at 17 and then did graduate study at Columbia University. By that time he was using a gift for facile writing of fiction to turn out potboilers for cheap magazines. Often he wrote 8,000 words a day by dictating to stenographers.

His industry simply continued when he advanced to writing not just for money; the rest of his life he wrote for a better world. Garrulous, tireless, and usually angry for change, he became a social historian of his times. Before he turned to socialism, he wrote in *The Journal of Arthur Stirling* (1903): "The world which I see about me at the present moment, the world of politics, of business, of society, seems to me a thing demoniac in its hideousness; a world gone mad with pride and selfish lust; a world of wild beasts writhing and grappling in a pit."[8]

Reading such fictionalized tracts as that one, critics give Sinclair a low score for literary merit. They admit though that Sinclair possessed energy and courage, said what he thought, and stirred things up. Two examples will illustrate. In *The Jungle* his socialism emerged from a tale about the shocking life of a Slav immigrant in Chicago. That man learned how to deal with modern horrors, but only after suffering at the hands of foremen, real estate sharks, and political bosses. In him readers saw a man descend into the cave of crime and emerge a socialist. That's why Jack London called the book the *Uncle*

Tom's Cabin of wage slaves.

Another novel called *King Coal* (1917) again developed out of first-hand investigation of bad conditions, this time in coal mines of Colorado. As Sinclair's protagonist, a rich young college man assumed the name of Joe Smith, went to work in the mines, and became a mule tender and then a miner's helper. He promptly busied himself reforming the system. Improvements touched safety, working conditions, and unionization. In Sinclair's hands, Joe's rewards included self-respect, popularity, and a girl. For readers, a reward was revelation of how coal companies ruled much of Colorado.

News like that was the point of Sinclair's novels. About those books he said many times that he meant to appeal to the longing in every heart for justice between man and man. After 1940 he broadcast that appeal to readers in 11 so-called planetary novels. They trace America's growing international involvement from 1913 into the 1950s. In order to give coherence to this sweep, he has Lanny Budd, illegitimate son of a munitions maker, take part in historical events, such as the Spanish Civil War. Budd even became confidential agent for President Franklin D. Roosevelt during Hitler's gaining power.

One of the Lanny Budd novels, *Dragon's Teeth,* won the Pulitzer Prize for 1942. Like many winners, it lacked substance as fiction but offered popular views. Maybe the prize was awarded for good service to liberal causes. Whatever the reason, probably few people go back to the Lanny Budd series now. The absence of good characterization was there as damaging as in his other books. Sinclair's characters were either sinners or saints, neither of them interesting for long. Mencken once hit a basis for this weakness: "When he [Sinclair] started out he loomed big. . . .Today he is going the road of. . .all who began as artists and ended as mad mullahs."[9]

The madness showed in Sinclair's setting up, in Mencken's view, as a world-saver, a professional messiah. Such a goal didn't attract Mencken. It is not surprising then that he helped nurture the opposite goal of becoming solely a professional writer in the second of these Baltimore streetwise novelists, James M. Cain. Like Sinclair, Cain wrote a lot, but never a didactic social novel.

Although both Sinclair and Cain abandoned the East Coast and worked in California, their careers could hardly have been more different. In the Golden West, Sinclair wrote to sell his views. He complemented his writing by forming a coalition of progressives under the name EPIC (End Poverty In California). With that group he won control of the Democratic Party there, and ran unsuccessfully for governor four times. He almost won once, and a follower did win in 1938.

By contrast, James M. Cain stuck to writing. The decision to make a career of writing was made for Cain in a strange way. One day he was sitting on a bench in Lafayette Square opposite the White House. The idea came, he said, right out of the blue Washington sky. He had, in fact, tried writing fiction unsuccessfully earlier, and had taught writing. But that decision in Washington led to his creating a shelf of bestsellers that also made successful movies. Among them were *Past All Dishonor* and *Mildred Pierce*.

Twenty-two years before that, Cain had been born in the Paca-Carroll house (ca. 1830) on St. John's College campus, Annapolis. (His father, a Yale graduate, was teaching there.) He grew up at Washington College, Chestertown, Kent County, where his father was president. After graduating from St. John's at 17, Cain bumped around from job to job. He also studied voice in Washington with the idea of making singing his career.

Luckily for literature, Cain's genius was not with notes but with words. He became a student of language, a writer who cared about style. At his death, a friend wrote of Cain's feeling for language and for a style he "imbued with elegance that he hid under an offhand" manner of speaking and writing.

Cain's manner may have rubbed off on him from the city rooms of the *Baltimore American* and the *Sun* where he first worked in 1918 as a reporter. He also edited his army company newspaper in France (1919). After World War I, he returned to the *Sun*, tried unsuccessfully to write a novel, and began writing for H. L. Mencken's *American Mercury*.

That magazine printed a series of satirical dialogues, most of them later collected in *Our Government* (1930). Those pieces showed Cain's gift for humor and for writing a dialect he had heard on the Eastern Shore of Maryland. When one of these, "The Governor," appeared in *Subtreasury of American Humor*, he wrote the editors that it was one of the few pieces he had true affection for. Those sketches supported his contention that writing had to have roots, that "it can't wriggle down from the sky, as Alice did, in Wonderland."

Mencken recognized Cain's gifts and rootedness, and provided him with both an editor and an audience. It was fitting that one Baltimore realistic writer should have discovered the other. Their partnership began in Baltimore when in 1924 they met for lunch at Marconi's on Saratoga Street, one of Mencken's favorite restaurants.

As a result of that luncheon Cain wrote an article for the first issue of Mencken's new magazine *The American Mercury*. In it Cain gave such an unflattering picture of a labor leader that the printer's union shop refused to print it. So it appeared in the second issue, printed by a new printer. Of the *Mercury* Cain later said that it was the only publication that gave him that curious excitement that a writer ought to get from seeing his work in print. And Mencken returned the compliment by saying that Cain's pieces were possibly better than any others he had printed. High praise that.

Mencken and Cain became friends because they loved writing, particularly realistic writing, and also because they loved music. Cain often joined Mencken's musical club's Saturday evenings. And once Cain added humor by having club members denounce Mencken with mock formality for giving them an ineffective cure for hangovers. That jesting fits the comment by a friend that Cain had a face usually wrapped in a grin "indescribable to anyone who has not seen it on the homely, craggy, unforgettable face of Jamie [Cain]."

But having Mencken and camaraderie in Baltimore couldn't hold Cain. When he was 32 he began writing for the *New York World*, a job Mencken helped him find. He wrote editorials for Walter Lippmann and a Sunday column with sketches like the ones he was printing in the *Mercury*. When the *World* changed hands, Cain became managing editor of *The New Yorker*. There he worked with another staff that was legendary for talents such as E. B. White, James Thurber, and Harold Ross.

Then in November 1933 Cain abandoned New York to make money writing movie scripts in Hollywood. The next year Cain advised Mencken to come write in California. (Mencken at the time was afraid of losing his money.) Cain told him that there was more money to be made there, for less effort, than anywhere on earth. He added that he guessed that he was going to do some writing for Metro for a few weeks: "I got cleaned out in Baltimore and have to make a little money."[10]

Although Cain made plenty of money as a screen writer, he was unhappy. He later told an interviewer that he had worked hard for the big salaries he had earned—up to $2,500 a week. He also said, "I parked my pride, my esthetic convictions, my mind outside on the street." Then he added, "[But] even working in a whorehouse, the girl has to like the work a little bit, and I could not like pictures."

While writing for the movies, Cain did a prodigious amount of writing that was congenial to his goals. Between 1933 and 1948 he wrote seven novels, six magazine serials, two plays, and more than

24 short stories. Those works gave him his place among American realistic writers. Nothing he wrote after he returned at 56 to live in Maryland matched some of them.

The earlier Maryland years, of course, helped Cain's writing. Just how much is open to speculation. Cain did occasionally use Maryland settings. Three examples are *Galatea* (1953), *The Magician's Wife* (1965), and *The Institute* (1976). He also put Eastern Shore characters in a number of early fictional sketches and dialogues. Usually these pieces began "Down in the country they used to. . ."

Cain's life in Maryland also emerged in his novels. His attempt to make a career in music helped him in *Serenade* (1937), *Mildred Pierce* (1941), *The Moth* (1948), and *Career in C Major* (1943). His work for the State Roads Commission made it easy to write about construction work in *Past All Dishonor* (1946), *Mignon* (1962), and *The Moth*. Work for an insurance company helped in *Double Indemnity* (1943). His experiences with people in Southern Maryland led eventually to realistic portraits in *Galatea* and *The Magician's Wife*. And were brothel visits on Raborg Street, Baltimore, put into *Past All Dishonor* (1946)?

Besides settings and experiences, Cain's language owed a debt to Eastern Shore vernacular. He later acknowledged a debt to what his ears had picked up from the speech of a bricklayer in Chestertown, Kent County, a man named Ike Newton. In early sketches, Cain seemed most comfortable when writing inside the mind of an uneducated character like Ike and narrating in his dialect. Characters said *heared* for *heard,* and lines such as "And I wasn't hardly up there than I seen. . ."

Even though later Cain invented better-educated narrators, he still told stories about what his mother called low life. He peopled his fiction with what he called thorough-going heels. One reason was his dislike of big American novels with heroes. His own fiction was short and offered scenes that his mother certainly didn't like. What would she think if she knew that recently a dealer bought at auction her copy of *The Postman Always Rings Twice* for $3,400? It bore Cain's inscription to his mother saying that he knew she wouldn't like the book but that she would probably like to have it.

Cain's mother perhaps understood that his great inspiration for that book and his other best novels was life in Southern California. He knew that too. And he had left Hollywood reluctantly to do research on a novel at the Library of Congress and settled in a Washington suburb. Later he thought of moving back to California,

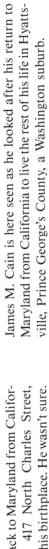

James M. Cain is here seen as he looked after his return to Maryland from California to live the rest of his life in Hyattsville, Prince George's County, a Washington suburb.

When Upton Sinclair moved back to Maryland from California, he visited the house at 417 North Charles Street, Baltimore, that may have been his birthplace. He wasn't sure.

Monument Square, Baltimore, ca. 1903, with the Continental Trust Building at far right. There Dashiell Hammett worked as operative for Pinkerton's. In front of that building was the Baltimore *Evening News*, where Mencken worked in 1906. At left is the old Post Office facing the Battle Monument.

James M. Cain and his first wife lived in what was then a proper address, the boarded up house at center, 2418 Linden Avenue. He was then working for the Baltimore *Sun*. Just a few doors away were the Bachrach relatives with whom Gertrude Stein lived.

Jacket design of the Grossett & Dunlap reprint shows the stars of a second film version of *The Glass Key*, 1942, looking not at all like Hammett's Baltimoreans with their distinguishing marks of social class.

Here is Dashiell Hammett in his familiar dapper pose about the time he wrote *The Glass Key*, his Baltimore novel. He was then writing in Hollywood, living a life far different from his Maryland boyhood and youth.

but didn't. His attitude towards Maryland at one point made him call it a "churlish little state from which I fled."

Despite that feeling, he continued to live in a rented house outside Washington in Hyattsville, Prince George's County, until he died on October 27, 1977. He was still writing then at 85 — writing his memoirs. During his final 30 years in Maryland he had published seven novels, the last two in 1975 *(Rainbow's End)* and 1976 *(The Institute)*. Publication of his historical novel *Mignon* in 1962 came after many years of research. It was not well received by critics or readers.

Those final years there were years of decline, both physically and professionally. He felt the pall cast by the long illness and death of his fourth wife — they had been so happy together. Another dark event was his friend Mencken's years of infirmity following a stroke. When Mencken died, Cain attended the small, stark farewell gathering, the only belletristic writer present. Cain's attendance was fitting because Mencken as mentor had taught him such things as passionate care for accuracy in fiction. Mencken also praised that fiction, and once defied anyone under the rank of archbishop to read ten pages of Cain and then quit before reaching the end.

Such confidence in the power of Cain's fiction proved justified. Long before Cain's death he enjoyed a revival of interest in his books. Since his death several films have been made from his novels, including a remake of *The Postman Always Rings Twice.* Both films have won a following, and the paperback edition is selling in its second million.

The jury of critics is still out trying to assess the merits of his work. Literary critics of the 1930s usually judged novels such as *The Postman Always Rings Twice* as slick offshoots of Ernest Hemingway's fiction. Some readers said he pandered to tastes then met only by books sold in drugstores on sex and also by murder mysteries. Certain readers connected Cain's writing with Hemingway's understated style and questioning of traditional values. His game, one critic decided early on, was to outrage readers mischievously — "but never to perplex [their] mind[s]."

Recent critics such as Tom Wolfe praise Cain. They make a case for his success in putting a reader inside an egocentric heel and making him or her care about him. Wolfe also liked the momentum of the narratives and said that fast pace resulted from a complex technique. Thousands of readers have raced to the end of *Double Indemnity.* Cain's fullest biographer ranked him just under Hemingway and William Faulkner as "master storyteller of the hard, dark minds and adventures of our times."

The present rise in Cain's reputation goes along with that of Dashiell Hammett, the third of the realistic novelists treated in this chapter. The work of these two writers did have the common denominator of the tough-guy tradition. They both knew the seamy side of Baltimore and drew on it in fiction. And they both were pioneers in realistic writing.

Today one significant difference in their reputations is that Hammett's depends more on people's curiosity about the man himself. For one thing, all we know about Hammett is odd. Strangeness touched even such a trivial matter as his name: in Maryland *Dashiell* is a fairly familiar name and is pronounced with an accent on the second syllable, *Da-Sheel.* In Baltimore he was called Sam, and his wife called him Samuel because he was christened Samuel Dashiell Hammett.

His career was odd, too. It whisked him from a narrow rowhouse in West Baltimore to a rented 42-room mansion in Beverly Hills, California, a house complete with ice cream parlor. His writing fiction lasted only a decade. After that, political activities — some with the Communist Party — led to governmental inquiries, jail, and black-listing by Hollywood film companies. After he wrote *The Thin Man* (1932), his sole literary achievement came from being advisor to his lover Lillian Hellman. That work began with *The Children's Hour* (1934), based on an idea that he provided. Later he wrote the movie script based on her *The Watch on the Rhine* (1939).

At the end of his life, Hammett was notorious and poor, poorer than he had been as a boy in West Baltimore. Readers know a great deal about those final years. But his biographers have so far devoted little space to his formative quarter century in Maryland. One reason for their oversight may lie in a scarcity of facts. Hammett himself failed to help fill in facts because he told stories about his early years to amuse rather than inform. Future literary sleuths will doubtless turn up evidence of the kind offered in this chapter about *The Glass Key's* being founded on a Baltimore election.

Here is a summary of what we do know about Hammett's Maryland life. His roots go back to the 18th century and to traditions of the Dashiells as sailors and the Hammetts as farmers. Biographers give this writer and his father, Richard, characteristics of their Southern Maryland clan — irresponsibility, drinking, gambling, and woman-izing. His father was a Catholic, a politician of sorts, and a failure in business. Richard carried with him from that old-fashioned place an ideal of the Southern gentleman. From that model, Dashiell may well have learned principles of loyalty and of keeping his word, two themes in his books.

Both father and son could look like Baltimore gentlemen dandies when in good clothes; both were tall and handsome. When the son became a celebrity, all the young, bright reporters in Baltimore copied his dapper pose from a portrait on the jacket of *The Thin Man*: soft felt hat, handkerchief smartly showing in the chest pocket of a tweed jacket, cane in hand. Thus Hammett joined a line of Baltimore dandies going back to the earlier novelist John Pendleton Kennedy, who was famous for his red-lined cloak. Although Hammett could look like an aristocrat, he couldn't create one in fiction. His blue-blooded Senator Henry in *The Glass Key* is a stick.

Hammett's mother contrasted with his father: she was more practical and tough. The daughter of a Protestant minister, she was an aloof woman who was called "Lady" by her in-laws, perhaps because she disapproved of them. Living among them in rural Southern Maryland, she bore her first child, Samuel Dashiell Hammett, on May 27, 1894. The birthplace was an unpainted weatherboard farmhouse in the longest-settled part of the state, St. Mary's County. The farm was on Sanner's Pond Road, just north of the site of Point Lookout prison camp for captured Confederate soldiers and sailors. (Both Sidney Lanier and John Banister Tabb had been incarcerated there a generation earlier.)

The name of the farm, "Hopewell and Aim," probably suited Hammett's young mother because she aimed to move her family to Baltimore, where she had relatives. When Hammett was six they moved in with her mother at 212 North Stricker Street. There he grew up. Until he was 26 he lived with his family there and nearby at 1417 West Lexington Street.

As a youngster he evidently felt proud of being a Baltimorean because he boasted to Southern Maryland cousins about his city's marvels. The city he meant was the one Mencken was reporting, a port offering an education not given in schools. After only a year in high school, Hammett had to pick up his learning in streets, bars, and brothels. As one result, by age 20 he had his first case of venereal disease.

All the while, Hammett was picking up a rare education away from the streets. One source was a nearby branch of the public library. (It was probably Mencken's branch on Hollins Street.) His mother scolded him for staying up so late reading that she couldn't get him off to work in the morning. This omnivorous reading remained a lifelong habit. It made his mind unusual for tidiness and accuracy.

Books, of course, weren't the only forces shaping Hammett's outlook then. A case might be made that those years in a crowded, rented rowhouse pointed up a chasm between classes. For contrast with a poor home, all he had to do was look through the rotogravure of the Sunday *Sun*. There he could have found models for his character Janet Henry in *The Glass Key*. As daughter of an aristocratic U.S. Senator, she appeared too often — so said the main male character. Doubtless she posed for pictures like other young women of her class all dolled up for tea dances and the like.

Tea dances were not for the Hammett family. Their need for money caused 14-year-old Hammett to drop out of high school. Later his younger brother explained that when their father became ill, the oldest son Dashiell was forced to run the small business. (That business employed blacks to sell fish from horse-drawn carts, a Baltimore street tradition, with the peddlers called Ay-rabs.) After that business collapsed, young Hammett became what he described later as "the unsatisfactory and unsatisfied employee of various railroads, stock brokers, machine manufacturers, canners, and the like." He added that he usually was fired![1]

One firing he later recounted to friends to show how independent he had been then. Although the employer fired him for being late every day in one week, Hammett's cool manner persuaded him to offer to rehire him if he would promise not to be late. That the young Baltimorean couldn't do. So impressed was the employer with such an honest reply that he let Hammett keep the job.

As chief support for his family, Hammett at 21 (1915) leaped at the offer of a job with Pinkerton's National Detective Agency. He stuck with them as private detective until 1922. Then he quit that job for writing about detectives. As operator he first worked in the Chesapeake region and shadowed men in Washington and less exotic spots such as the Havre de Grace racetrack, Harford County. Among other cases, he said he knew a man who had stolen a ferris wheel.

His base was the Continental Trust Building at the southeast corner of East Baltimore and South Calvert Streets. From this place he took the name of his first major detective, the Continental Op. Although the name of the building has been changed, passersby today can still see over the door and first-floor windows a set of ornamental black birds. Some local readers imagine those birds as ancestors of Hammett's Maltese falcon. (They appear to be eagles.)

Hammett may have been a fine Pinkerton operative, though we have no evidence. (Records supposedly were burned.) In his writing he capitalized on first-hand sleuthing. He drew not only on tracking criminals but also on strike-breaking. The ideal detective, he wrote, had to be hard and shifty—capable of beating both criminal and client. One of the oddities about Hammett was his being such a loyal follower—of the Pinkerton code and later of communism—and at the same time a hater of people in authority. Some readers think that paradox explains his detectives' growing more and more like the criminals.

Curiously, Hammett's first published writing did not rely on his career. Instead, it was a 100-word anecdote "The Parthian Shot," published October 1922 in *The Smart Set*. That sophisticated magazine launched many another writer, too. Four other pieces by Hammett appeared within a year, including the seminal "From the Memoirs of a Private Detective." Mencken, as editor, may have encouraged him to write for a new pulp magazine called *Black Mask* that Mencken and his co-editor George Jean Nathan created. They founded it in 1920 to make money, but sold it soon because, Mencken said, such enterprises begin as good sport but then bore. He did make money on it, however. And Hammett found in that magazine a vehicle for most of his fiction. Moreover, within its pages he revitalized the detective story almost singlehandedly.

Through his New York magazines, Mencken thus established Hammett as a major writer of realism in fiction. The younger Baltimorean (Hammett) growing up in Mencken's neighborhood hadn't known what an influence that editor would have. Nor did the neophyte detective gauge the significance of James Wright, assistant superintendent of the Baltimore branch of Pinkerton's. Wright served as model for the Continental Op, a fat, little, literate man and a tough-talking professional. Hammett gave him immortality as the Op and then as private eye Sam Spade in *The Maltese Falcon*.

With aid from Wright as well as Mencken, Hammett latched onto his subject and also found his style. Based on lower-class speech, his language suited a brutal people and their violence. His sentences were short—they average 13 words in early stories. Instead of a Latinate vocabulary, he fueled sentences with Anglo-Saxon-rooted words. His verbs pushed his prose along. That's why his stories raced to the end. Hammett also caught readers with dialogue.

Here is a sample exchange in "The Assistant Murderer" between the private eye Alec Rush and the crook, who speaks first:

"You ought to want to know what I'm doing hanging around 'em. I ain't tight. I'll tell you. I've been slipped half a grand to bump off the girl—twice. How do you like that?"

"I hear you," said Alec Rush. "But anybody can talk that knows the words."

"Talk? Sure it's talk," Zeipp admitted cheerfully. "But so's it talk when the judge says 'hanged by the neck until dead and may God have mercy on your soul.' Lots of things are talk, but that don't always keep 'em from being real."

"Yeah?"

"Yeah, brother, yeah!"

Set in Baltimore, this tale presents a private eye who does what Hammett proposed: he is not an erudite solver of riddles in the Sherlock Holmes manner; he is able to take care of himself and to get the best of anybody.

Rush is called "the ugly" man because of his cauliflower ears and two solid rows of gold teeth, the lower lapping the upper—souvenirs of his pugilist's career. No one doubts that he is tough. Rush has taken up private work after having been kicked off the police force for list of trumped up crimes that, he said, would stretch from here to Canton Hollow. He hints at blaming politics for his fall. We can believe him in view of *The Glass Key's* revelations about Baltimore politics.

This novelette tells of Maryland money and a complicated Maryland will, of a headstrong beautiful Baltimore girl living on Charles Street Avenue and her murder of a rich bachelor uncle living on Cathedral Street. Not one character is likeable, except perhaps the hired killer named Scuttle. But the tale satisfies because it is romantic, and the detective does get his man (or woman). When he does, he "screwed up his savage red eyes, nodded his head in a satisfied way, and with one finger described a small circle in the air."[12]

Detective Rush's success was deserved. Like other Hammett detectives, he was man fit for adventure. According to a rival writer of mysteries, Raymond Chandler, Hammett's private eyes have a startling range of awareness: "If there were enough like him, the world would be a safe place to live in, without becoming too dull to be worth living in." Hammett's detective made the Continental Op stories classics of what has come to be called hard-boiled detective fiction. The best hold up well today: sophisticated readers still admire such stories as "The Big Knockover."

Partly out of admiration, subtle literary critics dissect these Continental Op stories. They show how the Op goes into a situation and stirs things up. In doing so, he de-constructs the fictional reality cooked up by the criminals. His job is to reveal the fiction. To do so he uses whatever tools come to hand because detecting is a hard business. No matter how hard the job is, Hammett's detective gets his reward from doing it well. (Under Pinkerton rules, no agent could collect a reward.)[13]

Another intriguing trait of these detectives is their philosophic side. Sam Spade, for example, in *The Maltese Falcon*, tells a story to a beautiful female criminal to show the ethical irrationality of life. An additional charm of Sam Spade and the other detectives is their wit. One of them, Nick Charles in *The Thin Man*, spreads a surface of glitter over a bleak set of values, much bleaker than Agatha Christie's, for example. In doing that Hammett recognized early that he was working a different side of the mystery street than Christie and Conan Doyle. The hard-boiled American school of detective fiction gives the reader a world in which motives are mixed, crime is everywhere, and society, hostile.

To understand Hammett's achievement, readers can compare his fiction with the English "puzzle mysteries." Neither Rush nor any of the other Hammett detectives was capable of restoring order to the world as Agatha Christie has her Miss Marple do to her English village in *Murder at the Vicarage*. Such books as hers flourished after World War I. They contrasted not only with Hammett but also with other postwar books, as in the skeptical mood of T. S. Eliot, James Joyce, and Ernest Hemingway.

Those "puzzle mysteries" of Christie gave us the unchanged world of English country houses filled with servants and weekend guests. Its world was innocent and optimistic. Its detective always had superior intellect like Lord Peter Wimsey's, for instance, that puzzled out whodunits and thereby restored order to the community. In such stories as *Gaudy Night* (1935), by Dorothy Sayers, the criminal always had a definite motive.

Across the Atlantic in Maryland, Leslie Ford treated criminals like theirs and in stories of the same genre. Among her mysteries with local Baltimore settings were *The Girl from the Mimosa Club* (1957), and *Trial by Ambush* (1962). Ford was the nom de plume of Zenith Jones Brown, wife of a professor at St. John's College, Annapolis. In her many novels (more than 60) she entertained a generation of fans, particularly those who could recognize authenticity of setting.

Like Ford, Hammett used Maryland characters in a Maryland setting when he wrote *The Glass Key* (1931). His story bore an even deeper local stamp because it treated corrupt politics. Readers today can supply notorious examples from the 50 years since Hammett wrote his novel: Vice President Spiro Agnew brought disgrace on himself; so did U.S. Senator Daniel Brewster, and most recently Governor Marvin Mandel made a third in a trilogy of corruption.

Times were possibly even worse before those three added to the bad odor of Maryland politicians. Into his fictional politics, Hammett wove strands from political gangs before 1919. The violence was greater then, it seems, and the street murder of a close relative of a boss for political reasons seemed made to order as opening to a plot.

The plot of *The Glass Key* turned on the murder of the son of a high-born but corrupt U.S. Senator. The Senator's name, Ralph Bancroft Henry, echoed with literary ironies — Ralph Waldo Emerson, George Bancroft, Patrick Henry. Hammett's character was a Maryland gentleman, but his election depended upon a political machine.

In that machine a chief aide emerged as contrast to the Senator. He was Ned Beaumont, a man with no past and no pretensions to gentility. Although generally cynical, Ned remains loyal to his own friend and boss, a grafter. That man, Paul Madvig, was a power broker who warred with a bootlegger, Shad O'Rory. Against O'Rory, Beaumont fought by faking alibis, planting evidence, and covering up for the guilty. Eventually, his goal was simply survival. At the end, according to the blurb of an early edition, he had smashed a gang faction and "given the city officials a bad case of the shakes." The trail to that end was "brutal, violent and breath-taking."[14]

The glass key of the title became symbolic, as a dream at the end explained. A glass key opened a door that had kept out evil. Once the door was unlocked, the glass key shattered. The door could no longer be locked, nor could evil be prevented from spreading. In the last line of the novel, Beaumont simply watched an empty doorway through which his friend had left, all loyalty broken.

What biographers have not shown was how that glass key fitted the door to a particular Baltimore political struggle and to a murder that was part of it. But a student of mine, Michael Pluhar, has recently done just that, and he is planning to publish a full account. Here I give but a sketch of his findings. He followed clues from the novel to newspapers and other accounts of Baltimore politics during the first 20 years of this century. The coincidence of history with fiction turned out to be great. Pluhar even plotted movements of Hammett's characters through downtown Baltimore, and every step was supported by Hammett's accurate memory. (For example, the headquarters of the boss, the Rennert Hotel, was indeed eight blocks from the railroad station, just as in *The Glass Key*.)[15]

Hammett had been in Baltimore at the time of the political battle between bosses, and he made that struggle the facts of his novel. He also introduced its antagonists and its crisis. Being a novelist, Hammett, of course, filled in facts when needed and telescoped time. He also invented a characteristically clipped dialogue, beefed up the violence, and focused on brutal characters. He had done that before, using his days as a Pinkerton Op; now he did it in Baltimore. Biographers believe that his stories usually had basis in fact. Now they can be sure that *The Glass Key* was founded on real people and events in his native city.

Hammett evidently picked up a lot from word-of-mouth accounts in town about power plays within the Democratic Party machine. Also, his father, who had fancied himself a politician long before he moved to Baltimore, probably brought home plenty of news from the battlefront. Also word about the so-called Royal Family of political bosses appeared in newspapers.

John J. (Sonny) Mahon (1851-1928) was king. He was born of Irish immigrant parents in a tiny house on Frederick Street. As a street-gamin he recalled tossing bricks with a mob that attacked the 6th Massachusetts Regiment that famous April 19, 1861, when the first blood was shed in the Civil War. As boss he took money for what he called "legislative purposes." From officials of Havre de Grace race track, for instance, he received $10,000 annually as "adviser." He told reporters that he certainly did like to see the horses run.

Occasionally squabbles broke out between this king and another member of the royal family, Frank Kelly. Just such a split lay at the center of *The Glass Key*. In life, Kelly was a large grotesque Irishman, bald and red-nosed. Another important real-life character was "Big Bill" Harig, a lackey of Royalty. He had the reputation of being a slugger and a political tough all his life. So said one of his victims, who added, "He is a man who has been living in recent years on his reputation as a bad man."[16]

That comment came out after Harig was arrested for the shooting death of James M. (Jimmy) Mahon, brother of Sonny and an illegal bookmaker himself. That killing opposite City Hall happened the day after a raid on an alleged bookie joint, a raid staged by Captain Henry of Central district. In a trial Harig was acquitted on grounds of self-defense, although witnesses did not substantiate his defense.

Taking those characters into a fiction, Hammett's novel opened with the murder of a U.S. Senator's son, a man mixed up in illegal traffic. No witnesses came forward. Hammett proceeded to build a plot on finding the murderer. He cleverly changed names just enough to avoid incrimination. As the name of his chief political boss, for instance, he created *Madvig*, borrowing from both the real boss *Ma*hon and the killer Har*ig*. The rival boss *Kelly* became the equally Irish *O'Rory*. The historical Baltimore Police Captain *Henry* gave his name to the U.S. Senator. And a politician named *Broening* became simply *Roan*.

Hammett did not find a model for his protagonist Ned Beaumont in Baltimore, although Ned resembles Hammett himself physically. Both were tall, thin, and tubercular. But Ned was neither a detective like Hammett, nor a man like the Continental Op with whom readers could identify. Rather, he was a heel: he was a gambler, a bookie, and righthand man of political crooks. Like everyone else in the novel, he was corrupt. Also, he was very smart. Through his eyes, readers see into elegant faces on North Charles Street and scruffy ones on Thames Street, and note the evil in both. All classes of Baltimoreans were caught up in dirty politics; violence dominated City Hall as well as speakeasies.

Hammett's fictional portrait of Baltimore offers little to admire. The facade of neat red-brick rows of houses simply covers hypocrisy. As the book ends, however, readers have the satisfaction expected at the conclusion of all murder mysteries, a murderer uncovered. Also, the protagonist does go off with the upper-class woman for a new life in New York. And Baltimore gains a new, less corrupt administration, just as it did in the 1919 election. But in history the improvement didn't last. What has endured all these 50 years is Hammett's fictional Baltimore. It is something for a town to live on and on, portrayed no doubt just as she was in 1919. At least just as she was in two or three of her many facets. A true valentine, that![7]

The Glass Key turned out to be Hammett's best valentine for his home state. Of other stories set in Maryland only the unfinished *Tulip* may reflect Hammett's years in St. Mary's County. In that story is the isolation and the nearness to nature that Hammett liked. We also come upon fragments of his own early life in the return after World War I of the veteran as well as the return of an ex-prisoner. There too we find Hammett the hunter and the crack shot, a man who got on well with simple country people.

Among his unpublished manuscripts at the University of Texas only a few were set in Baltimore. These include a story of migratory workers in a Baltimore cannery and one about a railroad ticket agent, a character close to the B & O years in Baltimore. In a published Op story "The Girl With The Silver Eyes," a female character ships her things to 215 North Stricker Street, the address of an orphan asylum — in the story and in fact.

No scene in that story is as precisely located in Baltimore, however, as was one in Harlem Park in *The Red Harvest*. In it the Op dreams of sitting, facing the tumbling fountain there next to a veiled woman whose name he had suddenly forgotten and who was important to him. He recognized her only when she ran after the fire engines going out Edmondson Avenue crying "Fire!" He sought her down half the streets in the United States beginning with Gay Street and Mount Royal Avenue in Baltimore. That search carried the hero as far from Baltimore as Hammett's detecting for Pinkerton's did.

Like Sinclair and Cain, Hammett had to go away from home, it would seem, in order to write. Baltimore life and people gave them attitudes and raw material. But unfortunately that town's urban life, rich as it was, didn't generate high literary culture. That comes from exchanges of ideas and criticism. What Baltimore lacked were salons, publishers, and periodicals. And, most of all, it lacked freedom from a fixed social hierarchy. Also the city never could boast a Greenwich Village with an atmosphere nurturing to writers. Instead, it seemed to offer only hard geometry of square houses and circle lives, as Hammett had complained.

Without high literary culture, Maryland couldn't hold talented young writers such as Hammett. Yet the Old Line State holds up its head among literary centers because its influences have shaped writers of distinction. It is still doing so with superior talents like Russell Baker's and Adrienne Rich's — even if those writers don't stay home.

The return of the exiles, however, deserves a note. A surprising number have come back to live, or die, or be buried in Chesapeake soil. Cain and Sinclair moved back to Maryland, and Cain died there![8] Hammett was buried on a hill above the same Potomac River he was born on. Also near that river F. Scott Key Fitzgerald lies buried with his wife Zelda in a family plot near ancestral acres of Montgomery County. Appropriately, on his grave is carved a famous line from his novel *The Great Gatsby*. Thus it closed both his most popular book and his life. It also serves as a curiously suitable epitaph for this chapter's three other Maryland novelists-in-exile:

SO WE BEAT ON, BOATS AGAINST THE CURRENT, BORNE BACK CEASELESSLY INTO THE PAST.

XI
Gilded Butterflies
With Excellent Credentials

Echoes of the Jazz Age in F. Scott Fitzgerald's *Tender Is The Night* and *The Crack-up* and in Zelda Fitzgerald's *Save Me the Waltz,* books written in their Maryland home.

LAMP IN THE WINDOW

"Do you remember, before keys turned in the locks,
    When life was a close-up, and not an occasional letter,
That I hated to swim naked from the rocks
    While you liked absolutely nothing better?"[1]
— F. Scott Fitzgerald

September 9, 1935:
    "Baltimore is warm but pleasant. I love it more than I thought — it is so rich with memories — it is nice to look up the street and see the statue of my great uncle [Francis Scott Key] and to know Poe is buried here and that many ancestors of mine have walked in the old town by the bay. I belong here, where everything is civilized and gay and rotted and polite. And I wouldn't mind a bit if in a few years Zelda and I could snuggle up together under a stone in some old graveyard here. That is really a happy thought and not melancholy at all."[2]
— F. Scott Fitzgerald

Wearing his French beret, F. Scott Fitzgerald seems to be acting a part for his young daughter and neighboring Turnbull children at La Paix.

F. Scott Fitzgerald's triumph today astounds people who knew him during his "crack-up" in Baltimore. Who would have guessed when he left town for good in 1937 that his books would sell nine million copies? Also, since his death in 1940, twenty-one new volumes of his writings have appeared, and his books circulate in 35 languages. A stream of biographies and critical studies continues. One of the fullest and best books concludes, "F. Scott Fitzgerald is now permanently placed with the greatest writers who ever lived, where he wanted to be all along. Where he belongs."[3]

A decade ago I took a gamble on Baltimoreans' agreeing with the world's high estimation of Fitzgerald: Baltimoreans should certainly be proud that their city had served as refuge for such a distinguished writer. Or so I thought in 1975 when the time came to name a park newly created near where the Fitzgeralds had lived on Bolton Hill. Surely (I thought) that park should be named Fitzgerald Park to honor an important writer and his local associations. The naming, I discovered, was a privilege of the city's Park Board. To approach that group with a strong voice, I gathered support from our local improvement association. Everything seemed in order.

Then, to my dismay, the day before the hearing, word came by the municipal grapevine that my author was "too controversial," that he probably would not pass muster. "What!" I thought, "Was his past rising to haunt him — all the drinking, the rudeness and fighting when drunk, the tales of his womanizing, his novels about incest and infidelity?"

I called a well-known local writer, Louis Azrael, to help, and he did. In his youth he had known and liked Scott. Here is what he wrote to the Park Board: "Fitzgerald was a great distinction to the town and the neighborhood. He was of course one of the outstanding literary figures of the past 50 years. He had roots in Baltimore, and he loved it, and Baltimore, of course, ought to recognize him."

On the appointed day I appeared before the Park Board to give my speech. I had barely started when a Board member interrupted me. He moved for unanimous approval of my proposal. So a park had a name, and F. Scott Fitzgerald had added another laurel to his crown.

From that episode I realized that Baltimoreans had needed 40 years to change their minds and accept Scott's belonging among them. And belong he does now. Back in the 1930s neither he nor his wife Zelda looked as though they could ever be part of an old-fashioned place like Baltimore. They alighted there like gilded butterflies with excellent credentials.

Their gilt was tarnished. Scott at 36 no longer looked like the handsome youth in a collar ad that he had when *This Side of Paradise* (1920) made him famous. Nor was Zelda still a Jazz Age flapper with honey-colored hair. Tarnished though their brightness was, they came as celebrities. But they also came in great need of a refuge.

Among other things, that is what they found. The Fitzgeralds made their last home together in Baltimore, and lived through what he called the real dark night of the soul. There too he wrote enduring literature. Maryland proved a useful place for the last of the novelists (as he called himself).

In Maryland, where Scott had deep family connections, he proceeded to spend one quarter of his career. Three years later he died in California but, as he wished, was buried in Rockville, Montgomery County. This chapter surveys what he and Zelda did and what they wrote between 1931 and 1938 and shows why their life in Maryland was significant to literary history.

Living in that place they found more time to work and fewer distractions than they had in Paris, Cannes, and New York. Out of the Maryland period came Zelda's novel *Save Me the Waltz* (1932) and her string of essays. Scott too wrote some of his best nonfiction, including the essays in *The Crack-Up* (1945), and added to his notebooks. In addition, he polished and published *Taps at Reveille* (1935), his largest collection of short stories, some written in Baltimore. Also, both wrote remarkable letters.

The master work of the period was his psychological novel *Tender Is the Night* (1934). Its themes well suited a backward-looking province like Maryland, where a fixed ideal of conduct had only slightly eroded during the Jazz Age just past. That novel intoned an elegy for the Jazz Age. Unfortunately, the book seemed a failure. Afterwards Scott suffered a crisis of confidence that he so well described in *The Crack-Up*. But all during that difficult time he was developing his gifts.

Moving to Baltimore was important not only to his writing, but also to the Fitzgeralds' living through troubles. They moved to Baltimore for practical reasons. Zelda needed psychiatric care, Scott wanted a congenial, cheap place to write, and Scottie, their 11-year-old daughter, required a proper background and education to prepare her for the upper-class college that proper young women of her generation then attended, and after that, a proper marriage.

In a curious way, all three found what they sought in those Baltimore years. Scott came to write and did, though hampered by debt, drink, and what he regarded as the care of two helpless people. Zelda did receive the best available treatment, although she sank permanently into schizophrenia. And Scottie suffered the usual traumas of the early teens, complicated by having a troubled family, yet she went on to matriculate at Vassar College, and afterwards to marry a Princeton graduate from a proper Baltimore family. But in sum, while in Baltimore none of them was happy, nor was happiness expected.

Scott apparently recognized just how hard growing up in Baltimore was for Scottie. He later wrote her that in an odd way she was an old-fashioned girl because she had lived half in the world of Old Baltimore, represented by their first landlady, Mrs. Bayard (Margaret) Turnbull. And indeed he liked her being old-fashioned. A reason he did was his disappointment with his generation of radicals and breakers-down who had never found anything to replace what he called the old virtues of work and courage. Nor had his group of revolutionaries substituted satisfactorily for lost graces such as courtesy and tact.[4]

In letters Fitzgerald picked out what made him feel that he belonged among people who retained those graces. One time he wrote, "Baltimore is very nice and with plenty of cousins and Princetonians, if I were in a social mood, and I can look out the window and see a statue of the great-great uncle [Francis Scott Key, author of "The Star-Spangled Banner"] and all three of us like it here." Another time he added that there everything was civilized and gay and rotted and polite. Those qualities suited him.[5]

They also suited the notion of Baltimore that some other people entertained — even the uncomplimentary word *rotted*. Certainly, the streetwise novelists, Sinclair, Cain, and Hammett, would have included that word. Much less negative were conclusions drawn by Sara Mayfield, a friend of Zelda's from Alabama. Baltimore had a delightful society, because, she noted, it lacked the rigid conservatism of Zelda's hometown of Montgomery, and also escaped the strident commercialism of New York. She concluded that it gave Scott both liberty and security.

Promises of security came with two rented houses — a country Victorian cottage of 15 rooms called La Paix and a town house at 1307 Park Avenue, Bolton Hill. Both properties belonged to well off and "Proper" Baltimoreans and gave Scott the social tone he liked. At La Paix their brown-shingled caravansari stood on a 28-acre estate with the newer residence of the landlord, Bayard Turnbull.

There the Fitzgeralds dwelled among the rich, well-connected Valley Set, a leisure class in the hilly country north of the city. That group reputedly was devoted to horses, dogs, and rye whiskey. After renting La Paix from May 20, 1932 to November 1933, the Fitzgeralds moved into the city to Bolton Hill, the only downtown place where the socially elite could live, except Mount Vernon Place.

Along with social cachet, both rural and urban addresses gave the Fitzgeralds literary connections. For instance, the wife of their first landlord, Margaret Turnbull, loved literature and had read Scott's books. Also her in-laws had created the Turnbull Lectureship on Poetry at Johns Hopkins University. Since the family always entertained the lecturers, they invited Scott to dine with the 1933 lecturer T. S. Eliot. After dinner, Scott read Eliot's poetry aloud, and won the author's approval.

A second literary connection: Bayard Turnbull's father had owned a Baltimore publishing house and edited a magazine *The New Eclectic.* His mother had founded the city's Women's Literary Club, and had written *The Royal Pawn of Venice* and other historical romances in the manner of Mrs. Humphrey Ward, a popular English author of the late Victorian period. Contrasting with isolated La Paix, Bolton Hill provided Scott with a crowd of creative spirits. People said that you couldn't throw a baseball down any street there without hitting a musician, artist, or writer. Among the writers there in the 1920s and 1930s were James M. Cain, Gerald W. Johnson, Huntington Cairns, Letitia Stockett, Hulbert Footner, William Force Stead, and, earlier, Gertrude Stein.

Both rural and urban residences made Fitzgerald feel at home. A reason perhaps was an atmosphere that once made an English reporter say it seemed always late afternoon in Baltimore. That quiet air suited an author who felt his noon was past.

How easily the Fitzgeralds fitted such a place when they arrived in 1932 has been touched on in a spate of biographies but never through this book's perspective of those Baltimore years. Most anecdotes given here have not been published before, especially those about Bolton Hill. Fresh accounts enrich the story of what the Fitzgeralds did in Baltimore.

When they arrived they found a welcome in "Proper" circles. According to the son of their Bolton Hill landlord, Dr. Richard Shackleford, Baltimore society was hungry for people with academic standing and wealth. He said that Scott's Princeton connection put them in the Blue Book, and that his being an established writer gave entrée to anybody pretending to culture.

One irony was that although Scott had indeed made a place for himself in literary culture with *The Great Gatsby* (1925), he had not published a novel since. Another irony was that his income in 1932 was his lowest since before he published his first novel. But he drove a fancy car — a used Stutz. And his good address at La Paix had been found for him by a fellow Princetonian impressively named Edgar Allen Poe, Jr. (distant kin of the poet).

Fitzgerald buffs already know what Scott did at La Paix because Andrew Turnbull, son of their landlord, wrote a full account. Turnbull was 11 when the Fitzgeralds moved next door. He remembered Fitzgerald's gift for entertaining children and for inspiring them to aim high. Sometimes the boy interrupted Fitzgerald busily pacing the lane to work out scenes in *Tender Is the Night*. Then Turnbull noticed, "the illumination of his eye, the sensitive pull around the mouth, the wistful liquor-ridden thing about him, the haunting grace of motion and gesture, the looking at you, through you, and beyond you — understandably sweet — with smoke exhaling."

Turnbull also described Fitzgerald dressed for writing: he wore saddle shoes, pink shirt, and black Shaker-knit sweater. He had a "trenchant, mobile face" and "gray-blue eyes, faraway and full of the pathos of burned-out desires."[6]

Turnbull's mother, Margaret, became Scott's friend despite a contrast he noted between her strict Presbyterian standard of conduct and his conformity to an unflinching rationality. He admired her. Occasionally he read his writings to her, including a tribute to Ring Lardner. She was a good listener always, and kind. She helped make Baltimore home for the father and daughter. That winsome pair (as Turnbull called them) were lucky in 1932 to have Margaret Turnbull and her children welcome them — butterflies from exotic worlds with their French governess and international fame.

When the Fitzgeralds decided to move into the city from La Paix, they rented a house just down the street from the old Turnbull mansion on Beethoven Terrace. Their street displayed a picture book of Victorian architecture, charmingly set along a hilltop above downtown. At 1307 Park Avenue they lived in a spacious red brick house of classic Baltimore rowhouse design, with white marble steps and simple arched doorway. It was distinctive in not being part of a row. A 25-foot lot permitted adding a bay window on one side of the 20-foot-wide house. (That lot was twice as wide as many rowhouse lots.) Another distinction was its overlooking a small park around the Italianate Rolando-Thom villa. Out back, wide verandahs onto a garden also prevented any feeling of being hemmed in.

Fitzgerald used to pace the second floor verandah opening off his bedroom. He also paced the large second floor front room, his workroom, shaping sentences. Visitors in the double parlor under that room could hear him plainly because the rooms were so cavernous that sounds echoed. Sparsely furnished as it probably was during Fitzgerald's tenancy, the house must have been eerie at night. One overnight guest, a school friend of Scottie's, got a scare she hasn't forgotten. She recalls being startled when Scott suddenly appeared downstairs in the parlor that evening with a shotgun. He told her that he was going to kill the cockroaches.

With or without cockroaches, respectable residences surrounded 1307. Indeed, Bolton Hill was just the kind of place to appeal to a writer looking for urbane neighbors. Probably it appealed also to Fitzgerald because its values were chiefly historic and genealogical. For decades almost everyone who was really important in Baltimore lived in that district.

By the 1930s, a free-lance writer observed facetiously, residents were often "dubious persons, not felons, but the kind at whom a sound business man must look a little askance — doctors, Johns Hopkins professors, newspaper writers, musicians from the Peabody Conservatory, even, God save the mark, a librarian, a portrait painter, and a free-lance writer!"[7]

That's what Bolton Hill was like when the Fitzgeralds alighted in their second Baltimore home. Some "dubious" residents still talk about what they did there. One Sunday afternoon recently my wife and I entertained several neighbors who had known the Fitzgeralds. Our guests had stories to tell.

A guest of Scottie's age, David Roszel, volunteered that his Aunt Elizabeth Lemmon had become very friendly with Fitzgerald in 1934. She was one of the well-bred, intelligent women who solaced Scott's loneliness then. Scott liked to visit her at Welbourne, the Lemmons' antebellum country place near Middleburg, Virginia. Together they toured Civil War battlefields, and he entertained her when she visited relatives on Bolton Hill. Her nephew made a remark that showed how well Scott had met the family standards: "I always heard that Fitzgerald was a gentleman born and acted as such, and that Hemingway wasn't."

Alcohol and wasted lives were a central topic of our conversations about the Fitzgeralds. One story was told by Mrs. Fendall (Jane) Marbury, who lived a block west of them at 234 West Lafayette Avenue. Jane Marbury had been a girlhood friend of Zelda's, and she had had a brother in the same Princeton class and club as Fitzgerald. She had met Scott in 1918 when he came to Montgomery as a second lieutenant and fell in love with Zelda. "Yes," she said, "he drank always." And, as if to explain, she added, "Prohibition didn't do anybody in my generation any good. I could once name ten men in that group who were ruined by liquor."

One day in 1933, she recounted, Fitzgerald appeared on her doorstep in a state that she phrased as "a little cheered up." He asked, "Do you know who my landlord is?" I said, "I think I do. It's Mr. Shackleford." "Well," he proceeded, "The truth is we've had a little fire, and I think I had better get hold of him." I said, "I really think you better!" Earlier a fire at La Paix, set by Zelda, had made news when reporters thought that valuable manuscripts had been destroyed. (None were).

Jane Marbury continued reminiscing with a picture of Zelda. Back in 1928 or 1929 the Marburys had visited the Fitzgeralds at Ellerslie, their rented house near Wilmington, Delaware. There, meeting after years apart, Zelda greeted her by saying, "Jane, do you remember the time when you thought you were the smartest one in the high school, and I thought *I* was?"

Zelda had been authentically beautiful as a girl — and completely natural, and she seemed natural later, too. But before she came to Baltimore, she was already a wreck. One time as an excursion boat passed on the river, Zelda said, "I love to hear the boats go by and the music and to think of the young people dancing." Her friend's comment was, "She was then all of 28 — and already old! I thought it was so sad."

That old friend of Zelda's remembered being told then that the Fitzgeralds had left New York and come 150 miles south because so many people used to come out to their place on Long Island. Out there at Great Neck guests had drunk a lot and stayed for days. After the Fitzgeralds had been at their Delaware place a while, Scott observed, "I don't think we've come far enough."

According to Baltimore gossip, drinking wasn't Fitzgerald's only sin; womanizing was another. An anecdote illustrates how his reputation had spread. He once invited a young, attractive female camp director, Marian B. Millard, to come to 1307 Park Avenue and discuss sending his daughter to her camp. Well aware of his scandalous reputation, she had persuaded a male colleague to drive her to 1307 and to wait in the car out front. Her distress signal, they decided, would be the descent of a window shade.

Going inside, she was piloted past a merry luncheon party in the big rear dining room onto the back porch, and seated on a double swing with her host. Discussion of the serious matters of camp fees was memorably interrupted by Scott's looking at her and asking, "Did anyone ever tell you that your eyes are plaid?"

Then there came the polite escorting to the front door and out to the car. The driver rushed the car away from the curb and observed, "His fly was unbuttoned!"[8]

That lady has never forgotten the incident. Many other people have told of Scott's effect on them, because he had a talent for intimacy that enchanted the object of his notice. Once when his daughter was in some difficulty at Bryn Mawr School, he arranged to meet the headmistress, who also lived on Bolton Hill, and they took a stroll around the streets. Needless to say, his charm resolved the difficulty.

He also succeeded in charming a group of young men interested in writing. Of course, he always promoted neophyte writers such as Ernest Hemingway and John O'Hara. In Baltimore he promoted a young Irish writer Patrick O'Mara, and Charles Marquis Warren, author of a musical revue, *So What*? Fitzgerald collaborated with Warren on a film version of *Tender Is the Night,* for which Warren composed a musical score. It didn't sell.

Among local young men interested in literature, one that Fitzgerald noted in his ledger was Louis Azrael. Because Azrael evidently was such an enthusiastic reader, Fitzgerald offered him an informal education in fiction. One vital lesson took place Christmas Eve, 1934. Azrael saw lights burning in the front parlor at 1307 Park Avenue and stopped in. The two men chatted, inevitably about books. "He seemed surprised, even hurt, that I had not read Sigrid Undset's *Kristin Lavransdatter* and, rising to his book shelves, gave me a copy and ordered, 'Read it before you read another book.'"

Although Azrael rose to depart, conversation took another turn, and he sat down in an upholstered chair beside a floor lamp at the front of the room. Fitzgerald leaped up: "Don't sit in that chair!" he commanded. "Do you know who sat there this evening? Gertrude Stein. She was like a white light."

Azrael moved to another chair and listened to a long and eloquent lecture about Stein's influence on Scott, on Ernest Hemingway, and on other American writers during early days in Paris. (The incident of the forbidden chair appeared shortly in one of Fitzgerald's short pieces, as indeed so much that happened to him did.)

Azrael remembered that he had a lot of fun with Fitzgerald on many occasions. Sometimes they went to the theatre together, and once to the Princeton Triangle show. But mostly they just talked. Azrael stopped in on warm nights, they sat and talked on the back porch looking over the back yard and over neighbors' crape myrtle and roses.

Azrael recalled, "There were several friends of mine who also used to drop around, Evans Rogers and Purnell Hall. Rogers was a gifted and eccentric advertising man who worked for Joe Katz's agency, I believe, and was enormously interested in poetry. As a matter of fact, he gave some courses in certain poets — Gerald Manley Hopkins for one — and he wrote a novel that I don't think was ever published, an *extremely* good novel called *Deaf Heaven*. Purnell Hall was a very intelligent man. Others came too and we'd sit around and talk."[9]

Azrael added that though they had some very good times then, Fitzgerald usually did drink a lot of gin. He set a pace at an ounce an hour. Usually he got ahead of schedule and borrowed one ounce and then another.

Azrael of course wasn't the only protégé of Fitzgerald. Garry Moore, then only 18, worked with Fitzgerald on an idea borrowed from Grand Guignol to create an evening's entertainment by alternating Ring Lardner's nonsense plays with horror plays. One night he drove Scott home to Park Avenue by way of Eutaw Place. At the Francis Scott Key Monument there, Moore was startled by his passenger's jumping out of the car. "Fortunately I was driving very slowly. . . I got out and found Scott hiding under some bushes. 'Scott,' I said, 'what's the matter?' He said, 'Shhh! I don't want Frank to see me this way.'" Scott said he was descended from Francis Scott Key and felt embarrassed to have his illustrious relative see him drunk. "I had to stand in front of the monument to distract 'Frank' while Scott slipped by unseen."

Key and Fitzgerald were only second cousins, three times removed, but in calling Key his great-uncle the modern novelist enlarged a link with Maryland aristocracy as well as with a distinguished writer. Such enlargement also proved Scott's fascination with (in the words of his daughter) the poetic aspects of early times. On the wall of his workroom in Baltimore he had a "Histomap." He also wrote a suitably nostalgic "Foreword" for a collection of sketches by a local artist, Don Swann, *Colonial and Historic Homes of Maryland* (1939). In it Scott boasted that his own father had carried west with him memories of Maryland that predated Braddock's disaster.

Curiously enough, that nostalgia for Maryland's colonial past matched the feeling of one of his heroes, H. L. Mencken, then living only six blocks away. Their proximity in 1933 made for a great irony: those two authors were like colonels of some South American revolution — once victorious but now in quiet exile. Those Baltimore neighbors had indeed led a Jazz Age revolution in manners and morals.

That revolution past, the two men renewed acquaintance in February 1932 when Fitzgerald wired Mencken asking for the name of the top psychiatrist at Johns Hopkins. (Zelda was suffering a mental breakdown.) Mencken supplied the name of Dr. Adolph Meyer, a Swiss who directed the Henry Phipps Psychiatric Clinic there for almost 30 years. He pioneered techniques of psychiatric examination and of accurate recording of case histories. At the time when Zelda became his patient he was called the Dean of American Psychiatry.

When Zelda was given time away from the clinic, the Fitzgeralds and Menckens did see each other. But unfortunately for their friendship, Fitzgerald failed to charm Mencken's wife, Sara Haardt, a writer and a friend from Zelda's girlhood years in Montgomery. Because of her serious illness, she and Mencken lived quietly. Into that quiet household Fitzgerald frequently intruded with calls at all hours. So Mencken tired of him too and saw little of him. Mencken called him a charming fellow but not good company because (in Mencken's words) he gave himself too lavishly to the jug.

That was a sad epitaph for an old friendship. Mencken had launched Scott's career in the spring of 1919 by buying for *The Smart Set* his short story "Babes in the Woods." Quite in character, Scott spent the $30 check to buy white flannels for himself and a handsome, if useless, magenta feather fan for the woman he loved — Zelda. Also characteristic was his incorporating that fan in pieces he later wrote, and his cannibalizing the story in his first novel.

After that first commercial publication, Fitzgerald gave Mencken some of his best short fiction to print. In his inscription to Mencken's copy of *Tales of the Jazz Age* (now in the Pratt Library), Scott wrote: "For the notorious H. L. Mencken under whose apostolic blessing five of these things first saw the light." Among those masterly stories were "May Day" (July 1920), "The Diamond as Big as the Ritz" (June 1922), and "Absolution" (June 1924).

No matter how great the story, Mencken didn't pay more than $300. Fitzgerald sometimes complained about getting so little for a piece of writing that he had polished and polished, while *The Saturday Evening Post* paid $2,000 and more for a story written in 24 hours.

La Paix, Rodgers Forge, was rented by the Fitzgeralds as their first Maryland home and the work place in which Scott wrote most of *Tender Is The Night*.

Here is a newspaper photograph of the author at his La Paix desk.

Here is another publicity shot, this one of Scott obviously putting finishing touches on *Tender Is The Night,* published when he lived at 1307 Park Avenue.

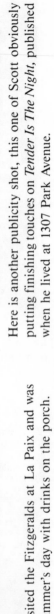

H. L. Mencken visited the Fitzgeralds at La Paix and was entertained one summer's day with drinks on the porch.

1307 Park Avenue was the second Maryland home of the Fitzgeralds and the scene of much of the breakdown Scott endured and then recounted in *The Crack-Up*. He wrote of pacing the second-floor back porch.

Zelda Fitzgerald posed to publicize her novel *Save Me The Waltz,* written mostly at Johns Hopkins Hospital.

Besides writing and ballet, Zelda took up painting during her mental illness in Baltimore.

Here Fitzgerald may be aping his friend Ernest Hemingway or he may simply be enjoying a sport practiced on Chesapeake Bay with special pleasure. He also went duck hunting once, another regional love.

The Cambridge Arms on North Charles Street, the third home of the Fitzgeralds in Maryland, was the beginning of Scott's bus-top journey in his story "Afternoon of an Author."

Graves in St. Mary's Roman Catholic Cemetery, Rockville, Montgomery County, of the Fitzgerald family, including Scott's and Zelda's—and his Maryland father's.

Although Fitzgerald was born in St. Paul, Minnesota, he absorbed ancestral Maryland from his father, Edward, who had been born at Glenmary, near Rockville, Montgomery County.

Still, Scott wanted the prestige of Mencken's seal of approval — and intellectual readers.

But for all this mutual admiration, the two writers often disagreed about literature, especially about Gertrude Stein's merits. Once in exasperation, Fitzgerald denied that Mencken was a literary critic at all, and he wrote Mencken, "You don't know what a writer goes through, what he fumbles for, you don't know the grace he searches for."[10]

Scott's last story to be published by Mencken appeared in the January 1932 *Mercury*. It was "Crazy Sunday," one of his best. The very next year was Mencken's last as editor of the magazine that, Scott believed, had created a favorable climate for his writing *The Great Gatsby*. That was Fitzgerald's tribute to a leading colonel in the literary revolution of the 1920s.

After "Crazy Sunday," the next important publication of the Fitzgeralds (by then in Baltimore) was Zelda's novel *Save Me the Waltz* (1932). Its appearance brought unhappiness to both wife and husband. She had wanted the book to assure her of a place as a writer. But she was disappointed that it didn't sell well (1,400 copies of an edition of 3,010), and critics pounced on the over-rich style and other weaknesses. The novel is still in print, read more, it seems, for its revelations of the Fitzgeralds than for merit as fiction. Zelda put in her falling in love with a French naval officer. Also, she noted odd sensations such as hotel lobbies that smelled of orchids, plush, and detective stories.

Its publication also made Scott unhappy. One reason was that Zelda produced her novel in only six weeks of concentrated writing, and he hadn't been able to bring off his novel in six years of trying. Another reason for his anger was her using the very materials of their life together that he was exploiting in his own novel. Yet, luckily for him, she hadn't brought in her mental illness, and that became a major part of his *Tender Is the Night*.

To make matters worse from his point of view, Zelda sent off her novel to his editor at Scribner's, Maxwell Perkins, without his knowledge. At that, Scott rushed up from Montgomery, Alabama, where he and their daughter were staying, to work over her manuscript before publication. How much changing he did we don't know. We do know that when he worked on other writings of hers he added detail and sharpened focus. His editing of this novel posed special problems: he told her doctor that her mixture of fiction and fact was intended to ruin what was left of him — and her. In his anger, he expostulated, "My God, my books made her a legend."[11] And they had.

In her novel Zelda ran through her married years in order to understand her illness. She looked back a dozen years to her wedding a brilliant writer: she was 19 then, and he was 23. For the world they then came to epitomize the gaiety of the Jazz Age. With the large sums he earned with writing short stories for popular magazines, they lived wild, good times.

They were celebrities wherever they went. They rented quarters in and around New York, in his hometown (St. Paul, Minnesota), in her hometown (Montgomery, Alabama), on the Riviera, in Paris, near Wilmington, Delaware, and in Switzerland. Zelda had one daughter and aborted other children. They both drank a lot, and when drunk turned to dangerous games such as diving from cliffs into the sea at night. All that became part of the Fitzgerald legend, but not all of it was incorporated in her book.

Even so Scott wanted Zelda to give up writing. To divert her energies, he encouraged her painting. Despite those efforts, she wrote a dramatic farce called *Scandalabra* that fall. She submitted it to a Baltimore repertory company, the Junior Vagabonds, whose productions met high standards and were well patronized. They produced it the following June in their theatre, a converted stable on West Read Street.

During a dress rehearsal that ran five hours, Zelda called in Scott to cut the script. He then read aloud to the cast, cutting lines as he went. One report has it that he doctored the play after opening night and through the first days of the run. We catch a glimpse of his role at the time from the following letter. It was sent to Isaac Benesch, a local businessman with a theatrical bent. (It has never been published):

My dear Mr. Benesch: *July 10, 1933*

The other night at the Vagabonds in a state of great excitement and discouragement I was guilty of a misconception and a consequent silly rudeness to you, and I feel that proper amends should be made. My wife and I were on the stage having a little post-mortem on her play when we came in on a discussion between you and Bob Dobson about quite another play. In a hypersensitive mood I applied your remark to the vehicle upon which we were laboring and thought that maybe we were meant to overhear, and naturally blew up.

Please accept my sincere apologies which have been forthcoming ever since I realized next morning that I was absolutely in the wrong.

Very sincerely yours,
F. Scott Fitzgerald[12]

Scandalabra didn't please local critics, who said it was confusing and static. To help promote it, Scott stood out front of the theatre before curtain time and praised it. Nothing seems to have come of his publicizing or of that production, though it has since attracted curious readers and one revival by another Vagabond troupe.

The spring following *Scandalabra,* Zelda published two essays, "Show Mr. & Mrs. F. to Number —" and "Auction — Model 1934." They appeared in a series of personal pieces that both husband and wife wrote during their Baltimore period. Most were nostalgic. Some of hers like those two essays appeared in print under both his and her names to take advantage of his greater fame.

Certainly he worked over her writing and sometimes added words. For instance, the auction piece listed useless accumulations, each filled with memories. One such item was a darned white sweater that he had worn when the house got cold after the heat went off at night. The memory it recalled was of 65 stories forced through the meshes of the sweater. But Zelda also had a gift for writing and had by then written enough for a book. In June 1934 Scott told her of his attempts to persuade Scribner's to publish a collection of her pieces. The collection never came out.

All during that time, Scott was also continuing to jot down his feelings and observations in notebooks. After he moved to Maryland he for the first time had a secretary type these notes in useable form. As headings for some of the 23 sections he listed such items as "Conversations," "Things Overheard," "Rough Stuff." He jotted down ideas for stories, and he copied segments from stories to use later.

In one note Fitzgerald said that sometimes he read his own books for advice: "How much I know sometimes — how little at others." Another time he decided that nobody can write a good biography of a good novelist because he is too many people. Also, he wanted to save phrases such as "the glitter of the hard and emerald eyes" or to recall "a little 14-year-old nymph in the Vagabonds." Once he noted, "Mencken forgives much to the Catholic Church — perhaps because it has an index." Another local note: "The sky that looks like smoke on Charles Street."[13]

These notebooks appeared in a volume with "The Crack-Up" in 1956, and helped fill out a picture of what Fitzgerald called those "terrible" years. One reason they were bad, both Ernest Hemingway and Mencken said, was that Scott had married the wrong girl. Zelda was jealous of his work and wanted to compete with him and, they said, ruin him. And the ruination of a talent became the theme of

Tender Is the Night. Its plot followed Scott's own decline. It also drew on Zelda's illness and her treatment at Hopkins Hospital while he was writing during the last part of 1932 and all of 1933.

Using these two experiences — his and hers — he junked earlier plots and manuscripts that he had brought to Baltimore. About all he salvaged was an account of Dick Diver's beating in Rome. Certainly the novel as we have it was written in Baltimore.

Even the title underwent a long evolution in Baltimore from *Our Type* to *World's Fair* to *The Drunkard's Holiday* to *Doctor Diver's Holiday: A Romance.* The final title came from "Ode to a Nightingale," by the English Romantic poet John Keats. Fitzgerald never read without crying the lines "Already with thee! tender is the night... / ...But here there is no light, / Save what from heaven is with the breezes blown / Through verdurous glooms and winding mossy ways." These lines read in the complete poem set a mood of disenchantment that Fitzgerald also created. That mood fitted the lives of the Keats-loving author and his wife in Maryland.

Scott recorded in his notes then that his novel was planned, "never more to be permanently interrupted." It was to tell the story of a natural idealist rising to the top of the social pyramid but losing his idealism in the progress and sinking to dissipation and drink. His idealist turned out to be a Johns Hopkins-trained doctor, Dick Diver. Scott promised that the background would be a glamorous world of the leisure class at its best.

During 1933 Fitzgerald carried through his plan for *Tender Is the Night* with constant enriching of diction and much polishing and tightening of sentences. He wrote the first draft in pencil on unlined white legal pads. Then Mrs. Isabel Owens, his secretary, typed (triple-spaced) a ribbon copy and two carbons, all of which the author revised. She typed the revised version and that in turn he revised, and so it went until he was satisfied or a deadline forced a halt. He was still revising the book when the novel was being serialized in *Scribner's Magazine.* So intensively was he working that when a fire damaged part of the house, he wouldn't permit interruption for repairs.

Out of such concentration emerged a rich texture. Fitzgerald wove Maryland threads into his elaborate fabric, threads doubtless pulled from his feeling for local history. He was always fascinated by his father's background in Tidewater Maryland squirarchy. His protagonist Dick Diver was blessed — and handicapped — by the same upper-class gentlemen's heritage.

All Scott's feeling for Maryland history may well have come into focus just the year before he moved to Baltimore. In late January 1931 Fitzgerald had returned from Europe alone to bury his father, Edward Fitzgerald, in the family plot of St. Mary's Roman Catholic Church cemetery, Rockville, Maryland. In the novel Dick Diver made the same journey. Through the novelist's moving account, we learn the discrepancy between Dick's life abroad and what his life should be.

When Dick accompanied his father's body on a local train, he identified once more with his Chesapeake homeland: he saw a familiar star and a cold moon bright over Chesapeake Bay; he heard "the lovely fatuous voices, the sound of sluggish primeval rivers flowing softly under soft Indian names"[14] — Potomac, Patuxent, Anacostia. That land was home.

In the churchyard Dick thought that it was very friendly to leave his father with many relatives — "These dead, he knew them all, their weather-beaten faces with blue flashing eyes, the spare violent bodies, the souls made of new earth in the forest-heavy darkness of the 17th century. 'Good-by, my father — good-by, all my fathers.'"

Again and again Fitzgerald associated his idea of moral vision with his father and the Chesapeake region. That vision, combined with Scott's command of a fine style, made *Tender Is the Night* a classic. Then weaving into his vision threads of old Maryland gave the book both color and truth. Dick Diver, for instance, was the only American male in his expatriate world who had repose. It came from his father's example. And the father learned courtesy, tact, and consideration for others from the Confederate widows who reared him.

Again, as part of a moral vision Fitzgerald also saw to it that Diver took his medical training at Maryland's premier institution, Johns Hopkins Medical School, Baltimore. There under the hospital dome all doctors — including the fictional Dr. Diver — had to pass a huge marble statue, filling the great space, of Christ the Healer, emblem of old values. Dick Diver failed to be true to that example.

Sales of Fitzgerald's novel, too, failed to live up to the author's expectations. Readers in 1934 preferred buying a fat historical romance, *Anthony Adverse* by Hervey Allen.[15] Scott's book appeared briefly on best-seller lists, but barely sold 15,000 copies. A local story may explain: a Bolton Hill neighbor, Mrs. Slingluff Downs, received a copy from Scott, read it, and threw it in the trashcan. She found it unsuitable for her teen-age daughter, a friend of Scottie's, to read. After all, she said, this novel brought up incest, excessive drinking, and extramarital sex. Never mind that these errors are condemned in the novel and that the characters are pathetic — the novel must be censored.

Despite a tepid reception for his novel, Fitzgerald followed his custom of publishing a collection of short fiction just after a novel. He called it *Taps at Reveille*. In 1934 he had 50 stories to choose from, some from his Baltimore years. Choosing among them he recognized that his time for writing stories like those was ending. He sensed exhaustion of resources. Looking back 15 years to 1919 and his first stories, he counted a steady production. They had given him his livelihood.

At the time of that assessment he wrote that he had asked much of his emotions in writing these stories, 66 for *The Saturday Evening Post* alone. The price exacted from him was high, he said, because he put something into each story more intimately him than his blood, tears, or semen. That something had been the extra he had. But by 1935 it was gone.

Although he had called writing stories for 5¢ magazines "whoring," readers today do not call the results hack work. Some of them, such as "Babylon Revisited" (1931), remain among the best fiction of the century. Certain stories we now see as exploratory runs that preceded a full race in his novels. Also, sometimes he moved parts of stories into novels, as he did from "One Trip Abroad" and "The Swimmers" to *Tender Is the Night*. But the great benefit was that just having to keep writing gave a discipline needed to perfect his skill. For he was always developing — all through the Baltimore period.

True, some writing suffered because Fitzgerald did not take time to polish. He needed money badly then and in his haste produced at least nine inferior stories that did not sell. But ten of his Baltimore articles and essays, and up to 40 short stories, did sell.

As usual with Scott, the line between the non-fiction and the fiction was fuzzy, because he was such an autobiographical novelist. He had to have personal emotional involvement in the event he wrote about. That's why one of his best was a story called "Financing Finnegan" (1937). It treated a promising writer's financial dependence on an editor and agent. The plot echoed Fitzgerald's desperate situation before he subordinated his hatred of Hollywood to eating. A whole year before he left Maryland for California, he had not been able to sell a story except to *Esquire*. That magazine paid him their standard $250 for "Financing Finnegan."

Absence of such personal emotional involvement also doomed Scott's historical novel about a 10th-century soldier of fortune,

Philippe, "Count of Darkness." Into that hero, he put the personality of Ernest Hemingway and his own knowledge of an era that he insisted was the most interesting century in history. Even so, the editors of *Red Book* stopped serial publication of the novel in 1935 after only four episodes. The story lacked Fitzgerald's magic.

Recently Louis Azrael told how Scott worked on that story. One midnight Louis saw a light in the front room of 1307 Park Avenue and thought that maybe Fitzgerald could use some help: inside, he found Fitzgerald down on the floor maneuvering little wooden blocks, children's wooden blocks. "I thought this was some sort of drunken activity, but I asked him what he was doing." The reply was that the author was laying out the city about which he was writing — "where the old city wall was, where the moats were, where the castles were, so he could visualize the city and write about it better." Azrael added, "He was a very meticulous worker. No matter what condition he was in he had professional integrity."[16]

Next Scott recorded his own history woven into the history of the Jazz Age that he had named and, in certain ways, personified. Still readable and still evocative of that era are "My Lost City," "Echoes of the Jazz Age," and "Early Success." Just before he moved away from Baltimore for good he published "An Author's Mother," "An Author's House," and "Afternoon of an Author."

The best of these was "Afternoon of an Author" about a ride down Charles Street from 33rd Street on the top deck of the double-decker bus that used to make that run into the city's heart. The author in the story impresses the reader with the fragility of art and the poignancy of the life of the artist as writer. He also makes Baltimore look lovely with its bucolic Johns Hopkins Homewood campus and Attic shape of a railroad station — and girls in charming dresses.

Today we enjoy reading that piece distilled during what Fitzgerald called the practically arctic night of 1934. At the time he protested that the mood of terrible depression and despair was not going to become characteristic of him, but the mood persisted. Other people liked those autobiographical pieces, too, and editors at Simon & Schuster wanted to collect them in a book. His editor at Scribner's, Max Perkins, suggested that Scott use his legacy from his mother to get free from hack work and write his autobiography. Nothing came of either idea.

One of Scott's most admired Baltimore pieces was his memorial to Ring Lardner in *The New Republic*, September 1933. At that time Fitzgerald was completing *Tender Is the Night*, and creating a character based on Lardner, Abe North. North too suffered from alcoholism and died young, his genius unfulfilled. Doubtless Scott also saw a parallel between Ring and himself. In the essay, he noted Ring's dozen years of "impenetrable despair." Only a decade had passed since the two writers had been great friends living near each other on Long Island. The last time they met Ring was simply "six feet three inches of kindness stretched out ineffectual in the hospital room."[17]

A year later in *Esquire* Scott published a series about his own decline — his "crack-up." The titles used in the magazine were "Sleeping and Waking" (December 1934), "The Crack-Up" (February 1936), "Pasting It Together" (March 1936), and "Handle With Care" (April 1936). Publishing such confessions in his lifetime was daring because they made him appear broken down. Right away Fitzgerald was attacked. His rival and sometime friend Ernest Hemingway said that the series was cowardly. Another friend, the novelist John Dos Passos, told Scott to get a reporting job or write a first-rate novel about the Depression, but to stop spilling out little pieces for *Esquire* about his going to pieces.

As a description "going to pieces" was not tragic enough for what Fitzgerald saw happening to him then. In one low moment he recorded in his notebook: "Then I was drunk for many years, and then I died." Another time he imagined himself a mended plate with the crack plainly there but a plate good enough to serve humbly still in the pantry. On the positive side, he defended himself by saying that his sacrificing his talents in pieces preserved its essential value. And that method had, in his words, some sort of epic grandeur. He hadn't given up.

In "Sleeping and Waking" he tells of how, wakened at two-thirty A.M. in Bolton Hill, he endures the hellish insomnia: "The *real* night, the darkest hour, has begun. I am too tired to read unless I get myself a drink and hence feel bad next day — so I get up and walk. I walk from my bedroom through the hall to my study, and then back again, and if it's summer out to my back porch. There is a mist over Baltimore; I cannot count a single steeple. Once more to the study, where my eye is caught by a pile of unfinished business: letters, proofs, notes, etc. I start toward it, but No! this would be fatal."

Then, after two revivals of old fantasies of heroism, he goes back to the rear porch, ". . .and conditioned by intense fatigue of mind and perverse alertness of the nervous system — like a broken-stringed bow upon a throbbing fiddle — I see the real horror develop over the roof-tops, and in the strident horns of night-owl taxis and the shrill monody of revelers' arrival over the way. Horror and waste — . . ."[18]

At that time Fitzgerald had an experience with Louis Azrael that has not been reported. The experience was similar to one a 19th-century Baltimore newspaperman had with Edgar Allan Poe. In Poe's case the writer died. Here is Azrael's recollection:

That was in the fall. I remember walking on Baltimore Street near Calvert and I saw Scott. It was not a cold day, but he had on an overcoat with the collar up, and he looked haggard and under stress, so I accosted him and said, "Scott, what's the matter?" He obviously was in a very bad state, and he asked me if I'd get him a cup of tea or some hot drink. So I took him across the street to the Emerson Hotel and I got somebody there—somebody I knew—while we just sat in the lobby to bring him some tea, which he drank.

Seeing the condition he was in, I asked him who his doctor was and he said, "Louis Hamman." His office was on Chase Street somewhere between Charles and Cathedral. I put him in a taxi and delivered him there. This was in the daytime. Several days after that I got this note (I'd do anything to have it now!) in which he said he was sitting on the sundeck at Hopkins and he was feeling much better and just wanted to thank me because, "It's just possible you saved my life. I don't know what would have happened to me wandering about the streets in that condition."[19]

Azrael doesn't date that close call, but it could have happened in the fall of 1934 or 1935.

By March 1935 Scott felt that he was living in a vacuum: "If I have anything in common with a man [in Baltimore] intellectually here our pasts seem to have been very different, and if, on the contrary, our pasts have been the same, there is no intellectual meeting ground. I feel like the old maid...who 'grew less desirable and more particular.'"

The year before, Zelda had written him how sad she thought it was that he had so many worries to make him unhappy when his *Tender Is the Night* should have been making him feel happy. She added that she hoped that the house at 1307 Park Avenue didn't seem desolate and purposeless, and that maybe he should invite Hemingway to visit there.

What Scott did instead was to give up that house and move to an apartment in the Cambridge Arms. From there he overlooked a fine mansion of 1800, Homewood, and the campus of Johns Hopkins University. When his daughter finished the school year at Bryn Mawr School, she moved on to boarding school and college. By then Zelda had already settled in a North Carolina mental hospital. And Scott himself left town for good when he went to California to write for the movies.

After he had decamped to Hollywood in 1937 Fitzgerald looked back on episodes such as the sorry one on Baltimore Street that Azrael recounted. He wrote his favorite cousin Ceci Taylor that health and morale had miraculously returned after three terrible years. He had triumphed over the double collapse in Baltimore of his health and his capacity to create. His triumph showed in his making capital out of those disasters in his writing.

Perhaps his secret was his tough Irishness or else what he called a New England conscience developed in his Minnesota youth. Or maybe the social comforts of Baltimore sustained him. Whatever the reason, out of his lengthy meditation on a crack-up in 1935, he derived a lesson of how to live with despair and without illusion.

Literature benefited because his learning those lessons led him to write a strong if bleak prose. Always, as his friend Edmund Wilson had recognized years before, Scott had a gift for turning language into something iridescent and surprising. The gift never stopped maturing during hard times in Maryland.

As Fitzgerald admitted, however, he never became part of Baltimore. One reason was his being too much an internationalist to be content there forever. But he did say that he liked Baltimore better than any city except New York. He loved the place, he told a friend, and was grateful to what he called the town's general urbanity and sophistication.[20]

Baltimoreans, in turn, have come to acknowledge the truth of Louis Azrael's telling the Park Board that just having F. Scott Fitzgerald in Baltimore gave the town great distinction. Back in 1932 Baltimoreans knew merely that a somewhat tarnished gilded butterfly had alighted, but one with social credentials. In their city he found a useful atmosphere and ideas for classic books. By 1937, when he left, Fitzgerald had proven that his credentials surpassed the social, that the tarnish on his wings but briefly hid a literary brightness of purest gold.

XII
Gertrude Stein "And Other Such Fakes" And Forward-Movers

The chance gathering in the Baltimore-Washington region of such innovators as Gertrude Stein, John Dos Passos, Ogden Nash, and Jean Toomer.

"...nothing really can stop any one living and feeling as they do in Baltimore."[1]
— Gertrude Stein

"When they came to see us the relations, from...Baltimore and they said they loved to read we were always surprised that they had not read anything."[2]
— Gertrude Stein

"In my book reviews I carried on a steady war against academic standards, and whooped up all the newcomers of any merit, but I was always opposed to Greenwich Villagism. We never printed [in *The American Mercury*] William Carlos Williams, Gertrude Stein or any other such fakes."[3]
— H. L. Mencken

Gertrude Stein's buddha-like image fascinated artists, including Picasso and
Jo Davidson, who created this sculpture in 1923.

F. Scott Fitzgerald died at the beginning of World War II, and after the war H. L. Mencken's serious stroke ended his career. Both men were writing their best work at the end. Yet they were already old-fashioned. "The last of the novelists" (Fitzgerald's epithet for himself) and "the sage of Baltimore" (not Mencken's epithet for himself) belonged to the first half-century.

Just how much Mencken did is revealed in an anecdote from his friend Huntington Cairns:

In 1945 Johns Hopkins University put on an international symposium of literary criticism with leaders of the field—Richard Blackmur, Henri Peyre, John Crowe Ransom, Herbert Read, and Allen Tate. Even the dean of aestheticians, Benadetto Croce, sent a paper. Since most of those critics were old friends of Huntington Cairns, he gave luncheon parties during the proceedings. At one of them, Cairns recalls, the subject of H. L. Mencken naturally came up. While some of the men had written against him, and they were still not in his camp, they nevertheless admired him. They wanted to meet him if it could be arranged.

So Cairns went to the phone and invited Mencken to lunch.

Mencken: "Those men are all against me."

Cairns: "Henry, I wouldn't ask you out here if I didn't know their respect for you. They may disagree with you critically, but they do respect you. If you'd like to join us, I know they'd be delighted. I promise you, you will have a good time and no difficulties."

So Mencken came. Summing up what happened, Cairns said, "He took over the luncheon, and it was a very gay luncheon." Then Cairns added, "You see, he was not in touch with those men. They were all oriented towards [T. S.] Eliot. And he missed that generation, critically."[4]

"That generation" included experimenters and writers who could be called forward-movers. Their glitter and fame make bright splashes to end this literary history. Brightness comes from writers of international shine such as Gertrude Stein, John Dos Passos, Jean Toomer, Ogden Nash, and Katherine Anne Porter. Yet for all that world scope, they belonged in one way or another to the Chesapeake-Potomac region.

They also shine here at the end because they match in spirit the contemporaries, who enter these final pages with them. Gertrude Stein even claimed that she invented our 20th century, and boasted that her Baltimore story "Melanctha" was the first step away from 19th-century literature into 20th. She and the other forward-movers experimented with language and pioneered form. Their advanced ideas created novels such as Dos Passos's *U.S.A.,* Toomer's *Cane,* and Stein's *The Making of Americans.*

In spite of their advanced ideas, that group exhibited a familiar Maryland interest in the past. It showed in titles such as *The Days Before* (Katherine Anne Porter) and *I Wouldn't Have Missed It* (Ogden Nash). Their predilection for history still receives little notice. Neither does their association with the Chesapeake region, although that was significant.

Gertrude Stein was a Baltimorean. She was also, she said, a genius. Whether or not she was a fake as a writer (as Mencken said), she has reigned for 75 years as a genuine literary celebrity. Everybody has quoted such lines of hers as "Rose is a rose is a rose is a rose" — usually misquoted with an extra "A" at the beginning. To readers and non-readers alike she has stood as a curiosity like Simon Rodia's bizarre Watts Towers, in Los Angeles, or Antonio Gaudi's wild architecture in Spain.

Not only were Stein's books odd, modern, and experimental, but she herself also illustrated the shrinking modern globe in the way she spanned the ocean: she settled abroad, and yet retained her Baltimore base. She even refused to call herself expatriate. Though she had lived in exile for 43 of her 72 years, Gertrude Stein declared herself in her last will and testament as domiciled in Baltimore, Maryland, U.S.A. That was because, she said, all her people came from there. She had been born in Allegheny, Pennsylvania (now part of Pittsburgh), but she asserted that Baltimore was "where we were born longer and that was because after all everybody has to come from somewhere."

Being "born longer" in Baltimore had its influence on Stein's work: it gave her understanding of family life, and it gave her material for specific characters and situations. She boasted, for instance, that she had described Maryland relatives well in *The Making of Americans.* Of kin, her mother's family held themselves superior because they had arrived in town before her father's. That was the way with Balti-moreans, some of whom still set great store by how long a person has lived in their city. As Stein tells it, the mother's family were "always there" and, though father's people were rich, and mother's were not, still father's were not quite equal to mother's.[5]

Such insights helped when Stein talked with French people who lived in the provinces. She "perfectly understood their family life and their feelings of differences and what happened to everyone because that was the way they lived in Baltimore." Her understanding of that way of living and feeling went into the making of specific characters from people Stein knew. Her servants, for example, inspired parts of *Three Lives*.

After the Stein children were orphaned when Gertrude Stein was 18, she moved from her family home in Oakland, California, to live with her mother's sister Fanny Bachrach at 2408 Linden Avenue, Baltimore. With her came her older brother Leo. She often described how strange it was to come from the rather desperate inner life that she had been living to the cheerful life of her Baltimore aunts and uncles.

When Gertrude Stein went to study at Radcliffe, she told of that experience in the first thing she wrote. While at college she was in and out of Baltimore visiting the enjoyable flock of "little aunts" (as she called them). After college in 1897 she settled in Baltimore and matriculated at Johns Hopkins Medical School. In her class she was one of the few women.

In Baltimore, Stein suffered a romantic disappointment that she soon would weave into fiction called *Q.E.D.* There too she branched out from the German-Jewish social circle that she had known well. That expansion came about partly because she lived apart from Baltimore relatives, first at 215 East Biddle Street and then nearby at 220 East Chase Street.

By her final year in medical school, Gertrude Stein had tired of medicine and was ready to try something new. She failed four courses. When she was offered a chance to make up the grades and take her degree, her friend Marion Walker pleaded with her to stay. According to Gertrude Stein the plea was, "But Gertrude Gertrude remember the cause of women, and Gertrude Stein said, you don't know what it is to be bored."[6]

Although Gertrude Stein lingered in Baltimore a while, in 1903 she followed her brother Leo abroad. She lived the rest of her life in Paris. Within a decade after leaving town, she wrote much of her pioneering work. Major books were *Three Lives* (begun in 1905, finished in 1906, but not published until 1909 as her first book), and *The Making of Americans* (begun in 1903, worked on again in 1906, completed in 1911, and published finally complete in 1925). In origin both were Baltimore books.

Gertrude Stein's moving to France avoided the parochial perspective of being just a Baltimore author telling Baltimore stories. She did narrate Baltimore stories beginning with *Three Lives*. But those fictions showed an international strain, too. She put into "Melanctha," for example, what she called poignant incidents noticed along her walk to pose for Pablo Picasso in Paris.

Today both the Picasso portrait and her story belong to America. Picasso's painting, a seminal work in modern portraiture, is in the Metropolitan Museum of Art. And her tale "Melanctha" stands at the head of serious literary treatments of blacks. A notable black novelist Richard Wright, for one, praised her story for opening his ears to the "living words that swirled around him, the deep, pure Negro dialect of his black grandmother."[7] He began then to write from that source himself. Since Wright in turn led others to write from that source, it can be said that Stein and her story about black women in East Baltimore blazed a trail still being followed by black novelists such as Alice Walker and Toni Morrison.

Other post-Baltimore writings included her first portraits, *A Long Gay Book, Two: Gertrude Stein and Her Brother,* and *Tender Buttons.* Her novella *Q.E.D.* she completed in the fall after withdrawal from Johns Hopkins Medical School. It was her earliest sustained work save for *Fernhurst.*

Stein's body of work connected Baltimore with a major experimenter as well as a unique personality. Through Picasso's portrait and others', both readers and non-readers came to know Stein's buddha-like image. For at least half a century she has represented the liberated spirit — like a red balloon sent aloft in church. Perhaps that reputation explains why more of Stein's writings are in print now than in her lifetime. But how much she is read remains a question. Admirers have praised her free invention and her desire to express the rhythm of the visible world. Non-admirers laugh. Neutral observers usually feel the way the 18th-century critic Dr. Samuel Johnson did about the poet Thomas Gray: Stein was dull in a new way and that made some people think her great.

Though her experimental pieces are difficult to read, her autobiographies are not. They are fun to read. Even in those books she seems to be posing as the wise child: certainly, she was always the conscious artist. During those walks to pose for Picasso, she "meditated on, and made," sentences. In her *The Autobiography of Alice B. Toklas,* Stein told of writing after 11 at night and of planning *The Making of Americans,* "struggling with her sentences, those long sentences that had to be so exactly carried out. Sentences not only words but sentences and always sentences have been Gertrude Stein's life long passion."[8] Such a passion is, to say the least, unusual.

One critic explained Stein's experiments after leaving Baltimore as an "iconography that would describe reality with such pervasive force that it would assume an aesthetic importance within the composition equal to that of the figures or objects being described. Gradually, this insistent iconography becomes not merely the element that subsumes the composition but itself the primary element out of which the composition is made."9

As if that iconography were not handicap enough, many pages make her sound self-absorbed. Other times, some readers say she sounds like a strong-willed Baltimore matriarch of a German-Jewish clan laying down the law. Other readers suggest that her books memorialize her attempt to assert her identity. In her stories we find her personal feelings, trivia, sidelights from her experiences — all mixed to make her *our* representative — everybody's — asserting the identities of all of us. Hence she used the title *Everybody's Autobiography* (1937) for an account of her American lecture tour in 1934.

At that time with old age in sight, Stein wrote that book and another popular autobiography called *The Autobiography of Alice B. Toklas* (1933). They made her a celebrity. Here was *la gloire*, what she and her brother Leo had longed for — fame as an originator of a literary style, as a pioneer of Modernism, as a promoter of the art of Picasso and Matisse, as a mentor of Hemingway and Fitzgerald. She made a mark more significant perhaps than Marylanders know.

Nearing 70, Stein became popular with American soldiers in France at the end of World War II. G.I.s loved their amusing compatriot. She told a story about how the Southern accent of a soldier named Duncan baffled Alice B. Toklas, who came from California. Since all Stein's people came from Baltimore, Gertrude Stein understood Duncan's funny stories perfectly; the two of them — the G.I. and the old Baltimorean — shouted with laughter.

No wonder Gertrude Stein said that France did not take away what was important. It was, she asserted, just the place where she made what she made, her books. Abroad, Gertrude Stein enjoyed the freedom Paris always offered foreigners with advanced ideas. She benefited by living 3,000 sea miles from Johns Hopkins patients, little aunts, and the Maryland class system. That system underlay *Ida: A Novel* (1941), a story about an upper middle class Baltimorean, Wallis Warfield, who became Duchess of Windsor when she married ex-King Edward VIII. That same upper class provided Baltimore gossip for her earliest fiction, *Fernhurst*. The gossip tattled the defection of a beloved housemate of M. Carey Thomas, then president of Bryn Mawr College and the brains behind Bryn Mawr School, Baltimore.

The defector left the president's house for a professor, a married man.

Like most of Gertrude Stein's writings, *Fernhurst* was published posthumously. But her experimental techniques had won her a reputation by December, 1934, when she lectured at the Baltimore Museum of Art. That was her only visit to Maryland since leaving at age 25. She found the town changed, but said she could find her way anywhere there. Baltimore was still Southern — more so, it seemed to her, than Richmond. When she delivered her lecture, the response was like that of one Baltimore artist, Florence Hochschild Austrian, who knew her and her family: the lecture was incomprehensible nonsense. That same listener also found her, 30 years later, unchanged: "Gertrude Stein is one of those people who get away with murder."[10]

Gertrude Stein and others recorded what she did in Baltimore then besides lecture. Gertrude and Alice were made to hang up their Christmas stockings when they stayed with Stein relatives at Pikesville, just northwest of the city. Among the gifts she delighted in were square little books from the ten cent store *(Flash Gordon* was one). She said they and the Ford car were examples of the romantic thing about America — that the best designing and the best material went into the cheapest thing.

During her tour, one Baltimore house she visited was 1307 Park Avenue, last home of Scott and Zelda Fitzgerald. There she admired Zelda's paintings enough to ask for two works to add to her collection. Zelda had already promised one of them to her doctor and substituted another painting. Afterwards Scott wrote her in the fulsome manner he always assumed with her; he praised her wise mind and handsome face and — echoing her earlier praise of his prose — her sentences that never leak.

Fitzgerald's admiration went back to Parisian days of 1925, when he read *The Making of Americans.* Immediately he had been eager to learn from that novel. Unfortunately for her, he couldn't persuade his publisher Charles Scribner's Sons to publish that novel because, he wrote her, old man Scribner's mind was too old.

Later in 1932 Fitzgerald wrote from Baltimore that whenever he sat down to write he thought of the line that Stein had drawn for him and told him that his next book should be just *that* thick. To her he wrote later, "So many of your memorable remarks come often to my head, and they seem to survive in a way that very little current wisdom does."[11]

To him as to other admirers she was an assuring rock. Her confidence came from her belief that she was a genius, that she was at the perfect place (Paris) to invent the modern consciousness, and that she was always right. No wonder Scott Fitzgerald found her talk the talk of an angel and her laugh so warming. He always remembered what an old covered wagon she was.

For all Fitzgerald's praise in that image, Baltimoreans were lucky that Gertrude Stein remained abroad because she could be destructive. Certain remarks in her autobiographical books showed how she saw Baltimoreans. She edged with irony her summation, "Baltimore is famous for the delicate sensibilities and conscientiousness of its inhabitants."[12] Anything but complimentary was her example of those qualities. She told a tale of how a Baltimore friend, Etta Cone— "rather lonesome and rather interested"—faithfully typed *Three Lives* letter by letter rather than commit the indiscretion of reading the text without Stein's specific permission. Stein then gave permission. Years later their friendship ended when Stein wrote to Etta in Baltimore offering to sell that typescript to her for $1,000. Etta, of course, hadn't charged a cent for her typing.

Doubtless Gertrude Stein had lost that delicate Baltimore sensibility, if she ever had it. Another writer in this chapter's international covey did develop a sensitivity—to the region and to its past. That was a sometime resident of Baltimore, John Dos Passos. Long before settling in that city, he had joined—with Fitzgerald and Hemingway—in what Gertrude Stein called "the Lost Generation." She meant men who had been in military uniform in World War I, and who had suffered disillusionment. Dos Passos had been with the French ambulance service.

Lost or not, Dos Passos fits this chapter because he was a forward-mover, an experimenter with language. He has a place in local literary history because of lifelong returnings to Potomac River farms; Tidewater was home. Like his friend Ernest Hemingway, though, he gypsied wherever pleasure and excitement called—Cap D'Antibes with Zelda and F. Scott Fitzgerald, for instance, and Spain during the Civil War.

His mother, a Marylander, took him as a boy to live at Spence's Point, Virginia, near the mouth of the Potomac. Their farm was just across the river from Maryland. And, in fact, Maryland waters had washed the Virginia shore ever since before the boy's ancestor, Samuel Sprigg, was governor of Maryland in the early 19th century. Still we can't call Dos Passos a native: he saw himself as a dweller in no man's land. (But his daughter recently said that he really did belong to the Chesapeake domain.)

Whether or not his view was right, Dos Passos retained his link with the Chesapeake while he gypsied. Then, in his 50s, he returned to write at his riverside farm. He also wrote in Baltimore, where he lived during the 17 winters of his children's schooling. There in Johns Hopkins University, Peabody, and Pratt libraries, he wrote; many of his pages were historical — *Men Who Made the Nation* (1957), for example. In them he showed high regard for Founding Fathers and the colonial South. By the time he wrote those books, he had finished experimenting with prose and politics.

Though his popularity had waned by then, he had already secured a niche in America's literary pantheon for his early experiments in narrative. According to a recent critic, Dos Passos resembles certain Elizabethan playwrights in being less a great artist than one of several hinges operating the same great door.

A decade of experimenting began with *One Man's Initiation — 1917* (1920). Then in *U.S.A.* (1930-1936) technical innovations and social conscience created his master work. In it Dos Passos relied on fictional devices that created the effect of collage: (1) "The Camera Eye," stream-of-consciousness passages giving his point of view on the decay of American society, (2) "Newsreel," snippets of popular songs, advertisements, and newspaper articles (headlines, too), that catch the immediate time of the fictional episode, and (3) self-contained capsule biographies of important Americans, who make ironic counterparts to characters. The resulting panorama of the years 1900-1930 stressed corruption and loss.

Dos Passos worked some of those devices into a novel of his Maryland period titled *Midcentury* (1961). Here is a segment about a man who influenced coal miners of Western Maryland:

> *When John L. Lewis retired at eighty*
> *as President of the United Mine Workers,*
> *the heavyweight orator of American labor was universally*
> *acclaimed as the mightiest organizer of them all.*
>
> *Born in the shadow of a minetipple*
> *in Lucas, a miners' shantytown in southeastern Iowa,*
> *the eldest of eight,*
> *son of a classconscious Welshman on the black books of the*
> *coal companies for proselytizing for the Knights of Labor,*
> *and an Iowa schoolteacher,*
> *John L. was raised on righteous indignation.*[13]

Even passages like that didn't give *Midcentury* the success of *U.S.A.*
By the time he published the later novel, financial success had become
especially important to him. Like Fitzgerald, he supported a family
by writing. A widower at 53, he married Elizabeth Holdridge, a widow
with a son, at her brother-in-law's farm north of Baltimore. They had
a daughter Lucy, who with her step-brother was educated in Baltimore.
Other financial demands came from the old family farm on the
Potomac.

Dos Passos then joked about being poor: he and his wife, he said,
could always set up a stand on the Maryland side of the Potomac
River and call it "Dos and Betty's Eats and Gambling." (Maryland
traditionally tolerated such pleasures as gambling, and in St. Mary's
County it was legal then.)

The honest writer, of course, earned his money by writing a number
of books of popular history, and some journalism. Among them were
Chosen Country (1951), *Prospect of a Golden Age* (1959), *Brazil on
the Move* (1963), *Mr. Wilson's War* (1963). His *The Head and Heart
of Thomas Jefferson* (1954) proved, like the rest, to be well crafted.
Dos Passos moreover surpassed other biographers in freshness on
such matters as Jefferson's understanding of Palladio's architecture.
And, of course, he displayed a novelist's gifts for narrative and
character.

His shelf of books proved that settling down to family life in
Baltimore suited the turn he made from radicalism to conservatism
in politics. That transformation affected every book he wrote in
Chesapeake days. His novel *Most Likely To Succeed* (1954) satirized
Communist followers, and *Midcentury* (1961) supported free
enterprise. This conservative leaning lay behind his nostalgic essay
about Baltimore in *A Guide to Baltimore Architecture* (1973). He
recalled boyhood images of sailing on Baltimore-bound steamboats,
of arriving at crowded wharves along Light Street. He remembered
waking in his bunk on the stately steamboat *Three Rivers* to the
singing of roustabouts unloading guano. Then and later in Baltimore
he found what he called the historic dimension; it gave residents a
certain dignity whether they were conscious of it or not.

Writers who missed that historic dimension found Baltimore dull.
One such writer, Julien Green, here makes an international footnote
to local literary history. At the onset of World War II, Green came
to Baltimore from Paris. The son of Americans, he had been reared
in France, where his fiction was well received by Andre Gide and other
literary critics. In Baltimore he for a time taught English at Goucher

College. There he found the all-female student body very innocent.

At that time Green lived with his cousin, Mrs. George Weems Williams, on Blythewood Road, a quiet, proper address off North Charles Street. In her mansion he wrote *Memories of Happy Days* (1942). Writing it, he said, was his way of returning to Paris; he even wanted to call it *Before the Evil Days* — but his American publishers objected to the word *evil*.

Later Green created another book from his gray, linen-bound diaries that he recorded during his stay and stored in the Williams' attic. Those diaries became staples of French literature on a shelf with Albert Camus' *The Stranger,* Jean Paul Sartre's *No Exit*, and Green's own novel *The Transgressor* (1957).

His diary demonstrates that he would possibly have been happier in Washington with other emigré writers. For instance, of a dinner at neighboring Evergreen he wrote, "Nothing particular was said at dinner, or afterwards — we are not in France — not a thing to record — just a sort of well-bred good-fellowship. Nothing spiteful either and consequently, nothing amusing."[14]

That dinner was given by ex-Ambassador (to Italy) Robert Garrett and Mrs. Garrett. After dinner over port and cigars, Garrett must have shown Green the collection of rare books in the huge paneled library. One rarity there was the manuscript of Dr. Alexander Hamilton's *History of the Tuesday Club* (of 18th-century Annapolis), complete with the author's illustrations.

In that room Garrett frequently entertained the Literary and Political Club. Possibly Green was guest at their meetings. In all likelihood the agenda centered on the political half of the club's name because the membership included an editor of the *Sun,* John Owens, and a fellow Pulitzer-Prize winning *Sun* writer, Mark S. Watson. Still, literary guests must have been in order. From local literati, one guest of pure delight would have been Ogden Nash.

Unlike Julien Green, Nash was an immigrant who stayed. Like Dos Passos, he put down roots in Maryland; both established dynasties through children and grandchildren there. Nash came to Baltimore as a young man looking to a sociable weekend with a friend. There he met and fell in love with a young Baltimore lady of Eastern Shore lineage. They married, brought up two daughters, and lived a proper North Baltimore life. He noted in *Life* magazine that "The homeliest men, near Chesapeake waters, / Have a knack of fathering lovely daughters."

Again like Dos Passos, Nash found Baltimore a good place to

compose. During his many years in Baltimore he published voluminously — practically a book a year. Familiar titles were *I'm A Stranger Here Myself* (1938) and *You Can't Get There from Here* (1957). About his assured place among innovators, another humorous writer, Morris Bishop, wrote, "Free from flashiness, free from trashiness / Is the essence of ogdenashiness. / Rich, original, rash, and rational / Stands the monument ogdenational!"[15]

One basis for saying Nash stood like a monument was his verses to introduce an orchestral suite by Camille Saint-Saens called "Carnival of the Animals." His words have been read in concerts by performers as diverse as the First Lady, Nancy Reagan, and Noel Coward. Listeners who hear Nash's words always remember the elephants, whose "teeth are upside down, outside," and the old fossil's bone that winked at Nash.

Nash sometimes directed his lines locally too. During World War II, for instance, he escorted a debutante to the Bachelor's Cotillion, a special Baltimore social occasion sometimes called a "german." Afterwards he complimented the young lady with a poem. One line reminded her that, "It's better to come out at a german / Than have a German come out at you."[16] Or, again, in 1970 when he lived in the well-regulated confines of a sub-suburb, Cross Keys, he wrote "A Plaintive Plaintiff":

My viewing has a restricted view:
Channels 13, 11, 2.
I hope that some day ere my burial
I'll be allowed a rooftop aerial.

Another piece that he sent to the management of the Village of Cross Keys was called "Unfair! Unfair!" (This poem and the preceding one were printed in February 1970 in *Keynotes*, but not, so far as I know, elsewhere.)

I wish to scotch the rumor that
I am an enemy of the cat.
I guess that no one on this globe
Is less of an aleurophobe,
In spite of which I hate the feline
That for my warblers makes a beeline,
Whose owner turns it loose to prey
On nuthatch, cardinal, junco, jay,
Whose ancient hunting urge is stirred
By sight of dove or mocking bird,
Who spurns its Puss-in-Boots to speed

To where I've scattered sunflower seed.
Three cats there are which haunt the scene
At Number 30 Olmsted Green;
One gray, one black, one black and white,
All insolence and appetite.
Like witches at Walpurgis party,
To them "Scat!" simply means "Eat hearty!"
Here cats walk wild, but dogs on leashes.
Are cats a special privileged species?[17]

Those lines exhibit Ogden Nash the experimenter at the end of his life. By the 1970s he and and his verse enjoyed international fame. In the august *Oxford Companion to American Literature*, Nash appears as author of light verse—from acidulous satire and irresponsible good humor to the mildly mad (*Oxford's* words). His style, according to *Oxford's* editor, was characterized by "hyper-dithyrambic meters, pseudo-poetic inversions, gangling asymmetrical lines, extremely pat or elaborately inexact rimes, parenthetical dissertations, and unexpected puns."

The poet Archibald MacLeish pointed out the error of calling Ogden Nash a writer of light verse. First of all, Nash wrote rhymed *prose;* his form didn't depend upon the line, as verse does, but rather on the whole sentence. Rhymes merely push sentences into humorous couplets. And the rhyme words point up the meaning.

As for the lightness attributed to Nash's writings, MacLeish called that a misnomer too. Nash invented colloquial, funny couplets that look harmless, trivial, undisturbing. But in fact, MacLeish points out, Nash had probed the Nixon years with a "satirist's concern for the humanity of human creatures."[18]

Part of Nash's appeal to readers lay in his attitude towards 20th-century changes in belief and sensibility. Other writers avoided humor; he depended on it. Other writers chose techniques of ambiguity, compression, and detachment; he chose clarity and wit. And he introduced the violent changes in the world—coming faster and faster—but didn't resort to themes of violence or alienation or absurdity.

In those ways Nash was close to another of that bright group of forward-movers—Huntington Cairns. Like Gertrude Stein, Cairns was much attached to Baltimore yet lived in exile—he in Washington. And like her, also, he promoted modern literature, though a different set of writers from hers. Cairns supported Robert Graves, James Joyce, the Morley brothers (of Park Avenue, Baltimore), and Ezra Pound.

Stein's residence on East Biddle Street, Baltimore (left center) was where she met the women who inspired *Three Lives*.

Gertrude Stein and her brother Leo came to live here at 2408 Linden Avenue, Reservoir Hill, Baltimore, and there experienced the happy times with her little aunts that she recalled in *The Autobiography of Alice B. Toklas*. The marker to the left of the door tells how the orphaned Steins found refuge there.

Gertrude Stein introduced her Baltimore friends Claribel (pictured in Matisse's drawings on the right) and Etta (on the left) to Picasso and Matisse (pictured in two poses at lower right). The Cones bought a number of items from Stein's collection, including the portrait in oil of Stein (left of center) by Felix Vallotton (1907), painted shortly after Stein began writing her Baltimore stories.

Johns Hopkins Hospital and School of Medicine looked like this at the time Gertrude Stein was a medical student there. The streetcar in the center probably was one that she rode across town from her apartment nearer the heart of Baltimore.

Katherine Anne Porter had lived and written many places, but longest in the Washington suburbs and in Georgetown. This photograph by Father Joseph Gallagher was taken at her 79th birthday party in Silver Spring.

John Dos Passos had ancestral ties with the Potomac-Chesapeake domain, and wrote for many years in Baltimore—mostly books that looked back.

Jean Toomer was a black native Washingtonian who joined the Harlem Renaissance and wrote about his city in *Cane*. Other talented black authors have lived in the capital, mostly because of Howard University or the Library of Congress.

Like so many Baltimoreans of his generation, he exuded a genial, yet quizzical, attitude. His early writing caught Mencken's attention, and the two men met frequently over lunch, even after Cairns took a job in Washington. He went as counsel for the National Gallery of Art. Working there, he said, left him Sunday free to write. Evidently his earlier lawyering in Baltimore had been a seven-day job.

In addition to Mencken, the Baltimore writers Cairns consorted with were Eli Siegel, a poet whose "Hot Afternoons Have Been in Montana" won a big prize from the *Nation*, and V. F. Calverton (*nom de plume* of George Goetz), editor in New York of *The Modern Quarterly: A Journal of Radical Opinion.* Those two writers differed from other native Baltimoreans in their tastes, and they emigrated to New York.

Yet some other local readers such as Cairns did show advanced taste. For example, Hochschild Kohn (department store) sold them James Joyce's *Portrait of the Artist as a Young Man* (1916), and Remington (book seller) offered them his *Ulysses* (1922), even though importing it was prohibited. That novel went over the counter in the blue paper edition with uncut pages. On a much larger scale, Cairns stimulated readers' intellects by inaugurating a discussion of great books on national radio, "Invitation to Learning" in 1940. One guest he tried, but failed, to snare was Mencken for a discussion of Aristotle.

Cairns's retaining Baltimore ties while working in Washington makes the two major regional cities seem close. And indeed the two have moved closer in time since William Wirt's wife complained of the eight-hour journey by coach between them. But Cairns held a Baltimorean's opinion of Washington. Of his native city on the Patapsco he said that, like San Francisco, it was unusual and charming. Of his adopted city on the Potomac he said little.

As for literary society in Washington, Cairns recalled that whatever existed in the 1930s and 1940s was dull and came to nothing. Another observer recorded in her Pulitzer Prize-winning history of the capital that even heady days of the New Deal lacked a superb chronicler. Certainly poetry and fiction didn't emerge from what that historian called the New Deal's engrossing business of remaking American Civilization. Even a New Dealer of genius lacked time to transpose his or her mission into the Great American Novel or an epic poem. None has yet appeared![9]

The only specialty of the District was what came to be called the Washington Novel. Examples of it are being written today. A baker's dozen of them go back as far as 1861 and George W. Curtis's *Trumps.*

All of those novels center on politics, of course. Among the lot were unfamiliar novels such as two by Gertrude Atherton — *Senator North* (1900) and *The Fashionable Adventures of Joshua Craig* (1909). More recent and more familiar were Allen Drury's *Advise and Consent* (1959, Pulitzer Prize), John Dos Passos's trilogy *District of Columbia* (1952), and Gore Vidal's *Washington, D.C.* (1967), *Burr* (1973), *1876* (1976), and *Lincoln* (1984).

After World War II prominent writers lectured at the Library of Congress. Some superior poets took turns acting as official Consultants in Poetry and gave readings there. From their works — and a few other poets' — an editor created *Washington and the Poets* (1973). Several poems there are very well known, poems such as Robert Lowell's "July in Washington," and Randall Jarrell's "The Woman in the Washington Zoo." That anthology focused on Washington as a city of government, not of people. One poem in the book even tells the reader that the capital is neither Rome nor home.[20]

One of the poets in that book, Archibald MacLeish, warned legislators of the power of writers. Here are a few lines from "A Poet Speaks from the Visitors' Gallery":

Have Gentlemen perhaps forgotten this?—
We write the histories.

Do Gentlemen who snigger at the poets,
Who speak the word professor with guffaws—

Do Gentlemen expect their fame to flourish
When we, not they, distribute the applause?
. . .

Gentlemen have power now and know it,
But even the greatest and most famous kings
Feared and with reason to offend the poets
Whose songs are marble
                    and whose marble sings.[21]

MacLeish served as Librarian of Congress (1939-1944), appointed to the post by Franklin D. Roosevelt. He also was part of the government later as Assistant Secretary of State (1944-1945). His writing at that time was prose supporting democracy in the war against Hitler and Mussolini. At the end of MacLeish's years in Washington, a fellow poet, Ezra Pound, was brought there a prisoner. His arrival raised questions for poets such as MacLeish, questions about the meaning of political treason, and about democracy and fascism.

Washington then became a center of controversy because Pound was confined by American authorities in St. Elizabeth's Hospital for a decade. He was declared mentally unfit to stand trial for treason, a charge based on his wartime broadcasts in Italy. In the hospital Pound received visits from local and visiting authors — T. S. Eliot, Robert Lowell, Edith Hamilton, Huntington Cairns, and H. L. Mencken were a few. Cairns saw to it that Pound received the Bollingen Prize in 1949, a tribute to that poet's art.

Cairns later reported that "As soon as Pound was locked in St. Elizabeth's, Henry [Mencken] got on the train and came over to see him — through a sense of duty — and brought him a present. He went that time because he was outraged [that Pound was being held there]."[22] Years before, Mencken had told Pound that in Pound's case a competent poet was spoiled to make a tin-horn politican. In the same letter he told Pound that six months back in the U.S.A. would straighten him out. If it didn't, then he would erect a bronze equestrian statue to Pound's memory alongside the one he was setting up in honor of Upton Sinclair.

Besides receiving visits from literati, Pound had visitors who read Chinese to him and one who brought Mathew's dictionary alphabetizing Chinese characters by romanized sounds. While at St. Elizabeth's, Pound published half a dozen books, including *The Cantos of Ezra Pound* (including the *Pisan Cantos*, 1949), *The Letters of Ezra Pound, (1907-1941)* (1950), and *Literary Essays of Ezra Pound,* with introduction by T. S. Eliot (1954). He had accomplished all that before he was freed April 18, 1958, declared permanently insane, and returned to his home in Italy where he lived until his death in 1972. Undoubtedly he was glad to get away from the city where he had been a most reluctant writer-resident.

Another writer, Jean Toomer, also endured the hardships of a prisoner, in a sense. He was a native, black Washingtonian — a poet in prose. Abroad or at home, he seemed never to escape the confinement of his native urban street. That ghetto for city blacks marked his novel *Cane* (1923). In it Toomer drew on people and places he knew growing up in the District.

As a grown-up, Toomer realized what his earlier experience lacked — true black riches. Those cultural riches he discovered when he went to Sparta, Georgia, with a white friend, Waldo Frank, to teach at the Georgia Normal and Industrial Institute. There he conceived the idea of *Cane*. In a place populated largely by black country people, he heard their folk songs. These words and music released a repressed part of his nature; it sprang suddenly to life "as spontaneous as gold and tints of an eternal purple."

Cane was written upon return to Washington and has a whole section set in that city. It opens on Seventh Street, "a bastard of Prohibition and the War. A crude-boned, soft-skinned wedge of nigger life breathing its loafer air, jazz songs and love, thrusting unconscious rhythms, black reddish blood into the white and whitewashed wood of Washington."[23] That section of Toomer's novel, according to Waldo Frank, was about "the threshing and suffering brown world of Washington, lifted by opportunity and contact into the anguish of self-conscious struggle."

Like the rest of that novel, the capital sections in it juxtapose prose sketches with poems. That combination was exotic, probably too much so for the tastes of the 1920s. Though the book won some favorable reviews, it dropped from notice until the 1960s. On first publication, a reviewer in the *New Republic* found it sometimes beautiful, filled with new ways of writing. Another reviewer, Paul Rosenfeld, decided that Toomer had unlimbered a soul, as he said, and given of its dance and music. The black leader W.E.B. DuBois declared that Toomer had hurled his pen to emancipate the Negro from the convention of sex. And Sherwood Anderson admitted Toomer's superiority to himself as a portrayer of Negro life in fiction.

When Toomer moved to New York, *Cane* became part of New York City's "Harlem Renaissance." He enjoyed success as part of that group of artists and writers. In Washington he had found no similar group to join.

Toomer left Washington for good after finishing *Cane*. At the time no literary life seemed open in the capital for anyone, least of all a black writer. A more congenial life opened to a white female writer 20 years later when Katherine Anne Porter moved to Washington. She settled down to a good life, to enjoy fame, love, money, and her favorite emeralds.

Katherine Anne Porter came to the Chesapeake-Potomac region after 50 years of wandering that more than matched the gypsying of Dos Passos. Like him she had the habit of being wherever history was being made. She was in Berlin, for instance, in the early days of Hitler and knew Goering. Naturally, she moved to Washington, D.C., when that city became the capital of the Western world during World War II. From 1944 until she died in 1980, she lived mostly in and around that capital, but with forays all over the map.

So, of a career of 46 years, Katherine Anne Porter spent about half in the territory of this literary history. Because she said that she felt at home in the South, she settled permanently on the border between North and South. By coincidence, before settling there, she had felt the luxuriance of the Maryland spring in *The Education of Henry Adams* with its woods of flowering dogwood and judas tree; that tree became symbolic in the story that made her reputation, "Flowering Judas."

At age 54 she made her first Washington home with Allan Tate, a poet and critic, and his wife Caroline Gordon, a novelist, in South East. Then she moved to P Street, Georgetown, where she stayed off and on for some years, mostly in a white, narrow house of character and some elegance. There she finished her novel *Ship of Fools* (1962) and received reviews of it.

After that book made her rich, she bought a mansion in the nearby Maryland suburb of Spring Valley. Later she lived for a decade on the 15th floor at 6100 Westchester Park Drive, College Park, Prince George's County. At the end of her life she moved to Carriage Hill Nursing Center, Silver Spring, where she died. She had lived longer in Maryland than anywhere else.

Her years there were vintage years, with honors, money, friendships, and eventually the comforts of religion. When she lived near the University of Maryland, College Park, officials of the University of Maryland there awarded her an honorary degree. She was happy to accept both it and their offer of a three-room suite in McKeldin Library to house her library and mementoes. Today the Katherine Anne Porter Room there is furnished with her rose-colored Louis Quinze sofa and other furniture. There too are photographs of literary friends such as Hart Crane and Robert Penn Warren. Warren's is a memento of Katherine Anne Porter's introducing him to his wife, the writer Eleanor Clark, at the P Street house.

In 1973 another Maryland college awarded Porter an honorary degree, the College of Notre Dame of Maryland in Baltimore. She liked coming to services at the college and became friendly with nuns there. One was the poet Sister Maura Eichner, who wrote and read the citation: "Titles like 'Flowering Judas,' 'Pale Horse, Pale Rider,' 'Noon Wine,' and 'Ship of Fools' linger in the mind like bell sounds in quiet sunlight. Her fiction — exploring man's enduring themes — links her with the great company of classic story tellers. She believes in the young. Because she is young of heart, she invited us all to time-lessness in God, she is our flowering branch, our spring renewal."[24]

Other honors came during her last Maryland years, among them the Gold Medal for Fiction from the American Academy of Arts and Letters. Then, for her *Collected Stories* (1965) she won both the National Book Award and the Pulitzer Prize for Fiction. Again, a big reception at the University celebrated publication of *Collected Essays and Occasional Writings* (1970). She was 80 then, and bedecked herself with her favorite jewels, a 22-carat emerald ring, diamond-and-emerald spray pin and a double strand of pearls with a diamond-and-emerald clasp.

Those collections of fiction and non-fiction followed publication of a long novel, *Ship of Fools.* Porter had worked on the manuscript for many years and finished it in Washington. The book became a bestseller and made her rich, both then and when it was made into a movie. A literary critic, F. O. Matthiessen, praised the "searching originality of the content."[25] He noted how much a modern she was, with clear influences from Ezra Pound and Sigmund Freud. Other critics always praised her style for the precision and clarity of a fine crystal goblet.

As a woman she was just as stylish. When she was in her 80s, a newspaper reporter noted how she conjured up magical images like a high priestess of some private cult. She spoke in a voice, high and firm, as "oddly metallic as if created by a toymaker to a Byzantine emperor." He noticed the large emerald — it became famous — gleaming, he said, like the fulfillment of long-deferred desire.[26]

Another man, Father Joseph Gallagher, a priest who visited her often, described her at 90 propped up in bed under a gilt-edged painting of the Madonna and Child. She was very tiny, but her face was still "marvelously alive, and crowned with elegant silver-white hair." He was struck right away by what he called her engulfing smile and "her ingratiating Southern voice, her wit, and her feistiness."[27]

A contrasting evaluation belongs next to Gallagher's. A contemporary novelist Doris Grumbach noted how complex and also elusive Porter was as a personality: "She was a capricious, self-centered, selfish, vain woman with many lovers and husbands but few real loves. What she wanted was recognition for her work, but she was too lazy, too aristocratic in her tastes, too involved in social life, to do very much of it."[28]

Certainly Katherine Anne Porter left a modest number of pages after a lifetime of writing. But the quality, most critics agree, was high. For example, when Father Gallagher wrote a memorial for the *Sun*, he praised her artistic vision of the roots of human tragedy. A high point of that vision was the only passage in *Ship of Fools* that was italicized: *"What they were saying to each other was only, Love me, love me in spite of all! whether or not I love you, whether I am fit to love, whether you are able to love, even if there is no such thing as love, love me."* Gallagher added that love was italicized in Porter's own life and gave an anecdote in proof: someone told her, "Katherine Anne, wherever you have lived, there have always been people who loved you." She replied, "Well, I always loved them first, and that sort of helped them get used to the idea."

Out of her vision of what Father Gallagher called the roots of human tragedy, Katherine Anne Porter made literary art. And of art, she wrote Gallagher, ". . .only the work of saints and artists gives us any reason to believe that the human race is worth belonging to."[29]

The death in 1980 of Katherine Anne Porter concludes both this chapter and this history of Maryland authors. Contemporaries are proving how right she was about artists making the human race worth belonging to. Some of these contemporaries who have national reputations appear in pictures here. As a local literary historian advised in 1911, we readers appreciate them for carrying on the work of older authors, who "by charm of style, purity of ideals, loftiness and range of subjects, interpretative faculty and power of illumination have glorified the vocation of literature and made it honorable."[30]

Katherine Anne Porter's death at the beginning of the 1980s broke a strong link of our younger contemporaries with earlier writers, for her life spanned almost a century. When she was born, Whitman was still alive, and so was Frederick Douglass, Colonel Richard Malcolm Johnston, Father Tabb, and Harriet Beecher Stowe. Porter was 20 when both Julia Ward Howe and Mark Twain died, and 28 when Henry Adams died, and his *Education* was first published commercially.

Time is compressed, then, when we look at local literary history from the end of this book. Looking back, we see the brevity of that history in such facts as Poe's corresponding with all early and mid-19th-century authors, and Mencken's being in touch with all the rest up to mid-20th-century. Rarely have two men spanned so much of a regional literature.

This telescoping of literary decades reveals literature's late start in the Chesapeake and Potomac region. Belles lettres there suffered for lack of an early city such as Boston. When in the 1790s Parson Weems wrote Washington's biography, Baltimore was still small. A generation later when Poe arrived it was a boom town and second largest in the whole country. Generations were so close that Weems could have stood godfather to Poe. And if Poe had lived to old age he could have done the same for Mencken.

Coming to the present, Mencken was in fact godfather of a contemporary Baltimore poet, Clarinda Harriss Lott, and could have godfathered Adrienne Rich had her father, Mencken's friend, been of that mind. In her turn, Lott today sponsors numerous local writers by printing their work and by arranging public readings.

Clarinda Harriss Lott has written about those up-to-date women and men and echoes the great Menckenean theme — that Maryland makes a good home for writers. She often comments on how the settled life in Baltimore leads to casual encountering of local writers in grocery and bar. No one is a celebrity; no one is pursued by autograph hounds. That would please Mencken.

The region is still the good work place for writers that Mencken said it was. Earlier poets had found it so — Poe and Lanier — and Frederick Douglass produced all but the brief first version of his memoirs there. And in Baltimore F. Scott Fitzgerald was able to write his long-planned novel *Tender Is the Night.* More recently Maryland has served well as work place for creative writers as diverse as Cynthia Voight, prize-winning author of children's books, and John Waters, whose films *Pink Flamingo* (1972) and *Polyester* (1981) made him "Sultan of Sleaze."

Besides living and filming in Baltimore, Waters exploits local character — the side that aids him in creating an ironical portrait of Middle America. His picture of his city contrasts markedly with that held by Walter Lord, another native writer (but one long resident elsewhere): "A pleasant civilized place where nobody ever seems to be in a hurry."[31] Another exile, Holmes Alexander, has "A pleasant image of [Maryland's] social and sporting and political traditions," but also "a darker image of its social climbing and in-fighting, considerable shallowness but many depths of empathy."[32]

What Lord and Alexander remember seems to fit Baltimore of 30 years ago and more. In 1935, for instance, Gerald W. Johnson noted that he lived what he called the dullest life in the dullest street in the dullest city in America. And that suited him and his writing just fine.[33] In a world of rapid change, he and other writers found security; in a time of uncertainty they found comfort in Chesapeake crab feasts and Mencken's talk.

Yet such comforts don't give everything a writer needs. If working in a placid pool were all, then Johnson could have written just as well in the village of New Baltimore, Ohio. Clearly he benefited from living in the middle of a large city, and one with the Chesapeake stamp. Even though some of Johnson's contemporaries fled Maryland's quiet, they retained the stamp. A classic example is Dashiell Hammett. He moved to California to invent a streetwise Baltimore detective, the Continental Op. Also, as freshly revealed in these pages, Hammett's *The Glass Key* depends for plot and character on Maryland's pride in class and Baltimore politics.

Today, 60 years after Hammett left town, a native poet, Daniel Mark Epstein, says, "It's an illusion that there's no 'literary scene' in Baltimore. During the mid-seventies, when the Maryland Writers Council still had its own building, with a bookstore and presses and readings, there was really a very intense literary community." Epstein adds that in the 1980s things are still lively. Certainly they are for him, winner of both a Prix de Rome and a Guggenheim.[34]

Epstein's friend Andrei Codrescu, a Roumanian-American poet, confirms the liveliness in an anecdote: "The center of town near the Washington Monument has occasioned a number of adventures. In 1981, poets Daniel Mark Epstein, Rodger Kamenetz and I climbed to the top of the Monument and shared a bottle of brandy while an electrical storm broke out and a furious rain kept us there for hours. When we came out we met the great schizophrenic poet Dan Curley who psychoanalysed for us the building on Monument where the Psychoanalytical Society of America was formed."[35] Codrescu's taking note of a founding is quite in keeping with the local penchant for history. Although he was resident for only a few years, he gave a typical local reply when asked what image he associated with Baltimore: "Dead poets. Poe. F. Scott Key."

Did Codrescu really feel the pull of the past as so many other Maryland writers have? We don't know, but certainly the habit of looking back comes through in Maryland book after Maryland book, new and old. The past seems more divine than the future in regional novels as different from each other as Christopher Morley's *Thorofare,* Gertrude Stein's *The Making of Americans,* and John Pendleton Kennedy's *Rob of the Bowl.*

For certain contemporary writers the past is indeed present. The novelist Anne Tyler, for example, finds that the Baltimore suburb of Roland Park satisfies her fantasy of being in a time machine. It is always 1910 there. And that fact lends depth and color to her fiction. Besides Tyler, a host of native-born Marylanders keep up the memoralizing tradition. Among those writers appearing regularly in local publications are James H. Bready, John Dorsey,   Ben

Herman, Carleton Jones, Jacques Kelly, Franklin Mason, and Carl Pohlner, Jr. Two outstanding books also come in the same genre, Murray Kempton's *Part of Our Time* (1955) and Russell Baker's *Growing Up* (1983). Together they count among key books about the 1930s Depression, an era the authors lived through as boys in Baltimore.

Compared with all those indigenous littérateurs, Washington writers come up short, as they have throughout history. Washingtonians always contrast with the rest of the state. Not for them are the benefits or drawbacks of what Mencken called long habituation with Marylanders' ways and opinions. Instead, authors in the capital appear to be free of indigenous markings. That fits Scott Fitzgerald's observation that the District was a place where retired naval officers always were surprised to find themselves without a native town.[36]

Washington journalists, of course, never expect to find anything resembling a hometown there. Even so, that talented group has spun some fine prose out of politics and crisis. Edward R. Murrow, for instance, wrote moving accounts of World War II for radio broadcasting, some of the best published in *In Search of Light* (1967). John F. Kennedy, another sometime Washington writer, won a Pulitzer Prize for *Profiles In Courage* (1957).

National and international ties of other Washington Pulitzer winners are shown in memoirs by Henry Adams and Dean Acheson, and in histories by Bruce Catton and Daniel J. Boorstin. Two Nobel laureates in literature also alighted in Washington: Juan Ramon Jimenez (1956) taught at the University of Maryland, College Park, Prince Georges County (1948-1951). And the 1960 laureate, St. John Perse, accepted a post at the Library of Congress under Archibald MacLeish in 1941, remained in Washington for 17 years, and married there.

Who can say how much the capital gained by attracting such distinguished literary residents? We know that Sir Kenneth Clark once applied what he called the outworn word *civilized* to social life in Georgetown. Still, most Washingtonians held a view expressed by a 19th-century English prime minister — that learning, literature and other arts constituted absurd interruptions to the business of politics.

Luckily, authors in the surrounding Chesapeake-Potomac domain disagreed. They left a full shelf, partly because they valued literature and partly because they loved Baltimore or wherever they rooted themselves in Maryland. Many contributors to that full shelf appear in the pages of this literary history. They make a rich chronicle. Above them all, though, are two belonging not just to literary history: they belong to literature — Poe and Mencken. They alone would serve to answer the question asked at the beginning of this book: did literary Maryland change from watery waste to flowering orchard? The answer is an emphatic yes. Great literary harvests have bloomed from what in the 17th century was just a rim of shore, a shell of mountain, and a noble arm of the sea, Chesapeake Bay.

Being informed of that harvest, the faithful reader may now wish to read a few or many of the books discussed in these pages. In the words of our master Shakespeare, "You do yet taste some subtleties o' the isle."[37]

THE PERCY GRAEME TURNBULL MEMORIAL LECTURES

Compiled by Richard H. Macksey

1891 Edmund C. Stedman, New York, "The Nature and Elements of Poetry" (8 lectures)

1892 Richard C. Jebb, University of Cambridge, "The Growth and Influence of Classical Greek Poetry" (8 lectures)

1893 Robert Y. Tyrrell, Trinity College, Dublin, "The Growth and Influence of Latin Poetry" (8 lectures)

1894 Charles Eliot Norton, Harvard, "Dante" (6 lectures)

1896 George Adam Smith, Free Church College, Glasgow, "Hebrew Poetry" (8 lectures)

1897 Ferdinand Brunetière, editor *Revue des Deux Mondes,* "French Poetry" (9 lectures)

1898 Charles R. Lanman, Harvard, "Poetry in India" (4 lectures)

1900 Charles H. Herford, University College of Wales, "English Poetry" (8 lectures)

1901 Hamilton W. Mabie, associate editor, *The Outlook,* "Poetry in America" (7 lectures)

1902 Emil G. Hirsch, University of Chicago, "Medieval Jewish Poetry" (8 lectures)

1904 Angelo de Gubernatis, University of Rome, "Italian Poetry" (9 lectures)

1905 George E. Woodberry, Columbia University, "Poetic Forms of Life" (8 lectures)

1906 Henry Van Dyke, Princeton, "The Service of Poetry" (6 lectures)

1907 Eugene Kühnemann, University of Breslau, "German Poetry" (8 lectures)

1908 A. V. Williams Jackson, Columbia, "The Poetry of Persia" (7 lectures)

1909 R. Menèndez Pidal, University of Madrid, "Spanish Epic Poetry" (7 lectures)

1911 Maurice Francis Egan, United States Minister to Denmark, "Typical Christian Hymns" (8 lectures)

1912 Paul Shorey, University of Chicago, "The Greek Epigram and the Palatine Anthology" (6 lectures)

1914 George Lyman Kittredge, Harvard, "The Poetry of Chaucer" (6 lectures)

1915 Sir Walter Raleigh, Oxford, "Poetry and Criticism of the Romantic Revival" (6 lectures)

1916 Paul Elmer More, Princeton, "Poets of America" (7 lectures)

1917 Edward Capps, Princeton, "Formative Influences in Greek Tragedy" (6 lectures)

1921 Charles Mills Gayley, University of California, "Contemporary English Poetry" (6 lectures)

1922 Emile Legouis, University of Paris, "The Poetry of Edmund Spenser" (6 lectures)

1924 Walter de la Mare, poet, "Three English Poets and Some Elements of the Poet's Art" (6 lectures)

1927 Albert Feuillerat, University of Rennes, "Shakespeare and Poetry" (5 lectures)

1930 Edmond Faral, Collège de France, "The Poetic Cycle of King Arthur" (6 lectures)

1931 George William Russell ("AE"), Irish poet, journalist, and statesman, "Some Personalities of the Irish Literary Movement" and "A Poet and Artist Considers Dreams" (2 lectures)

1933 (February) T. S. Eliot, poet, critic, editor, *The Criterion,* "The 'Metaphysical' Poets" (3 lectures)
(October) R. W. Chambers, University College, London, "The Continuity of English Poetry, from the Beginnings to Tudor Times" (5 lectures)

1935 Lascelles Abercrombie, Bedford College, University of London, "The Art of Wordsworth" (5 lectures)

1936 H. J. C. Grierson, University of Edinburgh, "Milton as Prophet and Artist" (5 lectures)

1937 Pedro Salinas, University of Madrid, "The Attitude Toward Reality in Spanish Poetry" (5 lectures)

1938 Robert P. Tristram Coffin, Bowdoin College, "New Poetry of New England" (6 lectures)

1939 Archibald MacLeish, poet, "Poets Now" (6 lectures)

1940 W. H. Auden, poet, "Poetry and the Old World" and "America is Where You Find It" (2 lectures)

1941 Joseph Warren Beach, critic, poet, novelist, "A Romantic View of Poetry" (6 lectures)

1947 (January) George Frisbie Whicher, Amherst College, "Emily Dickinson. The Making of an American Poet" (6 lectures)
(November) Robert Frost, poet, "Precepts in Poetry" and "Extravagances of the Spirit" (2 lectures)

1948 Donald H. Stauffer, Princeton, "Studies in the Lyrics of William Butler Yeats" (3 lectures)

1949 C. J. Sisson, University of London, "Shakespeare's Approach to Shakespeare" (3 lectures)

1950 Marie-Jeanne Dury, Professor à la Sorbonne, "De Victor Hugo intime à Victor Hugo mythique" and "La Poésie Française sous L'Occupation" (2 lectures)

1950 Henri Peyre, Yale, "Baudelaire as Critic"

1951 E. M. W. Tillyard, Cambridge, "The English Renaissance: Fact or Fiction?"

1952 Frank Percy Wilson, Oxford, "Elizabethan Drama"

1954 Pierre Emmanuel, "Poetry, A Vocation"

1957 Richmond Lattimore, Bryn Mawr, "Studies in the Poetry of Greek Tragedy"

1958 Poetry Festival, concurrent with First Bollingen Poetry Festival: R. P. Blackmur, Princeton, "The Poetry of Edwin Muir"; Yvor Winters, Stanford, "Poetic Styles, Old and New"; Marianne Moore, poet, "The Poetry of Dame Edith Sitwell"; Mark Van Doren, Columbia, "The Poetry of Thomas Hardy"

1961 "The Moment of Poetry": John Holmes, "Surroundings and Illuminations"; May Sarton, "The School of Babylon"; Richard Eberhart, "Will and Psyche in Poetry"; Richard Wilbur, "Round About a Poem of Housman's"; Randall Jarrell, "Robert Frost's 'Home Burial' "

1963 Yves Bonnefoy, Paris, "La Poésie Française et L'Expérience de L'Être"

1965-66 Roy Harvey Pearce, California-San Diego, "Whitman and Our Hope for Poetry"; Arnold Stein, University of Washington, "George Herbert's Lyrics: The Art of Plainness"; Wolfgang Clemen, University of Munich, "The Spirits in Shelley's Poetry"; T. B. L. Webster, University College, London, "Euripides: Traditionalist and Innovator"; Jorge Guillén, Harvard, "A Portrait of Pedro Salinas"; John H. Finley, Jr., Harvard, "Pindar's Beginnings"; George E. Duckworth, Princeton, "The 'Old' and the 'New' in Vergil's *Aeneid*"; Viktor Pöschl, University of Hamburg, "Poetry and Philosophy in Horace"

1966 Michel Deguy, Paris, "Poésie et Connaissance"

1968 Margit Frenck and Antonio Alatorre, "Poesia y musica del renacimento español," lecture and recital

1969 Northrop Frye, University of Toronto, "Romantic Poetics and Myth"; Irving Singer, M.I.T., "The Loves of Dido and Aeneas: Variations on a Theme: Henry Purcell: *Dido and Aeneas;* Hector Berlioz: *Les Troyens à Carthage*"

1970 A. Alvarez, London, "The Savage God: Sylvia Plath and Contemporary Poetry"; David Ray, University of Iowa, "The Light-Bound Space of the Mind: Remarks on Contemporary Poetry and Painting"; Dámaso Alonso, Madrid, "Hijos de la ina: Children of Wrath"

1971 Paul Valéry Centennial: Jackson Mathews, Gérard Genette, James Lawler, Michel Deguy, Elizabeth Sewell, Jacques Derrida

1972 Kenneth Koch, poet, "Poetry and Children"

1973 Eric Segal, Yale, "The Birth of Comedy"; Nathan A. Scott, Jr., University of Chicago, "Hope, History, and Literature"; William Heyen, poet and critic, "On Richard Wilbur: An Experiment in Criticism"

1974 Conference on the Genealogy of the Epic: Gregory Nagy and Richard Macksey, Hopkins, chairmen, Joseph Russo, Haverford, Albert B. Lord, Harvard, David Bynam, Harvard, Jenny Clay, Haverford, Hugh S. MacKay, Jr., Harvard, Douglas Frame, Paris, *et al.*

1975 Josephine Jacobsen, Poetry Consultant to the Library of Congress, "The Landscapes of the Imagination: Elliott Coleman at Hopkins" (commentary on a program of films and videotapes)

Louis Zukofsky, poet, translator, and critic, "Poetry and Poetics: An Objectivist Perspective"; Jacques Derrida, École Normale Supérieure, "La Question de Style"

1976 Philippe Lacoue-Labarthe, Université de Strasbourg, "L'écho du sujet: sur la compulsion autobiographique"

1977 Edwin Honig, Brown, "The Poet's Other Voice: Spontaneous Exchanges on Translation"; Harold Bloom, Yale, "The Sublime Crossing and the Death of Love"; Yves Bonnefoy, Collège de France, "Que peut encore la poésie?"

Symposium on John Ruskin, published as *The Ruskin Polygon: Essays on the Imagination of John Ruskin:* John Dixon Hunt, London, George L. Hersey, Yale, Jeffrey Spear, Princeton, Marc A. Simpson, Yale, William Arrowsmith, Hopkins, Garry Wills, Hopkins, Richard Macksey, Hopkins

1978 Paul de Man, Yale, "Baudelaire, Benjamin, and Translation"; Jean Starobinski, Université de Genève, "An Interpretation of Rousseau and Baudelaire"

1979 Ronald Paulson, Yale, "Constable's Poetics: The Suppression of Literary Landscape"; Frank Doggett, Stevens Centennial Lecture, "Wallace Stevens: The Making of Poems"; Francis Fergusson, California-Berkeley, "The Bathos of Experience: The Poetics of Edmund Burke"

1980 James Nohrnberg, University of Virginia, "Epic Comparison and Comparative Epic in *Paradise Lost*"; Michel Deguy, Paris, "La poésie en question"

1981 Paul de Man, Yale, "The Poetics of the Sublime"

1982 Arnold Stein, University of Illinois, "The Voices of the Satirist: John Donne"

1983 John Malcolm Wallace, University of Chicago, "*Timon of Athens, De Beneficiis,* and the Three Graces"; J. Hillis Miller, Yale, "The Difficulties of Reading William Carlos Williams" (Centennial Lecture)

1984 Joseph N. Riddel, California-Los Angeles, "An American Poetics"

Notes

(N.B. Place of publication is New York unless noted.)

As Their Land and Air Is

1. Gertrude Stein, quoted in James Mellow's *Charmed Circle: Gertrude Stein and Company* (Praeger, 1974), 396.
2. Russell Baker, "The Biggest Baltimore Loser Of All Time," *New York Times Magazine,* October 21, 1973.
3. H. L. Mencken, letter to Theodore Dreiser, May 12, 1916, *Letters of H. L. Mencken,* selected and annotated by Guy J. Forgue (Knopf, 1961), 81.
4. Russell Baker, note to Shivers, July 6, 1982.
5. Josephine Jacobsen, note to Shivers, July 7, 1982.
6. Adrienne Rich, note to Shivers, July 2, 1982.
7. George Steiner recently noted that there is "no objective measure for magnitude in literature," and that "blue chips have risen and fallen wildly on the bourse of taste and reputation." (*New York Times Book Review,* September 30, 1984).
8. Fortunately for a rural state, the first bookmobile in the United States was sent out by the Washington County Free Library staff in 1901.
9. Washington's single industry, government, attracts white-collar transplants and transients. The number of lawyers there exceeds the combined population of Maryland's Aberdeen, Havre de Grace, and Westminster — 30,300 (1980).
10. Anne Tyler, note to Shivers, July 6, 1982.

I. Literary Fames and Domains

1. F. Scott Fitzgerald, Foreword to Don Swann's *Colonial Historic Houses of Maryland* (Baltimore: Etchcrafters Art Guild, 1939), i.
2. Gerald W. Johnson, unpublished manuscript given to Shivers in 1978.
3. H. L. Mencken, Baltimore *Evening Sun,* June 13, 1921, quoted in "Mencken's Baltimore," *Sun,* September 8, 1974, 39.
4. John Barth, "Some Reasons Why I Tell the Stories I Tell the Way I Tell Them Rather Than Some Other Sort of Stories Some Other Way," *New York Times Book Review,* May 9, 1982.
5. H. L. Mencken, *The Smart Set,* May 1913. Maryland writers' antagonism towards New England literati predates Poe, who called them Frogpondians. Gertrude Stein pointed out the sterility, austerity, and individuality of the New England literary tradition.

6. H. L. Mencken, *Evening Sun,* February 15, 1926, quoted in "Mencken's Baltimore," 27.

7. This contrast between Baltimore and Washington echoes the one pointed out once by Virginia Woolf between Central London and Hampstead. In that case the distance was only four miles; the American cities are still 40 miles apart, although moving closer. (The Maryland countryside separating the capital from Baltimore is filling with people.) But the cities still contrast.

8. H. L. Mencken, *Happy Days* (Knopf, 1940), 239.

9. John Dorsey, "The Many Lives of the Pratt's Richard Hart," Sunday *Sun,* July 4, 1976.

10. H. L. Mencken, *Evening Sun,* May 11, 1931, quoted in "Mencken's Baltimore," 6.

11. Russell Baker, "The Biggest Baltimore Loser Of All Time."

12. John Dorsey, "The Many Lives of the Pratt's Richard Hart."

13. Julia Randall, "Maryland," *The Puritan Carpenter* (Chapel Hill: U of North Carolina P, 1965).

14. Adrienne Rich, note to Shivers, July 2, 1982.

15. Thomas Cooper, *Some Information Respecting America* (London, 1795), 21.

16. Henry B. Adams, *The Education of Henry Adams* (Boston: Houghton Mifflin, 1918), 268.

17. In 1973 when Agnew resigned from the vice presidency of the United States for wrongdoing, Baker treated his plight as characteristic of Baltimoreans.

18. Gertrude Stein, *The Autobiography of Alice B. Toklas* (Literary Guild, 1933), 100.

19. Anne Tyler, note to Shivers, July 6, 1982.

II. Annapolis Wits and Baltimore Bards

1. Quoted from "an old Maryland song" by Henry Callester in a letter of August 1, 1743, and printed at the front of J. A. Leo Lemay's *Men of Letters in Colonial Maryland* (Knoxville: U of Tennessee P, 1972).

2. Quoted by Carl Bridenbaugh in *Myths and Realities: Societies of the Colonial South* (Atheneum, 1976), 45.

3. George Alsop, *A Character of the Province of Maryland, A Critical Edition,* Harry H. Kunesch, Jr., ed. (Ann Arbor: University Microfilms, 1970), 65.

4. Ibid., 93-94.

5. Ebenezer Cook, *The Sot-Weed Factor* (London, 1708).

6. Moses Coit Taylor, *A History of American Literature, 1607-1765* (1878).

7. Alexander Pope, *Dunciad* (London, 1728).

8. Richard Lewis, "Description of a Spring. A Journey from Patapsco to Annapolis, April 4, 1730," *Pennsylvania Gazette,* May 21, 1731.

9. Brasseya Johns Allen, *Pastorals, Elegies, Odes, Epistles and Other Poems*

(Abingdon [Harford County], Maryland: Daniel P. Ruff, 1806).

10. James Sterling, *Epistle to Dobbs, the Hon. Arthur Dobbs, Esq.; In Europe From a Clergyman in America* (Dublin, 1732).

11. Richard Bard's poem was originally published as "Judge Bard's Narrative,"; quotations from *History of Frederick County,* by Folger McKinsey and T. J. C. Williams (Frederick: L. R. Titsworth, 1910), 46-52.

12. Alexander Hamilton, "History of the Tuesday Club" (manuscript at Evergreen House, Johns Hopkins University Library), I:345-346.

13. Lemay, 230.

14. Jonas Green, "Memorandum for a Seine-Hauling, in Severn River, Near a Delightful Spring at the Foot of Constitution Hill," *Maryland Gazette,* August 22, 1754.

15. Harold Kellock, *Parson Weems of the Cherry-Tree* (Century, 1928), 87-88.

16. Ibid., 141.

17. Thomas Jefferson, *The Complete Jefferson,* Saul K. Padover, ed. (Duell, Sloan & Pearce, 1943), 552-553.

18. John B. Colvin, "To the Public and Patrons of the Baltimore Weekly Magazine" (Baltimore: William Pechin, June 10, 1801).

III. Rising Glories of City and Nation

1. William Wirt, letter to his daughter Catherine, November 24, 1822, quoted in John Pendleton Kennedy, *Memoirs of William Wirt* (Philadelphia, 1849), I:130.

2. John Pendleton Kennedy, quoted in Charles H. Bohner, *John Pendleton Kennedy, Gentleman from Baltimore* (Baltimore: Johns Hopkins P, 1961), 112.

3. William Wirt, *Sketches of the Life and Character of Patrick Henry* (Philadelphia, 1838), 141-142.

4. Wirt's letters to his family and friends have not been published, although John Pendleton Kennedy printed excerpts in his biography of Wirt. Most letters are in the Library of Congress and Maryland Historical Society.

5. One explanation for the irony comes from Samuel Eliot Morison, a modern historian with Baltimore connections: what is known as Baltimore Society grew between 1800 and 1850 around a nucleus of 150 old Maryland county families. Descendants retain county ties.

6. John Pendleton Kennedy, *Swallow Barn* (Philadelphia, 1832), 183.

7. Bohner, 219.

8. Frank G. Carpenter, · *Carp's Washington* (McGraw-Hill, 1960), 129. Bancroft published his 10-volume history in 1834 and a revised edition in 1876 and 1883-1885.

9. John E. Semmes, *John H. B. Latrobe and His Times, 1803-1891* (Baltimore: Norman, Remington, 1917), 103. When Latrobe produced his children's books, a number of other local publishers also took advantage

of a brisk market created by new ideas of child development. Children's books came from presses of Edward J. Coale, Bayley & Burns, and William Raine. Most books were pirated from English originals, many were hand-colored, and hardly any announced an author (so little glory accrued to an author of a children's book). As for those books' popularity, we have a sampler as evidence, one worked by a Maryland girl of 1800: "Patty Polk did this and she hated every stitch she did in it. She loves to read much more." (Sister Monica Kiefer, "Early American Childhood in the Middle Atlantic Area," *Pennsylvania Magazine,* January 1944, 88:13).

10. John Neal, *Wandering Recollections of a Somewhat Busy Life* (Boston, 1869), 1.

11. James Russell Lowell, *A Fable for Critics* (1848).

12. Thomas O. Mabbott and F. L. Pleadwell, eds., *The Life and Works of Edward Coote Pinkney* (Macmillan, 1926), 120.

13. Frederick Gutheim, *The Potomac* (Rinehart, 1949), 265. Originally recorded by Maurice Matteson from the singing of John Feldman of Eckhart.

14. An owner of a Baltimore circulating library, Joseph Robinson, pleaded with subscribers after the British attack on the town's Fort McHenry: "He is almost certain that no one would intentionally detain a book of his, but he knows, from experience, that many mislay his books with their own, by which means he is kept out of them. Amongst others missing (supposed to be mislaid during the late distressed situation of this city) are a number of odd volumes, which make several sets imperfect. . . ." (Supplement to the *Federal Gazette,* Baltimore, June 1, 1815).

15. The first publication of the anthem bore instructions to sing it to the tune of "Anacreon in Heaven," a drinking song from England. Key already had that tune in mind because he had used it a decade earlier for a patriotic song called "When the Warrior Returns," which had the line, "By the light of the star-spangled flag of our nation."

16. In 1851 Payne complained about the powers-that-be in Washington for not giving him a job so that he could buy a home of his own. Then he was sent as consul in Tunis, where he died, still homeless.

IV. Irrecoverably a Poet

1. Russell Baker, "The Biggest Baltimore Loser of All Time." When Baker was a Hopkins undergraduate, he was on a panel for the Poe Society of Baltimore (January 19, 1947) to discuss "What the Contemporary College Student Sees in Poe."

2. Edgar Allan Poe to Isaac Lea, May 1829, written in Baltimore, *The Letters of Edgar Allan Poe,* John Ward Ostrom, ed. (Gordian Press, 1966), I:18-19.

3. Ibid.

4. Poe's grandfather held the rank of major and served as quartermaster general, but Baltimoreans brevetted him "general," for services to Lafayette, who called him "my friendly and patriotic commissary" (Arthur Hobson

Quinn, *Edgar Allan Poe: A Critical Biography,* Appleton-Century-Crofts, 1941, 15.)

5. William Henry Poe, "For the North American," quoted in *Collected Works of Edgar Allan Poe,* Thomas O. Mabbott, ed. (Cambridge: Harvard U P, 1969), I:516-517.

6. Ostrom, *Poe Letters,* I:29.

7. John Neal, quoted in *Collected Works of Edgar Allan Poe,* Thomas O. Mabbott, ed., I:540.

8. Anonymous, *The Musiad,* Floyd Stovall, ed., in *Edgar Poe the Poet* (Charlottesville: U P of Virginia, 1969), 68-70.

9. John E. Semmes, *J. H. B. Latrobe* (Baltimore: Norman, Remington, 1917), 558.

10. Ibid.

11. Bohner, 194.

12. Thomas O. Mabbott, ed., *Merlin, Baltimore, 1827, Together with Recollections of Edgar A. Poe,* by Lambert A. Wilmer (Scholars' Facsimiles and Reprints, 1941), 31-37 passim.

13. Arthur Hobson Quinn and Richard H. Hart, *Edgar Allan Poe: Letters and Documents in the Enoch Pratt Free Library* (Scholars' Facsimiles & Reprints, 1941), 9.

14. Letter from R. D. Unger, M.D., to Chevalier Reynolds, October 29, 1899 (Manuscripts Department, University of Virginia Library). Note that Unger wrote 50 years after he fraternized with Poe, and, therefore, his portrait may well be colored by Poe's posthumous reputation.

15. Anonymous, "A Dissertation on Our Literary Taste," Commencement Address, St. Mary's College, July 14, 1846 (manuscript in St. Charles College, Baltimore).

16. Mabbott, *Merlin,* 27-28.

17. Mabbott, *Collected Poe,* I:569.

18. Quinn, 643.

19. William Hand Browne, *Building Poe Biography,* John Carl Miller, ed. (Baton Rouge: Louisiana State U P, 1977), 71.

20. John Banister Tabb, quoted in *Father Tabb, His Life and Works,* by Jennie Masters Tabb, (Boston: Stratford Co., 1921), 36.

21. Browne, *Building Poe Biography,* 86.

22. Walt Whitman, *Specimen Days, Complete Writings of Walt Whitman,* Richard Bucke et al., eds. (G. P. Putnam, 1902), IV:286.

23. Ibid., 22.

24. Ibid., 285.

25. Thornton Wilder, letter to Henri Peyre, January 23, 1952 (Thornton Wilder Collection, Beinecke Library, Yale).

26. Mary E. Phillips, *Edgar Allan Poe: The Man* (Philadelphia: John C. Winston, 1926), I:342-344.

27. Estimate from Mrs. Teresa Johanson of Kelmscott Books, Baltimore, December 1984.

V. Dawn of a Fine Literary Day?

1. Poe, letter to N. C. Brooks, September 4, 1838, Ostrom *Poe Letters* I:111.
2. Ralph Waldo Emerson, letter to his wife in Concord, Massachusetts, from Baltimore, January 18, 1843, *The Letters of Ralph Waldo Emerson,* Ralph L. Rusk, ed. (Columbia U P, 1939), III:118.
3. Frederick Douglass, *Life and Times of Frederick Douglass* (Collier, 1971, from revised edition of 1892), 84.
4. Emerson, letter to his wife.
5. Poe, letter to N. C. Brooks, September 4, 1838, Ostrom *Poe Letters* I:111.
6. Poe, letter to Joseph Evans Snodgrass, Ostrom *Poe Letters* I:201.
7. Constance Rourke, *The Roots of American Culture* (Harcourt, Brace, 1942), 56.
8. H. L. Mencken, "A Sound, Honest History of National Letters," *Evening Sun,* August 15, 1925.
9. Anthony Trollope, *North America* (Knopf, 1951), 294.
10. See Henry Adams, *Education of Henry Adams* (Boston: Houghton, Mifflin, 1918), 44.
11. Poe, letter to J. Beauchamp Jones, Ostrom *Poe Letters* I:114.
12. Poe, letter to Snodgrass, Ostrom *Poe Letters* I:175.
13. Edgar Allan Poe, *A Chapter on Autography By Edgar Allan Poe,* Don C. Seitz, ed. (Haskell House, 1974), 56.
14. Lambert Wilmer, *Atkinson's Saturday Evening Post,* Philadelphia, August 11, 1838.
15. John Hewitt, *Shadows on the Wall: Glimpses of the Past* (Baltimore: Turnbull, 1877), 22.
16. William W. Smithers, *The Life of John Lofland With Selections From His Works* (Philadelphia: Wallace M. Leonard, 1894), 108.
17. T. S. Arthur, *Ten Nights in a Bar-Room,* C. Hugh Holman, ed. (Odyssey, 1966), 53.
18. Poe, *Autography,* 41.
19. Poe, *Autography,* 60.
20. William Henry Carpenter, reported in a letter from W. H. Browne, December 3, 1875, in *Building Poe Biography,* 79.
21. Theophilus Conneau, *A Slaver's Log Book, or 20 Years' Residence in Africa* (Englewood Cliffs, N.J.: Prentice-Hall, 1976). For decades the original manuscript lay hidden in the back room of W. H. Lowdermilk's book shop in Washington, in a pink cardboard box tied with orange woven tape and laden with dust.
22. John Hewitt, *Shadows,* 22.
23. Ann Newport Royall, quoted in *Maryland: A New Guide to the Old Line State,* Edward C. Papenfuse et al., eds. (Baltimore: Johns Hopkins P, 1976), 443. Two years after publishing that comment about Washington County women, Royall was tried and convicted in a Washington, D.C., court on the charge of being a common scold. Royall's newspapers *Paul Pry*

(1831-1836) and the *Huntress* (until 1854) made her, people said, the grandma of muckrakers. A story, probably apocryphal, had it that she conducted the first presidential press conference by accosting President J. Q. Adams swimming nude in the Potomac. She sat on his clothes until he agreed to talk to her. Though he called her a virago-errant, he added that she wore enchanted armor.

24. Mary Barney, *National Magazine, or Lady's Emporium,* May 1831, II:21.

25. Bohner, 139.

26. Gustav de Beaumont, *Marie or Slavery in the United States* (Stanford, Cal.: Stanford U P, 1958), 126.

27. William Lloyd Garrison, "The Free Mind, A Prison Sonnet, pencilled impromptu on the wall of my prison-cell in Baltimore, Maryland, April, 1830" (*American Literary Autographs,* Herbert Cahoon et al., eds., Dover and the Pierpont Morgan Library, 1977), 29.

28. Hewitt, 21-22.

29. Garrison, *American Literary Autographs,* 29.

30. Frederick Douglass, *Life and Times,* 78.

31. Ibid., 442-443.

32. Frances Ellen Watkins Harper, "The Slave Market," *Poems on Miscellaneous Subjects* (Boston, 1854), 14-15.

33. Countee Cullen, "Incident (For Eric Walrond)," *On These I Stand* (Harper & Row, 1947).

34. Margaret Perry, *A Bio-Bibliography of Countee P. Cullen, 1903-1946* (Westport: Greenwood Publishing Corporation, 1971). Mencken was furious at the refusal to admit Cullen to the Emerson Hotel, Baltimore.

35. Harriet Beecher Stowe did not substantiate claims that Henson modeled for Uncle Tom, although several ghost-written autobiographies changed his story to fit the novel.

VI. From Drum Taps to Confederate Diaspora

1. Henry E. Shepherd, *The Representative Authors of Maryland* (Whitehall, 1911), 1.

2. James Ryder Randall, "Maryland, My Maryland," the official state song, and one of the few state anthems worth remembering. This one upsets some natives who want to substitute less subversive lyrics.

3. Lizette Woodworth Reese, *The Old House in the Country* (Farrar, Rinehart, 1936), 48.

4. Also connected with Massachusetts, the novelist Louisa May Alcott was in Washington during the Civil War. As a nurse to wounded soldiers in Georgetown, she gathered material for her first book, *Hospital Sketches* (1863). The war also entered her *Little Women* (1868).

5. Mrs. E. Trail Mathias, Sr., of Frederick recently confirmed reports that old Barbara Fritchie was sick in bed at the time and that the heroine was in fact another woman in town who disputed with Confederate soldiers.

Fritchie was well enough to show the flag to Yankee troops when they reoccupied the town.

6. Walt Whitman, *Correspondence, 1842-1867,* Edwin Haviland Miller, ed. (New York U P, 1961), I:83.

7. Sidney Lanier, quoted in *The Times of Melville and Whitman,* by Van Wyck Brooks (Dutton, 1947), 359.

8. Wiliam Hand Browne, letter to Paul Hayne in South Carolina, July 19, 1870, quoted in Jay B. Hubbell's *The South in American Literature* (Durham: Duke U P, 1954), 707.

9. Susan Dabney Smedes, *Memorials of a Southern Planter* (Knopf, 1965), 189-190. At the time the author wrote her memorial she lived with sisters, most of them Confederate widows, at 1307 John Street, Bolton Hill, Baltimore. Her picture of the South, though somewhat romanticized, went through a dozen editions. Prime Minister William E. Gladstone saw to it that the book was published in England because he felt that something less than justice had been done to the South. Smedes herself said that she wanted the young to learn of a good master.

10. Sidney Lanier, letter to Bayard Taylor, quoted in Lewis Mumford's *The Golden Day* (Boston: Beacon, 1957), 82.

11. Col. Richard Malcolm Johnston, *Autobiography* (Washington: Neale, 1900), 85-86. "I have gotten very, very much solace to the sadness of long separation [from Georgia]. . . in recalling people, places, and occasions — once familiar — and imagining their like in new inventions." (73).

12. David C. Holly, "Baltimore in American Literature," (typescript, Maryland Room, Enoch Pratt Free Library, a thesis for Johns Hopkins University, May 1933), 170.

13. Innes Randolph, recorded in 1910 by John A. Lomax and printed in Jay A. Hubbell's *The South in American Literature,* 479. Randolph practiced law in Baltimore after the Civil War. He also wrote editorials and book and other reviews for the *Baltimore American.* With Lanier, he joined the Wednesday Club, and took a leading role in the club's production of an operetta called "Bombastes Furioso."

VII. No Peace and Claret

1. Henry Adams, *Education of Henry Adams,* 298.

2. John Banister Tabb, "From a Photograph," *Camera Work: An Illustrated Quarterly Magazine Devoted to Photography,* January 1903.

3. Logan Pearsall Smith, *Unforgotten Years* (Boston: Little, Brown, 1936), 286. Smith had numerous Baltimore cousins, including M. Carey Thomas, president of Bryn Mawr College.

4. Anonymous, quoted in David C. Holly's "Baltimore in American Literature," typescript (Maryland Room, Enoch Pratt Free Library, 1933).

5. Anonymous, untitled typescript labeled "The American, Volume 1," pp. 39-40, Maryland Historical Society Library. Its date is about 1885.

6. Dr. Bertram M. Bernheim, *The Story of The Johns Hopkins: Four Great Doctors and the Medical School They Created* (Kingswood, Surrey, England: The World's Work [1913], 1949), 31-32. The chief planner and architect of the new Johns Hopkins Hospital, John Shaw Billings, influenced writers everywhere when he left Baltimore to design, build, and direct the New York Public Library in Bryant Park. Before that he had created the best medical library in the world, the Surgeon General's, and became famous for establishing its Index Catalogue.

7. Henry James, Jr., *The American Scene* (Bloomington: Indiana U P, 1968), 311.

8. Samuel Eliot Morison, *Nathaniel Holmes Morison* (Baltimore: The Peabody Institute, 1957), 16. George Peabody had to prod Baltimoreans to accept his benefaction, and so his cultural complex didn't open until after the Civil War. People in other places were quicker: Yale and Harvard accepted museums; Nashville, his teacher-training college; London, his housing for the poor.

9. Lizette Woodworth Reese, *Victorian Village* (Farrar & Rinehart, 1929), 164-165.

10. Henry Adams, *Education of Henry Adams,* 19.

11. Ibid., 268.

12. Frank G. Carpenter, *Carp's Washington* (McGraw-Hill, 1960), 134.

13. In the 1880s the wife of General Philip Sheridan wouldn't let her daughters read novels until they were 18, and even then proscripted George Eliot's as being morally corrupting (or at least confusing). To Mrs. Sheridan, Tolstoy's *Anna Karenina* was undoubtedly the most pernicious of all novels. She, of course, had read it.

14. Published in Philadelphia by the Old Franklin Publishing House, 1879, in both English and German.

15. George Alfred Townsend, *Katy of Catoctin* (Centreville, Md.: Tidewater, 1959), 9.

16. Called Harlackenden Hall, the mansion served as summer White House in 1914 and 1915 for Woodrow Wilson, another sometime Baltimorean-Washingtonian.

17. Sidney Lanier, letter from Camp Robin, near Asheville, North Carolina, July 5, 1881, *Centennial Editon of Sidney Lanier* (Baltimore: Johns Hopkins P, 1945), X:321.

VIII. The Perfect Lady and a Sort of Devil

1. H. L. Mencken, *Evening Sun,* May 11, 1931, quoted in "Mencken's Baltimore," *Sun,* September 8, 1974, 6.

2. H. L. Mencken, "Good Old Baltimore," *The Smart Set,* May 1913, reprinted in *On Mencken,* John Dorsey, ed. (Knopf, 1980), 66.

3. H. L. Mencken, "Autobiographical Notes," 1925, Mencken Collection, Pratt Library, typescript, 187.

4. H. L. Mencken, letter of August 1940, quoted by Carl Bode in a brochure for the Mencken Society (1981).

5. H. L. Mencken, *Happy Days* (Knopf, 1940), 55.

6. H. L. Mencken, letter to Thomas R. Smith, July 30, 1935, *More Mencken Letters,* Carl Bode, ed. (Knopf, 1977), 361.

7. H. L. Mencken, *Evening Sun,* May 11, 1931, quoted in "Mencken's Baltimore," 6.

8. Mencken, *Minority Report* (Knopf, 1956), 292-293.

9. Mencken, *Evening Sun,* February 15, 1926, quoted in "Mencken's Baltimore," 26.

10. Theodore Dreiser, quoted in Isaac Goldberg's *The Man Mencken: A Biographical and Critical Survey* (Simon & Schuster, 1925), 378-379.

11. Ernest Boyd, *H. L. Mencken* (Robert M. McBride, 1925), 40-41.

12. Charles Scruggs, *The Sage in Harlem: H. L. Mencken and the Black Writers of the 1920s* (Baltimore: Johns Hopkins P, 1984), 182.

13. Victor Weybright, *The Making of a Publisher: A Life in the 20th Century* (Reynal & Co., 1966), 89.

14. H. L. Mencken, *Evening Sun,* July 12, 1910, quoted in "Mencken's Baltimore," 25.

15. Mencken, *Newspaper Days* (Knopf, 1941), 278.

16. Mencken, *Heathen Days* (Knopf, 1943), 116.

17. Gerald W. Johnson, *America Watching* (Baltimore: Stemmer House, 1976), 20.

18. Mencken, *The Vintage Mencken,* Alistair Cooke, ed. (Knopf, 1955), 162.

19. Ibid., 173.

20. Ibid., 223.

21. Ibid., 232.

22. Mencken, *Happy Days,* 84-85.

23. Mencken, "Notes to *Newspaper Days,*" Mencken Collection, Pratt Library, typescript, 4.

24. Gerald W. Johnson, "Henry L. Mencken (1880-1956)," *Saturday Review,* February 11, 1956, 39:12-13.

25. Huntington Cairns, interview with Shivers, 1982.

26. Richard Wright, *Black Boy* (Harper, 1945), 217-218.

27. Gerald W. Johnson, "Henry L. Mencken (1880-1956)," 13.

28. Mencken, *Newspaper Days,* ix.

29. Mencken, "The Fireplace," typescript in Bradford F. Swan Collection, Beinecke Library, Yale, part of autobiographical notes written in 1941.

IX. "Shallow, Kittenish Fellows" and Other Traditionalists

1. Guy J. Forgue, ed., *Letters of H. L. Mencken* (Knopf, 1961), 271.

2. H. L. Mencken, *A Mencken Chrestomathy* (Knopf, 1949), 497.

3. Hamilton Owens, *Baltimore on the Chesapeake* (Garden City: Doubleday, Doran, 1941), 1-2.

4. Charles Angoff, *H. L. Mencken; A Portrait from Memory* (T. Yoselof, 1956), 106.

5. Christopher Morley, *Kitty Foyle* (Grosset & Dunlap, 1939), quoted on the jacket.

6. Christopher Morley, *Thorofare* (Harcourt, Brace, 1942), 386.

7. Ibid., 369.

8. Memorabilia of Hamilton Chace Davis.

9. Richard H. Hart, "Poetry in Maryland," lecture, December 15, 1942 (Maryland Room, Pratt Library).

10. Folger McKinsey and T. J. C. Williams, *History of Frederick County* (Frederick: L. R. Titsworth & Co., 1910), 613.

11. Belle Caples Morris, *Songs of the Sassafras* (Athens, Georgia: U of Georgia P, 1940).

12. Hart, "Poetry in Maryland."

13. Elinor Glenn Wallis, *Natural World* (Prairie City, Illinois: James A. Decker, 1940), 14.

14. Josephine Jacobsen, "Arrival of My Cousin," *The Animal Inside* (Athens, Ohio: Ohio U P, 1953).

15. Julia Randall, "Maryland," *The Puritan Carpenter* (Chapel Hill: U of North Carolina P, 1965).

16. Baltimore *Sun,* May 6, 1941. As for literary culture, Baltimore private schools alone prepared a number of prominent contemporary authors, including Richard Hart, Walter Lord, William R. Mueller, Page Smith, and Warren H. Smith.

17. Laura Lee Davidson, *Winter of Content* (Abingdon, 1922), 1.

18. Edith Hamilton, *The Greek Way* (Norton, 1942), 16-17.

19. Cairns, interview with Shivers, 1982.

20. Doris Fielding Reid, *Edith Hamilton, An Intimate Portrait* (Norton, 1967), 38.

21. Lizette Woodworth Reese, "The White Fury of the Spring," *White April* (Holt, Rinehart & Winston, 1930). Another poem about Maryland springs, "Wild Peaches," by Elinor Wylie, was much more often anthologized than this one by Reese, perhaps because of its idyllic view of the Eastern Shore, or because Wylie was more glamorous and also well known in literary New York.

22. Hart, "Poetry in Maryland."

23. Louise Bogan, *American Poetry Achievement* (Chicago: Henry Regnery, 1954), 25.

24. Lizette Woodworth Reese, *A Victorian Village* (Farrar & Rinehart, 1929), 92.

25. Reese, *York Road* (Farrar & Rinehart, 1933), 47-48.

26. Appropriately, her own words are inscribed on her tombstone in St. John's Cemetery, Huntington, Baltimore: "The long day sped / A roof; a bed; / No years; / No tears."

27. Lizette Woodworth Reese, "Old Eli," *The Old House In the Country,* 45.

28. Sally Bruce Kinsolving, "The Poetry Society of Maryland," typescript, (Maryland Room, Enoch Pratt Free Library), 7.

29. Hart, "Poetry in Maryland."

30. William Force Stead, "Southern Idyll," *Festival in Tuscany and Other Poems* (London: Cobden-Sanderson, 1927), 29.

31. Facts from manuscript essays and letters in the Library of Congress and the James Marshall and Marie-Louise Osborn Collection, Beinecke Library, Yale.

32. William Force Stead, "I Closed My Eyes To-day and Saw," *Oxford Book of Modern Verse, 1892-1935,* William Butler Yeats, ed. (Oxford: Oxford U P, 1936), 234-235.

33. Stead, Osborn Collection, Yale.

34. Stead, ed., *Rejoice in the Lamb,* excerpted in *The Heath Guide to Poetry,* edited by Baltimore poets David Bergman and Daniel Mark Epstein (Heath, 1983), 57.

35. Ibid. Smart's contemporary critic Dr. Samuel Johnson felt that Smart's madness didn't hurt anybody, that he should not be put away, and that Smart's habit of falling on his knees in the street and praying was less mad than what most people did, which was not to pray at all.

36. Shivers collection.

37. Hulbert Footner, *Charles' Gift* (Harper & Brothers, 1939), 75.

38. Letitia Stockett, *Baltimore: A Not Too Serious History* (Baltimore: Grace Gore Norman, 1936), 117-118.

X. Square Houses, Circle Lives

1. Christina Stead, *The Man Who Loved Children* (Holt, Rinehart & Winston, 1965), 314. Some critics hold that this novel by an Australian who once lived in Maryland is not only a work of art, but also a fine portrait of the Chesapeake-Potomac domain.

2. Upton Sinclair, *American Outpost* (Columbia, Mo.: U of Missouri P, 1932), 196.

3. William F. Nolan, *Hammett: A Life at the Edge* (Congdon & Weed, 1983), 100.

4. Gerald W. Johnson, "Upton Sinclair: Not to be Dismissed," *Sun,* December 3, 1968.

5. Whistler's older brother married the daughter of Thomas Winans, a Baltimorean who, with his father, Ross, made millions manufacturing locomotives and building a railroad between Moscow and St. Petersburg for the Czar. Whistler worked for a time in Baltimore.

6. Upton Sinclair, *Autobiography* (Harcourt, Brace & World, 1962), 12.

7. Upton Sinclair, quoted in Leon Harris's *Upton Sinclair, American Rebel* (Thomas Y. Crowell, 1975), 10.

8. Upton Sinclair, quoted in Alfred Kazin's *On Native Grounds* (Reynal & Hitchcock, 1942), 118.

9. H. L. Mencken, *The Young Mencken,* ed. by Carl Bode (Dial, 1973), 102.

10. James M. Cain, letter inside Mencken's copy of Cain's *Our Government* (Mencken Room, Pratt Library).

11. Dashiell Hammett, quoted in Richard Layman's *Shadow Man: The Life of Dashiell Hammett* (Harcourt Brace Jovanovich, 1981), 3.

12. Dashiell Hammett, "The Assistant Murderer," in *A Man Called Spade* (Dell, n.d.), 130-131.

13. Allen B. Crider, "The Private Eye Hero: A Study of the Novels of Dashiell Hammett, Raymond Chandler, and Ross MacDonald," Dissertation Abstracts International, 34:722A-23A.

14. Jacket blurb on Hammett's *The Glass Key* (Grosset & Dunlap, 1942(?).

15. Pluhar proved to be a first-rate sleuth when he undertook solving the puzzle of what facts underlay *The Glass Key.* He is continuing his search and expects to publish a full report.

16. *Baltimore American,* "Downtown Slaying of 'Jimmy' Mahon Celebrated Case," January 27, 1952.

17. Did Raymond Chandler make a gesture to Hammett when his *Farewell My Lovely* (1940) ended with a Baltimore detective trusting a woman and ending up dead with her bullets in him?

18. Cain willed his body to a Baltimore hospital. He also instructed his friends to put on a happy party instead of a funeral. The party was everything he could have wished, according to guests who attended it at the University of Maryland, College Park, near his home.

XI. Gilded Butterflies with Excellent Credentials

1. F. Scott Fitzgerald, "Lamp In A Window," *F. Scott Fitzgerald In His Own Time: A Miscellany,* Matthew J. Bruccoli and Jackson R. Bryer, eds. (Kent, Ohio: Kent State U P, 1971), 73.

2. F. Scott Fitzgerald, letter of September 23, 1935, *The Letters of F. Scott Fitzgerald,* Andrew Turnbull, ed. (Scribner, 1963), 531.

3. Matthew J. Bruccoli, *Some Sort of Epic Grandeur: The Life of F. Scott Fitzgerald* (Harcourt Brace & Jovanovich, 1981), 495.

4. F. Scott Fitzgerald, *Letters to His Daughter,* Andrew Turnbull, ed. (Scribner, 1965), 57.

5. F. Scott Fitzgerald, *Letters,* October 4, 1934, 517, and the later one of September 23, 1935, 531.

6. Andrew Turnbull, *Scott Fitzgerald* (Scribner, 1962), 211.

7. Gerald W. Johnson, *North Carolina Authors* (Chapel Hill, 1952), 70.

8. Interview with Shivers, 1954.

9. Interview with Shivers, 1982 and Azrael's "Scott Fitzgerald, 1934," *Mount Royal Review,* February 28, 1966.

10. Charles Angoff, *H. L. Mencken,* 181.

11. Turnbull, *Scott Fitzgerald,* 207.

12. Unpublished letter to Isaac Benesch.

13. F. Scott Fitzgerald, *The Crack-Up,* Edmund Wilson, ed. (New Directions, 1945), "Note-Books," passim, 91-236.

14. F. Scott Fitzgerald, *Tender Is The Night* (Scribner, 1951), 267.

15. Hervey Allen is said to have bought an old farm on Maryland's Eastern Shore with his royalties. There he continued writing popular historical novels. Earlier he wrote *Israfel: The Life and Times of Edgar Allan Poe* (1926).

16. Interview with Shivers, 1982. Another Baltimorean, Huntington Cairns, recalled what an unhappy man Fitzgerald was then: "I was with him the night his copies of *Tender Is The Night* came. He opened them and inscribed one to me. It was a kind thing for him to do. But he was a kind and gentle person." (Interview with Shivers, 1982.)

17. F. Scott Fitzgerald, *The Crack-Up,* 34.

18. Ibid., 66-67.

19. Interview with Shivers, 1982.

20. F. Scott Fitzgerald, letter to Mr. and Mrs. Eben Finney, Spring 1937, *The Letters of F. Scott Fitzgerald,* 548.

XII. Gertrude Stein "And Other Such Fakes" and Forward-Movers

1. Gertrude Stein, *Everybody's Autobiography* (Random House, 1937), 251.

2. Ibid., 148.

3. H. L. Mencken, "Autobiographical Notes," 1925, Mencken Collection, Pratt Library, typescript, 112.

4. Huntington Cairns, interview with Shivers, 1982.

5. Stein, *Everybody's Autobiography,* 230-231. Katherine Anne Porter noted Stein's unusual animation when writing of early family life — "stories. . .as pretty and innocent as lizards running over tombstones on a hot day in Maryland." (*The Days Before,* Harcourt, Brace, 1952), 49.

6. Stein, *The Autobiography of Alice B. Toklas* (Literary Guild, 1933), 101.

7. Richard Wright, quoted in *Selected Writings of Gertrude Stein,* Carl Van Vechten, ed. (Modern Library, 1962), 338.

8. Stein, *Toklas,* 41.

9. Leon Katz, "Matisse, Picasso and Gertrude Stein," *Four Americans In Paris* (Museum of Modern Art, 1970), 60.

10. Florence Hochschild Austrian, interview with Lottchen G. Shivers, 1974.

11. F. Scott Fitzgerald, letter of April 28, 1932, Hotel Rennert, Baltimore, ms., Beinecke Library, Yale.

12. Stein, *Toklas,* 52. Through purchases by Etta and Claribel Cone of Eutaw Place, Baltimore, a fine part of Stein's art collection ended in the Baltimore Museum of Art. It almost seems that Stein had planned a memorial in her town.

13. John Dos Passos, *Midcentury* (Boston: Houghton Mifflin, 1961), 109-110.

14. Julien Green, *Diary, 1928-1957,* selected by Kurt Wolff (Harcourt, Brace & World, 1964), 99.

15. Morris Bishop, quoted in an American calendar, ca. 1978.

16. Anecdote told by Professor Raymond D. Havens, Wordsworth scholar at Johns Hopkins University, 1952.

17. Ogden Nash, poems published only in *Keynotes,* Village of Cross Keys, February 1970.

18. Archibald MacLeish, "Introduction" to Ogden Nash's *I Wouldn't Have Missed It,* ed. by Linell Smith and Isabel Eberstadt (Boston: Little, Brown, 1975), ix.

19. Constance McLaughlin Green, *Washington, Capital City* (Princeton: Princeton U P, 1963), 418.

20. Francis Coleman Rosenberger, *Washington and the Poets* (Charlottesville: U P of Virginia, 1977).

21. MacLeish, "A Poet Speaks from the Visitors' Gallery," *Washington and the Poets,* 1-2.

22. Huntington Cairns, interview with Shivers, 1982.

23. Jean Toomer, *Cane* (Boni and Liveright, 1923), 71.

24. Joan Givner, *Katherine Anne Porter, A Life* (Simon & Schuster, 1982), 493.

25. Ibid.

26. Carl Schoettler, "Katherine Anne Porter Reigns For Students," *Sun,* April 15, 1974.

27. Father Joseph Gallagher, "Katherine Anne Porter on Her 89th Birthday," *Evening Sun,* September 30, 1980.

28. Jacket of Givner's biography. Porter's glamorous female image certainly contrasted with that of the scientist Rachel Carson, her neighbor in Silver Spring, whose *Silent Spring* changed people's way of perceiving their environment. And Porter didn't aid future writers as did Sophie Kerr, editor and writer of fiction from Caroline County. Kerr bequeathed money for an annual award to a promising writer among seniors at Washington College. The prize is the largest undergraduate prize in the nation.

29. Gallagher, "Katherine Anne Porter on Her 89th Birthday."

30. Henry B. Shepherd, "Introduction," *Representative Authors of Maryland,* 9.

31. Walter Lord, letter to Shivers, July 21, 1982.

32. Holmes Alexander, letter to Shivers, July 2, 1982.

33. Gerald W. Johnson, *North Carolina Authors,* 70.

34. Lenora Heilig Nast et al., eds., *Baltimore: A Living Renaissance* (Baltimore: Baltimore Historical Society, 1982), 211.

35. Andrei Codrescu, letter to Shivers, July 5, 1982.

36. F. Scott Fitzgerald, *The Crack-Up,* 116.

37. Shakespeare, *The Tempest,* V:1:124. Appropriately, the great bard ends a literary history of a people who had the taste long ago to name Shakespeare Street in Fells Point. It still is lined with old, placid rowhouses.

Further Reading
A Selected Bibliography

After perusing the writers' canon, readers may like to look into books about the authors. Suggestions are given here by chapter. As in the notes, New York is the place of publication if no place is given.

No one has introduced a list such as this one better than Evelyn Waugh who said that it was not intended as "a display of industry nor as a guarantee of good faith" (*Edmund Campion,* 1935). I can only echo him in commending my list "to any reader who wishes to amplify details that I have stated too briefly, too vaguely, or too allusively."

Ball, Donald L. *Eastern Shore of Maryland Literature.* Lewis Historical Publishing Co., 1950.

Ferguson, Robert A. *Law and Letters in American Culture.* Cambridge: Harvard U P, 1984.

Hallstead, William F., "Literary Maryland," *Maryland Magazine,* 7 (June 1974), 15-20.

Holly, David C., "Baltimore in American Literature." Typescript, 1933, Maryland Room, Enoch Pratt Free Library, Baltimore.

Perine, George C., ed. *The Poets and Verse-Writers of Maryland.* Cincinnati: Editor Publishing Co., 1898.

Raley, Loker, ed. *300 Years: The Poets and Poetry of Maryland.* Henry Harrison, 1937.

Shepherd, Henry E., *The Representative Authors of Maryland.* Whitehall, 1911.

Steiner, Bernard, "Maryland Authors Who Have Lived and Worked in Maryland." Typescript, 1908 (?). Maryland Room, Enoch Pratt Free Library.

I.

Green, Constance McLaughlin. *Washington, Village and Capital.* Princeton: Princeton U P, 1962.

— *Washington, Capital City.* Princeton: Princeton U P, 1963

Harbaugh, T. C. *Middletown Valley in Song and Story.* Frederick, Md., 1910.

Jopp, Harold D. and Ingersoll, R. H., eds. *Shoremen: An Anthology of Eastern Shore Prose and Verse.* Cambridge, Md.: Tidewater Publishers, 1974.

Miller, Perry. *The Life of the Mind in America from the Revolution to the Civil War.* Harcourt, Brace & World, 1965.

Myerson, Joel, ed. *American Writers in New York and the South.* Detroit: Gale Research, 1979.

Rourke, Constance. *American Humor: A Study of the National Character.* Harcourt, Brace, 1931.

Thurston, Walter Cundiff, ed. *The Eastern Shore of Maryland in Song and Story: A Tribute from its Loyal Sons and Daughters to a Pleasant Peninsula.* Federalsburg, Md.: Stowell Print Co., 1938.

Turner, Frederick Jackson. *The Significance of Sections in American History.* Gloucester, Mass.: P. Smith, 1959.

II.

Bridenbaugh, Carl. *Myths and Realities: Societies of the Colonial South.* Atheneum, 1976.

Davis, Richard Beale. "The Intellectual Golden Age in Colonial Chesapeake Bay Country." *Virginia Magazine of History and Biography,* 78, no. 2 (April 1970), 131-143.

Kellock, Harold. *Parson Weems of the Cherry-Tree.* Century, 1928.

Lemay, J. A. Leo. *Men of Letters in Colonial Maryland.* Knoxville: U of Tennessee P, 1972.

Mayo, Bernard. *Myths and Men: Patrick Henry, George Washington and Thomas Jefferson.* Harper Torchbook, 1963.

Silver, Rollo G. *The Baltimore Book Trade, 1800-1825.* New York Public Library, 1953.

Smith, Mrs. Samuel Harrison. *The First Forty Years of Washington Society.* Ed. by Gaillard Hunt. Scribner, 1906.

Wroth, Lawrence C. *Parson Mason Weems, A Biographical and Critical Study.* Baltimore: Echelberger, 1911.

III.

Bohner, Charles H. *John Pendleton Kennedy: Gentleman from Baltimore.* Baltimore: Johns Hopkins P, 1961.

Brooks, Van Wyck. *The Age of Washington Irving.* E. P. Dutton, 1944.

Charvat, William. *Literary Publishing, 1790-1850.* Philadelphia: U of Pennsylvania P, 1959.

Davis, David Brion. *Antebellum American Culture: An Interpretive Anthology.* Lexington, Mass.: Heath, 1979.

Davis, Richard Beale. *Literature and Society in Early Virginia, 1608-1840.* Baton Rouge: Louisiana State U P, 1973.

—"Poe and William Wirt." *American Literature,* 16 (November 1944), 212-220.

Filby, P. W., and Howard, Edward G., comps. *Star-Spangled Books.* Baltimore: Maryland Historical Society, 1972.

Hubbell, Jay B. *Southern Life in Fiction.* Athens, Ga.: U of Georgia P, 1960.

Kennedy, John Pendleton. *Memoirs of the Life of William Wirt.* Philadelphia, 1849.

Ridgely, Joseph V. *John Pendleton Kennedy.* Twayne, 1966.

Semmes, John E. *John H. B. Latrobe and His Times.* Baltimore: Norman, Remington, 1917.

Shivers, Margaret Littlehales. "Whip Syllabub Genius: A Look at William Wirt Through Unpublished Letters." Typescript, May 1984, Maryland Historical Society and Yale University History Department.

Sullivan, Larry. "The Reading Habits of Baltimore Bourgeoisie: A Cross Cultural Analysis." *Journal of Library History,* 16 (Summer 1981), 227-240.

Taylor, William R. *Cavalier and Yankee: The Old South and American National Character.* Harper & Row, 1969.

Uhler, John Earle. "The Delphian Club: A Contribution to the Literary History of Baltimore in the Early Nineteenth Century." *Maryland Historical Magazine,* XX, no. 4 (December 1925), 305-346.

IV.

Allen, Hervey. *Israfel: The Life and Times of Edgar Allan Poe.* Simon & Schuster, 1926.

Mabbott, Thomas O., ed. *Poe's Brother: The Poems of William Henry Leonard Poe, etc.* George H. Doran, 1926.

Mabbott, Thomas O., ed. *Merlin, Baltimore, 1827, Together With Recollections of Edgar A. Poe, by Lambert A. Wilmer.* Scholars' Facsimiles & Reprints, 1941.

Mabbott, Thomas O., ed., "Annals," in *Collected Works of Edgar Allan Poe, Volume I, Poems.* Cambridge: Harvard U P, 1969.

Ostrom, John Ward, ed. *The Letters of Edgar Allan Poe.* Gordian Press, 1966.

Phillips, Mary E., *Edgar Allan Poe: The Man.* Philadelphia: John C. Winston, 1926.

Quinn, Arthur Hobson. *Edgar Allan Poe: A Critical Biography.* Appleton-Century-Crofts, 1941.

Stovall, Floyd, ed. *Edgar Poe the Poet: Essays New and Old on the Man and His Work.* Charlottesville: U P of Virginia, 1969.

V.

Brooks, Van Wyck. *The Times of Melville and Whitman.* E. P. Dutton, 1947.

French, John C. "Poe's Literary Baltimore." *Maryland Historical Magazine,* XXXII, no. 2 (June 1937): 101-112.

Garrison, William Lloyd. *The Letters of William Lloyd Garrison.* Ed. by Walter M. Merrill. Cambridge: Harvard U P, 1971-1973.

Hemenway, Robert. *Zora Neale Hurston: A Literary Biography.* Urbana: U of Illinois P, 1977.

Hewitt, John. *Shadows on the Wall.* Baltimore: Turnbull Brothers, 1877.

Hill, Patricia Liggins. " 'Let Me Make the Songs for the People': A Study of Frances Watkins Harper's Poetry." *Black American Literature Forum,* 15, No. 2 (Summer, 1981): 60-65.

Huggins, Nathan Irvin. *Slave and Citizen: The Life of Frederick Douglass.* Ed. by Oscar Hamlin. Boston: Little, Brown, 1980.

Preston, Dickson J. *Young Frederick Douglass: The Maryland Years.* Baltimore: Johns Hopkins P, 1980.

Seitz, Don C., ed. *A Chapter of Autography by Edgar Allan Poe.* Haskell House, 1974.

Smithers, William W. *The Life of John Lofland, With Selections From His Works.* Philadelphia: Wallace M. Leonard, 1894.

VI.

Canby, Courtlandt, ed. *Lincoln and the Civil War, A Profile and a History.* George Braziller, 1960.

Coyle, William, ed. *The Poet and the President: Whitman's Lincoln Poems.* Odyssey, 1962.

Edward, Herbert J. and Hankins, John E. *Lincoln the Writer: The Development of His Style.* Orono, Me.: U of Maine at Orono P, 1962.

Harbert, Earl N., ed. *Critical Essays on Henry Adams.* Boston: G. K. Hale, 1981.

Hubbell, Jay B. *The South in American Literature: 1607-1900.* Durham: Duke U P, 1954.

Johnston, Col. Richard Malcolm. *Autobiography.* Washington: Neale, 1900.

Kaplan, Justin. *Walt Whitman: A Life.* Simon & Schuster, 1980.

VIII.

Bode, Carl. *Mencken.* Carbondale, Ill.: Southern Illinois U P, 1969.

Bode, Carl, ed. *New Letters of H. L. Mencken.* Knopf, 1977.

Dorsey, John, ed. *On Mencken.* Knopf, 1980.

Forgue, Guy J., ed. *Letters of H. L. Mencken.* Knopf, 1961.

Manchester, William. *Disturber of the Peace: The Life of H. L. Mencken.* Harper, 1951.

Mayfield, Sara. *The Constant Circle: H. L. Mencken and His Friends.* Delacorte Press, 1968.

Nolte, William H. *H. L. Mencken: Literary Critic.* Middletown, Conn.: Wesleyan U P, 1966.

Stenerson, Douglas C. *H. L. Mencken: Iconoclast from Baltimore.* Chicago: U of Chicago P, 1971.

IX.

Beirne, Francis. *The Amiable Baltimoreans.* E. P. Dutton, 1951. (Reprinted Johns Hopkins P, 1984.)

Hahn, George. "The Hold of Victorian Baltimore on Lizette Woodworth Reese and H. L. Mencken." *Maryland Historian,* 11 (1980), 29-38.

Noble, Edward and Tubbs, Edward, eds. *Maryland in Prose and Poetry.* Baltimore: Lehmer Printing Co., 1909.

Oakley, Helen M. *Three Hours for Lunch: The Life and Times of Christopher Morley.* Searingtown, Pa.: Watermill Publishers, 1976.

Reid, Doris Fielding. *Edith Hamilton: An Intimate Portrait.* W. W. Norton, 1967.

Wecter, Dixon. *The Saga of American Society: A Record of Social Aspiration, 1607-1937.* Scribner, 1937.

X.

Harris, Leon. *Upton Sinclair: American Rebel.* Thomas Y. Crowell, 1975.

Hellman, Lillian. *An Unfinished Woman—A Memoir.* Boston: Little, Brown, 1969.

Hoopes, Roy. *Cain.* Holt, Rinehart and Winston, 1982.

Johnson, Diane. *Dashiell Hammett: A Life.* Random House, 1983.

Johnson, Gerald W. et al. *The Sunpapers of Baltimore.* Knopf, 1937.

Layman, Richard. *Shadow Man: The Life of Dashiell Hammett.* Harcourt Brace Jovanovich, 1981.

Madden, David, ed. *Tough Guy Writers of the Thirties.* Carbondale: Southern Illinois U P, 1968.

Nolan, William F. *Hammett: A Life at the Edge.* Congdon & Weed, 1983.

Sinclair, Upton. *The Autobiography of Upton Sinclair.* Harcourt, Brace & World, 1962.

—*My Lifetime in Letters.* Columbia, Mo.: U of Missouri P, 1960.

XI.

Bruccoli, Matthew. *Some Sort of Epic Grandeur: The Life of F. Scott Fitzgerald.* Harcourt Brace Jovanovich, 1981.

—*The Composition of* Tender Is the Night*: A Study of the Manuscripts.* U of Pittsburgh P, 1963.

Bruccoli, Matthew and Duggan, Margaret D., eds. *Correspondence of F. Scott Fitzgerald.* Random House, 1980.

Bruccoli, Matthew, Scottie Fitzgerald Smith, and Joan P. Kerr, eds. *The Romantic Egoists.* Scribner, 1974.

Mellow, James R. *Invented Lives: F. Scott and Zelda Fitzgerald.* Boston: Houghton Mifflin 1984.

Milford, Nancy. *Zelda.* Harper & Row, 1970.

Mizener, Arthur. *The Far Side of Paradise: A Biography of F. Scott Fitzgerald.* Boston: Houghton Mifflin, 1965.

Turnbull, Andrew. *Scott Fitzgerald.* Scribner, 1962.

Turnbull, Andrew, ed. *The Letters of F. Scott Fitzgerald.* Scribner, 1963.

Wilson, Edmund. *The Shores of Light.* Farrar, Straus & Young, 1952.

XII.

Brinnin, John Malcolm. *The Third Rose: Gertrude Stein and Her World.* Boston: Little Brown, 1959.

Brooks, Paul. *The House of Life: Rachel Carson at Work.* Boston: Houghton Mifflin, 1972.

Crandell, George W. " 'A Good Bad Poet': The Ogden Nash Collection." *Library Chronicle* of the University of Texas at Austin. New Series #16. Austin: Harry Ransom Humanities Research Center, 1981.

Four Americans in Paris: The Collections of Gertrude Stein and Her Family. The Museum of Modern Art, 1970.

Givner, Joan. *Katherine Anne Porter, A Life.* Simon & Schuster, 1982.

Green, Julien. *Diary, 1928-1957.* Selected by Kurt Wolff and translated by Anne Green. Harcourt, Brace & World, 1964.

Lott, Clarinda Harriss. "Poetry and Literature," *Baltimore: A Living Renaissance.* Ed. by Lenora Heilig Nast et al. Baltimore: Baltimore Historical Society, 1982.

Ludington, Townsend. *John Dos Passos: A Twentieth Century Odyssey.* E. P. Dutton, 1980.

Mellow, James R. *Charmed Circle: Gertrude Stein and Company.* Praeger, 1974.

Pollack, Barbara. *The Collectors: Dr. Claribel and Miss Etta Cone.* Bobbs-Merrill, 1962.

Index

Credits

Illustrations:

Enoch Pratt Free Library, Baltimore: 41 top, 59 top, 59 bottom, 61 left, 86 left, 88 left, 110 top, 111 right, 129 right, 174 top, 200 left, 200 right, 250 left, 253 left

National Portrait Gallery, Smithsonian Institution, Washington, D.C.: 2 center left, 42 right (gift of Mr. and Mrs. Paul Mellon), 60 right, 72, 100, 109 right, 129 left, 142, 150 left, 266, 282 left

Natalie W. Shivers: 2 top, 62 right, 83 left, 88 right, 149 top, 173 left, 173 right, 198, 199 bottom, 251 left

Private Collection: 238, 249, 250 right, 251 right, 252 top, 252 bottom, 253 right, 254 left

George Wend: 42 left, 87, 149 bottom, 176 top, 224 left, 279 left

Johns Hopkins University: 2 center right, 86 right, 131 top, 151 top (all The Ferdinand Hamburger, Jr. Archives), 34 (Evergreen), 62 left (Peabody Library)

Author's Collection: 197 top, 212, 224 right, 225 right, 281 top

The Edward L. Bafford Photography Collection, Albin O. Kuhn Library and Gallery, University of Maryland Baltimore County: 162, 174 bottom, 175 top, 176 bottom, 197 bottom

Library of Congress: 43, 110 bottom, 130, 151 bottom

Baltimore *Sunpapers:* 223 left, 249, 282

Maryland Historical Society: 52, 131 bottom, 152

The Peale Museum, Baltimore: 84–85 (Hambleton Collection), 199 top

William Amelia: 175 bottom

Baltimore Museum of Art: 280

Commission for Historical and Architectural Preservation (Baltimore): 83 right

Eileen Darby, Graphic House: 2 bottom right

Drawing by John Briggs Potter, printed in *Education By Uncles,* by Abigail Adams Homans, Boston: Houghton Mifflin Co., 1966: 150 right

Frontispiece, Shepherd's *Representative Authors of Maryland,* 1911: 2 bottom left

Father Joseph Gallagher: 281 bottom

Linda Lapides: 61 right

John B. Maclay III: 18

John Maclay: 279 right

Maryland Historical Trust: 41 bottom

Ann Miller: 188

Moorland-Springarn Research Center, Howard University: 111 left

Office of Tourist Development, Maryland Department of Economic and
    Community Development: 122
University of Maryland, College Park: 223 right
Walters Art Gallery: 109 left
Theresa Yenca: 254 right

Quotations:
The author gratefully acknowledges the following for permission to print
    or reprint unpublished or published materials (and these credits constitute
    an extension of the copyright page):
The New York Times: for excerpts from "The Biggest Baltimore Loser of
    All Time," by Russell Baker, copyright © 1973 by The New York Times
    Company; from "Some Reasons I Tell the Stories I Tell," by John Barth,
    copyright © 1982 by The New York Times Company.
Kathryn Johnson: for passages from unpublished manuscript by Gerald
    Johnson.
University of Virginia Library: for quotations from letter of R. D. Unger
    to Chevalier Reynolds (October 12, 1899) in the Poe-Ingram Collection
    (#38-135), Manuscripts Department, University of Virginia Library.
Richard Macksey: for his translation of Stéphane Mallarmé's "Le Tombeau
    D'Edgar Poe."
Collection of American Literature, The Beinecke Rare Book and Manuscript
    Library, Yale University: for excerpts from January 23, 1952 letter by
    Thornton Wilder to Henri Peyre, by permission of Donald Gallup,
    Literary Executor; from "The Fireplace" (typescript, copyright © 1941)
    by H. L. Mencken (Bradford F. Swan Collection).
Harper & Row, Publishers, Inc.: for "Incident" from *On These I Stand* by
    Countee Cullen, copyright © 1925 by Harper & Row, renewed copyright
    © 1953 by Ida M. Cullen.
Holt, Rinehart, & Winston, Publishers: for passage from "How Softly We
    Went in the Sunny Hall," from *The Old House in the Country* by Lizette
    Woodworth Reese, copyright © 1930 by Farrar & Rinehart, Inc.; from
    "The White Fury of the Spring," from *White April* by Lizette Woodworth
    Reese, copyright © 1930 by Lizette Woodworth Reese, copyright © 1958
    by A. Austin Dietrich; from *American Outpost* by Upton Sinclair,
    copyright ©1932 by Farrar & Rinehart, Inc.; from *The Man Who Loved
    Children* by Christina Stead, copyright © 1965 by Christina Stead.
Baltimore *Sunpapers:* for passages by H. L. Mencken reprinted by
    permission of The Baltimore *Evening Sun.*
Enoch Pratt Free Library: for excerpts from H. L. Mencken's "Notes to
    Newspaper Days" (copyright © 1942) and "Autobiographical Notes"
    (typescript © 1925), in the Mencken Collection, in accordance with the
    terms of the will of H. L. Mencken.
Alfred A. Knopf, Inc.: for excerpts from the following works by H. L.
    Mencken: "Good Old Baltimore," *The Smart Set,* May 1913, reprinted

About the Author

Frank R. Shivers, Jr., probably has just the right qualifications to write this book: he has roots in Maryland—his father was born in Somerset County, Eastern Shore—and he himself enjoys the perspective of two Yale degrees. Born near the historic Quaker town of Haddonfield, New Jersey, he has taught a generation, mostly in the English Department chair at the oldest Quaker educational institution south of Philadelphia. He loves literature and history.

As regional historian, Shivers has published *Bolton Hill: Baltimore Classic* (1978) and, as co-author, *Chesapeake Waters: Pollution, Public Health, and Public Opinion, 1607-1973* (1983). In the works is *Streetwise In Baltimore: A History of Baltimore Through Street Names*. He is proud of a Baltimore *Sun* award for readability.

In the community Shivers has served on boards of historical and preservation groups. He was a founder of his neighborhood newspaper, of Bolton Swim and Tennis, Ltd., and of A.I.M.S. (Association of Independent Maryland Schools). He, his wife, and four children are devoted to books and to Maryland.

The Baltimore and Maryland Books of Maclay & Associates Inc., 1981-1986

Those Old Placid Rows, by Natalie W. Shivers *1981*

The Grasshopper, illustrated by A. J. Volck *1981.*

Baltimore and the 19th of April, 1861, by George William Brown *1982*

Great Baltimore Houses, by Joanne Giza and Catharine F. Black *1982*

Early Manor and Plantation Houses of Maryland, by H. Chandlee Forman (with Bodine & Associates) *1982*

Port Tobacco, by Kim R. Kihl *1982*

Lost Baltimore Landmarks, by Carleton Jones *1982*

Baltimore: A Picture History, by Francis F. Beirne and Carleton Jones (with Bodine & Associates) *1982*

Baltimore Citygames, by David J. Peerless *1983*

Mount Vernon Place, by John Dorsey *1983*

Baltimore Deco, by S. Cucchiella *1984*

Baltimore in Old Engravings 1985

Maryland Wits and Baltimore Bards, by Frank R. Shivers, Jr. *1985*

Roland Park, by James F. Waesche *(1986)*

The publishers wish to express their thanks to all those who understood.